New Era Publishing

SHOE SHINE BOY

Written by:

Charles H. Belim

Published by:
New Era Books
1211 Atlantic Ave, Suite 303
Brooklyn, New York 11216
347-651-6366

First Printing: January 1, 2013

ISBN: 978-0-9844071-6-3

Typist/Editor: **Lisa Roma, Creative Women's Network**

Web site: www.newerabooks.net/
          www.newerapublication@aol.com

SHOE SHINE BOY

Charles H. Belim

New Era Publishing
Brooklyn, New York
Copyright 2012

Dedicated to

ଔଛୠଔଛ

Earline Crawford-Steed-Belim
Mother

William Gibbs
Father

Willie Mae Steed-McCant
Aunt

David K. Belim
Brother

Special Thanks to
Mary Hines/Maelou

Chapter 1 ~ Leaving Georgia

M y mother, Earline Crawford-Steed, Crawford belonging to the father she knew in name only, not by deed, was born on November 28th, 1928 in Manchester, Georgia to Grace Steed. It was fitting that she take the name of those who loved and cared for her, my mother's family, the Steeds of Manchester. Not once do I ever recall anyone using my grandfather's first name. It was as though my mother was conceived by virtue of *immaculate conception*. That is how far removed this man was from my mother's daily life and family.

Picking cotton had been the Steed family's main source of income when my mother was a child. The Steed Family were sharecroppers for a white family who owned the land. My mother would tell us stories and show us her hands with those marks on her fingertips from cotton picking. Cotton is very light in weight, so one has to pick plenty of cotton to fill up a Croaker-Sack-Bag.

One of my grandma's sisters, Mrs. Willie Mae McCant, whom we affectionately called Aunt Tee, or "Tee" for short, left Georgia and came North because her husband wouldn't stop drinking -- and cut in the fool. Her desire was for Uncle Josh to return to being an upstanding Christian filled with the Holy Ghost -- dipped in water. Aunt Tee left Uncle Josh and came up the country a few years behind Uncle Albert, who worked on a railroad as a Pullman Porter, a parlor car attendant and much sought after job by many Blacks all across the country, especially in the deep South, also known as "Jim Crow country." That position gave many single young Black men a way out of picking cotton or being lynched at the hands of "White Night Riders." It also gave others with families a chance to go North or West in search of a better life. My Uncle Albert and his wife were of those who took hold of hope and came North to Boston in the early 1930's. As to the exact year I am not sure, but I do know my mother wasn't yet in her teens. Aunt Tee came second, then Mom, and everyone else came in droves thereafter.

Earline came to Boston at age fifteen on a train from Manchester, Georgia in the Spring of 1943. She was met at South Station in Boston by the whole family, Uncle Albert, and Aunt Tee's cousins Jimmy and Rufus. Earline felt totally liberated just knowing no cotton fields could be seen or found nearby to remind her of Georgia. Nor were there any *"For Colored Only"* signs on the walls outside restrooms or *"For Whites Only"* signs near that cool stream of flowing water coming from the fountain a few feet away.

"Utopia" may not have been a part of my mother Earline's vernacular the day she stepped onto Massachusett's soil. But we can rest assured that those feelings of utopia and having reached it did exist deep within her heart and soul on the day she met her family. At age fifteen she was truly a Georgia Peach, tall for a girl back then, five feet ten inches, size ten shoe, long black hair flowing down her back and a copper tone complexion. Did I say "very pretty to look at?" She was "all that and a bowl of grits," as country folk would say about her back then.

Aunt Tee was the matriarch of those in our family who had come to Boston, 'though not the oldest. Uncle Albert's wife, Aunt Louvenia, was the oldest and the one who called the shots. She had assimilated well within the infrastructure of Black Bostonianhood through her church on Humboldt Avenue and Deckard Street. She held the position of Church Mother. It was already decided that Earline would stay at Tee's place, where she quite easily settled into the cozy two-bedroom walk-up overlooking Warren Street.

Aunt Tee worked as a domestic for some Jewish families in Brookline, Allston and Roxbury. There were times she was needed -- expected – to go to Cape Cod, or "The Cape" as it was called, to work in their summer homes. Aside from doing most of the cooking, she would have to get down on her hands and knees with soapy water and brush-scrub their floors. She washed clothes in a "Set-Tub." A Set-Tub was the connecting portion of a kitchen sink, and was usually very deep. Aunt Tee's other duties included bathing Mrs. Ann's baby girl "little Sara" and "bad ass Billy." Billy would always ask that question, "Why are you so Blaaack? God doesn't like youuuu!" My poor aunt would cry a thousand inward tears, for she knew he was taught those things by the family she cooked and cleaned for. Dear Aunt Tee held her indignations deep within, so long as she worked those floors on her hands and knees.

Many times Aunt Tee's weekly pay came to fifty dollars. To add insult, she would be handed old discarded white dolls, although they knew she had no children. Other times, much of her pay was split because of the leftover food she was given along with old clothes. Never one to frown, my aunt simply smiled and said, "Thank you, Ma'am / Miss Ann." She continued doing domestic work until she could no longer tolerate being down on her knees scrubbing floors.

Tee was almost 70 years old when she stood back up. Back in the late 1940s up to the late 1960s, domestic workers were paid in cash and perishables. No laws were in place to protect the worker, therefore, no employer set aside a dime for Social Security. They just weren't considered. Even in our current times, foreign domestic workers are dehumanized by their own countrymen and women, especially if they don't speak English or have any papers.

In 1969, I believe things began to change for people like my Aunt Tee. By then she was all used up, ready to be replaced by a "younger slave." Any takers, Earline being unskilled and with only a 10th grade education, her options were limited. One of her cousins suggested she try for a job at the GE Company in East Boston out by Revere, Massachusetts. War products were still in high demand. Many young Blacks from Boston as well as young Whites worked side by side during the war years doing their patriotic duty to support the war in Europe.

Earline worked as an assembly line worker. Health benefits weren't the best, overtime work was plentiful, and she was strongly encouraged to invest in US Savings Bonds, Series E, or War Bonds as they were sometimes referred to. In those days, that's where the American workingmen and women put their money for a rainy day. Earline fell right in line with many other young Blacks who believed a better way was to come for Blacks as a whole.

Social acceptability was a must back in the mid 1940's to late 1960's in my community. While Mom was employed at GE, she met and became friends with my Dad's niece's husband long before she met my Dad. His name was Lawson Riley. At that time he was attending school to become a mortician. Eventually he succeeded and opened his own business. It stands today bearing his name. I applaud his tenacity and drive. Many Blacks today lack that pertinacious attitude in my old community of Roxbury. The Riley Funeral Home stands as a testament. It is said, "If you can see success in the eyes of the mind, so can you make it a physical reality for all to see as well."

My Mom had a good voice, so did my Aunt Tee, as did other women in my family. Gospel music was their calling. Groups like the Five Blind Boys of Alabama, The Dixie Humming Birds, Swan Silver Tones, Mahalia Jackson, and Reverend James Cleveland could be heard singing "Peace Be Still." I can still close my eyes and see and hear Mom singing along with the radio. Mom and Aunt Tee oftentimes sang in church together.

When Mom first came to Boston, she would join my Aunt on Sundays and together they would sing in church. My Aunt's minister was Brother Joshua Adams of the Church of God and Christ. He and his wife were also from Georgia. Because of my Aunt's strong hold on my Mom, it prevented her from going to other churches, especially if they weren't considered the fire and brimstone type.

Now, there's something called "speaking in tongues." Simply put, it meant essentially that God and the individual were having a one-on-one heart to heart talk. Now, before you say, "I have no idea of the language," or what might have been discussed, all I know is, I was told it was God's language, according to my folks. Baptist churches and many others just didn't have the Holy Ghost in them so they missed the message.

The Church of God and Christ was very strong. Brother Adam's wife was the State Mother. She was even over my Aunt Louvenia's church. Bishop Crocket, who had the big church near the Warren Statue, his church has been gone for over 30 years. He also was a big wig in the Church of God and Christ. That is, when he wasn't creeping on 60 Sherman Street in a certain woman's house. I guess he was holding one of those one-on-one late night Revival Meetings, no doubt, when the poor sister went to speaking in tongues and he mounted the sister as a means to revive her. Funny thing took place. She had a "conehead-ugly pop-eyed baby boy" who could pass for Brother Crocket's twin. Them late night tongue talking sessions are real strong sessions.

My mother and aunt used to go to the Gospel programs at a local high school called "Technical High School." The social and political meeting place has historically always been the Black Church in our communities across this vast country of ours. Being a member of the politically correct church has always earned a political candidate the backing of those members and their friends. Look, if you will, at Adam Clayton Powell and Calvin Butts. The list goes on and on. Rev. Mike Haines was once the head, or at least the last voice, on the Massachusetts Board of Corrections. How do I know this? He gave me parole in 1972 from old Deer Island.

New Hope Baptist on Shawmut Avenue, Tremount Methodist on Tremount Street (it may be under a different name and leadership today), Rev. Mike Haines' church on Warren Street, and the many others, have played a much-needed role in the moving ahead of our communities. Because of the high rates of recidivism, drug usage, teen pregnancy and, last but not least, teens killing teens, the Black churches need to reach out more to their constituents who placed them on those elected boards, because it is *their* babies who are dying minute by minute.

Perhaps it wasn't the case in 1944 when my Mom was a teenager, but today this is the reality. Although it seemed as if Earline was really being welcomed into that little clique, she was really frowned upon because of her accent and "country-ness," as they called it back then. Many educated Blacks in Boston in the early 1940s were only one to two generations removed from that very same environment in the South that she came from. This stigmatization seemed to increase if any Georgia dust was thought to still be on your shoes. My father's family was of that same mindset.

In many ways, Black bigotry within our communities still thrives. In Boston, the newly arrived Black Southerner, male or female, is quickly labeled a "homie," which is meant in the negative sense, mind you. In the nation's capital you are labeled a "Bama." Again, it has a negative connotation to it as well. As you can see, neither are terms of endearment but rather seeds of the "Willie Lynch Syndrome" well planted and watered by our own ignorance. Earline was still able to step past that mindset.

My mother's cousin Rufus was known on the Hill as a bad MF with his hands, a knife, etc. He kept BS away from his young cousin, Rufus' brother Jimmy. In years to come, Jimmy's like for young boys would slip out. Rufus would serve a federal sentence in FCI Danbury long before it became a female facility. I, too, would be sent to Danbury in 1985 to serve three years for Credit Card Fraud.

My Aunt Louvenia ran a home-based day care business. Through that business is how she made many social contacts within the Roxbury Community back in the mid 1950's and early 1960's. My cousins Rufus and his brother Jimmy are now deceased. We can't pick or choose our families, we either accept them for who they are, or we don't. I've chosen to embrace all my family members, regardless of their shortcomings.

Earline assimilated and integrated herself well after awhile, in spite of the little petty actions by some of the people whom she met. One of those era's favorite hangout spots was a large Chinese restaurant on Mass Avenue. It was directly opposite the Christian Science Building two doors from where Danny's His and Hers Hair Salon was. The Donnelly Memorial Theater was another place. Its doors closed in the late 1960's. Many Black groups of that era and beyond were seen there. Places like the Old Boston Arena, Handy's Grill, the High Hat at the corner of Mass Avenue and Columbus where the Harriet Tubman Building now stands. The Patio Lounge was strictly a square bar for the after work crowd.

Those were some of the hangout spots of my parents and others, long before narcotics changed the demographics along with senseless murders of many unknown faces throughout Roxbury. Long before a "Dumpy-Stumpy firey Irishwoman" named Louise Day-Hicks came to power within the Boston Public School System, she may not have literally expressed it verbally, but her actions and demeanor said the following: To level the educational playing field within the Boston Public School System was to "keep them damn Niggers locked into those inferior schools deep in the bowels of Roxbury!" She's now gone to purgatory, "bless her little heart!"

The end of the war in 1945 brought hope to the hearts-minds-souls of many Blacks throughout America. Our fathers, uncles, brothers and sons had served their country well in the war in Europe. By doing so, hope was alive and kicking with both feet. Finally, people of color believed equality had come within their immediate grasp. However, those hopes and dreams became short lived. We soon found out we were still the last hired and first to be fired, on many occasions. Some, though, were able to "slip through the cracks," because of opportunity and education. Much of the work done by civilian Blacks in the North to support the war effort began to dry up. Yet again, many Blacks became increasingly disenfranchised.

As Blacks were eased out, or downsized, Whites returning home from the war in Europe were re-integrated back into those same jobs. Somehow, through all that, a tenth-grade Sweet Georgia Peach named Earline Steed managed to keep her job at General Electric in East Boston. Mom managed to stay on for a couple more years. In doing so, that gave Mom a sense of independence and self-worth as a person.

Chapter 2 ~ Meeting David Belim

I n 1946 my mother met a man a few years older than she through a mutual friend at her place of employment. Around this same time, my aunt was becoming concerned that my mother was becoming a bit too loose in terms of her coming and going. Aunt Tee was very old fashioned. She felt that unmarried women shouldn't be out late at night past 11:00pm. Her real issue with my mother was her not attending Sunday School each and every Sunday. Looking back on both personalities, especially my Aunt's fears, I can understand my Aunt wanting to protect her sister's daughter. Mom, on the other hand, was working daily, functioning as an adult by paying her own way, even though she had not yet reached the age of twenty-one.

What would really cause my aunt to go totally off on Earline was her smoking a cigarette near their apartment while tapping her foot and snapping her fingers. Cigarette in her mouth, transistor radio on, fingers popping on the other hand, everybody back home was called that evening from Uncle Albert's house. Tee wanted her on the midnight train back to Manchester, Georgia, bypassing Atlanta and all stops in between. It was decided Earline needed stern guidance. So, by week's end, my young mother moved into Reverend Adams' house with his wife up on Bower Street between Humboldt and Walnut Avenues, at the backside of the Lewis Jr. High School.

Rev. Adams had a huge home with many large rooms upstairs and downstairs. His house sat far back from the sidewalk and a long pathway ran from the front gate to the front porch of their home. The front porch was long and screened in with several lounge chairs and two small tables, so when company came they could all sit comfortably along with the house residents. Brother Adams worked for "The Railroad," as they called it. He cleaned the passenger cars in South Station after all the passengers came off the train. Also, he and his wife provided shelter to Vets who were "shell shocked" from World War II right up to the

Korean War. I do know those men that stayed with Brother and Sister Adams had some serious issues. A few of them shook like a man going to the electrical chair. The government must have paid them well because he kept at least five at all times.

Earline was now at the Adams' house where she had her own room. She didn't totally abandon church. She would still attend and even sing in the church choir. She was still employed at GE. She now was seeing this brother named David Belim from Florida who also worked at General Electric. He had been to Rev. Adams' home a few times to pick Earline up, always very respectful of the time. Never once did he keep her out past her scheduled curfew.

Rev. Adams was a respected minister and member of the community. On several occasions, he had accompanied Earline to church on Sunday. That act alone put everyone at ease. Aunt Tee insisted Mom bring him to dinner at Uncle Albert's big house. Their approval meant everything and she knew this. The rest of the family wanted to see him face-to-face, check him out and ask questions about his family, where he came from, whose plantation in or around Florida "owned your folks" back in the days of physical slavery.

Many men got turned down from ever marrying a certain sister based on who owned their folks. So-and-so owner had a bad name because his lot of slaves were not properly docile by the time freedom reached them. And that's how my folks did their thing; they'd ask the eldest what he or she thought or knew about the coloreds who came from so-and-so's land. Once Uncle Albert and Aunt Tee approved a thing, it was a done deal. Down South got the call from Uncle Albert and Aunt Tee that "Earline done found herself a man." Well, praise be to God/Jesus, to my folks they were the same person in many respects.

When I look back on those stories my family used to tell my brother and I, even down to my Mom sharing them with her granddaughter before her own death in 2001. That whole ritual had much merit. One needs as much background information on a soon-to-be lover, wife, or husband as they can gather. Had I not abandoned half of what I was taught, many problems I encountered with women, my first wife, especially, could and would have been totally avoided simply by avoiding that person altogether.

છ

Chapter 3 ~ The Rift

While Earline was living with Brother and Sister Adams, she was always respectful of time restraints imposed on her since she had agreed to accept lodging at their family home. Mom didn't want to venture too far from the Adams house whenever she did accept a date with this man David Belim, whom she was keeping company with on a regular basis. Whenever she and David would go out to a local movie theater it would be to the neighborhood theater on Warren Street near her Aunt's apartment. The movie "Cabin in the Sky" featuring the vibrant legendary actress-songstress Ms. Lena Horne was a must-see for Black Folks during my Mom's era. The movie was released in 1943.

Shortly after arriving at the Adams' residence from seeing "Cabin in the Sky," Earline had taken a quick shower and returned to the privacy of her bedroom. Her solitude was suddenly broken by a knock on the locked door, which momentarily startled and caused her to perspire. The second knock brought her back to consciousness and allowed her to ask, "Who is it?" The voice on the other side of the thick oak wood door surprised Earline when she heard Brother Adams announcing himself in a barely audible tone. "It's Reverend Adams, Earline."

Earline asked, "What's the matter, Brother Adams?" Brother Adams replied, "I need to speak with …" Earline quickly responded, "Can't it wait until the morning, Brother Adams?" Brother Adams' quick "NO" echoed through the thick oak door.

Reverend Adams had never once come to Earline's door, open or closed, before this night. Always Mother Adams would do the knocking or calling. Earline's thoughts immediately went to his wife, perhaps she was ill or they needed assistance with a sick war veteran.

Earline's room was large, yet sparsely furnished, with a small twin sized bed and two thick folded quilts stacked upon her freshly ironed white linen sheets. Over her bed hung an old picture of Brother Jesus at the historic Last Supper. Directly opposite her bed stood a rickety dresser that held much of what she owned at that time. On top of her dresser sat a mirror held together by a piece of peeling brown tape. Next to her bed on the floor was a "slop jar" to attend her personal needs at night so as not to disturb anyone with toilet flushing. One lone chair sat by the small closet, the chair that held the clothing she laid out to wear the next day.

Before opening her bedroom door to allow Reverend Adams to enter, Earline made sure her night robe was properly covering her body. Upon opening the door, she could easily see Reverend Adams heavily perspiring. Quickly, Earline offered to get him a glass of water from the pitcher that sat beside a neat stack of paper cups next to her transistor radio. Reverend Adams responded with a sharp "NO!" Feeling a bit awkward, Earline said, "Let me move these clothes from the chair so you can sit."

As she began to move the clothes from the chair to the bed, Reverend Adams sat down on the bed. Continuing to feel awkward, Earline set the clothes back on the chair. Reverend Adams started to mutter, "Lord Jesus, help me, help me!"

Not knowing what to do, Earline came closer to ask what the problem was. At that point, the minister snatched my mother's hand, pulling her off balance toward him and causing her to fall onto him as he sat on the bed.

This should not be happening! Earline could not believe what was taking place. Rev. Adams tried hard to get on top of her to assault her while pulling on her robe. He was a strong man, but Mom was a bit stronger and younger, a big strong tomboy country girl who could defend herself and didn't mind fighting. Rev. Adams kept saying, "Don't fight! I'm sorry! I'm sorry!" Yet, he would not let go of his grip on her robe. Somehow, Earline scratched him deep in his face, which made him loosen his grip on her. She had him on the defense, and whipped his perverted ass single handedly in that room, never once crying out for help.

That bastard ran out of the room like a whipped pup! Mom said about that incident that she was too hurt and disappointed to cry. She immediately locked her bedroom door and put the chair under the doorknob. She dressed herself and packed all her belongings, angrily awaiting daybreak, knowing it would be nearly impossible to get a taxi at that hour of the night on Humboldt Avenue.

All that night Earline stood by the window until it became light enough to leave. Once she felt safe, she picked up her things and walked out, leaving the doors wide open as she headed to her Aunt's house on Warren Street, still too angry to cry.

Aunt Tee was readying herself for work when Earline showed up, suitcase in hand. Upon entering Tee's kitchen, she broke down in a flood of tears in her Aunt's arms. Through her sobs, she told Aunt Tee the entire story, omitting nothing, for what seemed like an hour. Our Aunt just sat there totally stunned speechless. To Earline's dismay, she was disbelieved by the only woman whom she truly trusted in the city, her "mother's own sister!"

My Aunt's actual response was, "Earline, were you drinking and made this up? You know, you've been smoking cigarettes and listening to that un-Godly music on the radio. Why would you want to ruin a relationship with good God-fearing Christians like Brother and Sister Adams? Them *is* respectable church folk!"

Earline just sat there and cried. Still Aunt Tee stood up for Brother Adams, and Mom never returned for any reason. Tee never mentioned a word to Brother and Sister Adams. It is not known how Reverend Adams explained away the deep scratches on his face the next day, but as to why Earline left, he told his wife, "She missed her Aunt."

Within one week, Earline and David Belim had found a small place in the South End to stay, known as "Rutland Square." Things didn't not die that night, nor did they die because Mom and my brother's father moved in together. However, Earline turned very bitter on a personal level toward the faith she was born into. From 1946 until 1972, my mother would only enter a church twice, when her own mother died and when my great-Grandma passed away.

As children, we never quite understood why this coldness would always come over Mom whenever Bro. Adams' name came up between she and my Aunt. In 1966, the whole sordid story would finally come to a head. Mom would be locked up as a result of things she held for years deep within her heart. In the pages to come, all will come together in the truth. In 1947, Earline Steed married David Belim in Boston, Massachusetts. There was no church wedding, just a simple one at City Hall. Mom refused any sort of church wedding, or to be married by Rev. Adams, as the family had urged.

Cousins Jimmy and Rufus had no trouble accepting their cousin's story. Jimmy being a closet homosexual and Rufus being a certified tough guy who would kill a rock if it moved unexpectedly. Their varied lifestyles gave much insight into the mind of a man like Bro. Adams. Jimmy never openly came out of hiding except when he saw something of interest. (I had another family member much like Jimmy, he just wasn't blood to me directly, but he was still a true family member.) They called him "Jimmy-grease-em-up." Rufus, having been in the penitentiary, had good common sense, for you see all types in prison. Having been in the state and federal penitentiary myself, I've seen many types of freaks and perverts, both Black and White, and in between. What I've yet to see is a Muslim in jail for sexual assault. Let me be a bit clearer. They may very well be serving time for that charge, but they were not Muslims when they committed the act.

Christian clergy members seem to have a high propensity for having the Bible in one hand and the other hand up some small child's dress or in some young boy's pants. Look at what the Catholic Church went through in Massachusetts between 2000 and 2004. And here's the kicker -- in most cases, they were White victims as well as those charged. That's not to say Blacks are exceptions. Not so at all. We just do a better job at hiding the perversion. We are a people so quick to say Blacks don't do this or that. Bullshit! We do it and you good church going folks know I'm not wrong. In the penitentiary, all the child molesters and hardcore rapists "tote the Bible as a shield or badge of honor and protection."

That type of lewd and licentious behavior must be routed up and out of our communities. Those types of people have left their mark, not only on my Mom back in the 1940s. It also has touched two of my own daughters. Check out this irony, one of the assaulters wasn't in a clown suit with candy in one hand; he was a good-book-toter and a family friend, as well. I know first hand what that can do to a child and family.

On September 7th, 1948, my Mother gave birth to her first child, a boy whose name would be that of his father, David K. Belim, my big brother.

ഗ

Chapter 4 ~ No Staying Power

I guess the responsibilities of a young child and marriage overwhelmed the young father, David Belim. Far too many Black fathers, myself included, have conjured up all sorts of crazy rationalizations to justify walking away from our inherent responsibility of participating in our child's growth and development. I, too, accept blame for the same charge. Desertion, and dereliction of my duty, failing to be proactive in all of my children's lives, sometimes we must expose and accept our own character defects in order to be honest and objective. I call this admission on my part as self charged. I must be honest by laying myself bare to be self-charged, indicted and convicted. He and I both failed, he failed a wife and infant son. I, in turn, failed three women and five Beautiful Nubian Queens.

Collectively, we manufacture all types of cockamamie excuses for our ill-responsible attitude toward our responsibilities. Men, in the sense of its usage, transcend color. I refer to all men, here, not just those of color. We have little, if any, problem siphoning off that "Sweet Nectar" that lies deep within the folds of a woman's thighs that give us so much joy. But accountability to her and what comes out of her is what should be our main focus. All men are not being charged, only those whose feet fit easily into those shoes of abandonment. If it doesn't apply, then "please, let it fly."

Mr. Belim's reason for breaking camp, leaving my mother, was this. He claimed to have contracted "The Clap" – gonorrhea. The charge he leveled against my Mom was that she "gave it to" him. Wow! What? Not another betrayal! And this time it was her own husband. This indictment blew her young mind. Especially when he was the only man she had been with since they met. He used that lie to run back to his hometown in Florida and never return, even though he had other family living in Boston to this very day. There had been ample opportunity for him to have been involved in the lives of his son and grandchildren, as well as great-grandchildren. Naturally, my Mom had herself immediately checked out and she received a clean bill of health. After Mr. Belim left, she was forced to move back in with her Aunt on Warren Street. Only this time with an infant.

Mom was not working, due to the baby needing her care, so everything was on my Aunt's shoulders in terms of support. The WIC Program was still "light years away" in 1949. That $12 to $15, on a good day, depending on whom Tee worked for, along with the table scraps from those Jewish tables, is how they got by, including the help of other family members.

April 1949, my Mom and brother went home to Manchester, Georgia. Mom stayed about a month. My grandma had two sisters and brothers each. I knew all of them. My great-grandparents were called Momma and Daddy. They even addressed each other that same way. Mom's aunt, who lived in Atlanta, called her husband "Daddy Pa," and so everyone else did, for that matter. Before Mom returned to Boston, it was agreed that Kenny would remain in Georgia until Mom got herself together in Boston. With that all settled, she could return to Boston with ease because her son was in good hands.

ॐ

Chapter 5 ~ Starting Over

Now that her infant son was safe with his great-grandparents in Georgia, Mom could refocus on finding a job and a place for herself and son. Being back at Aunt Tee's didn't help in many ways. My Aunt made her feel as though she were still that 15-year old girl who had just stepped off the train at South Station back in 1943. She had surpassed that stage of her life, for in a few years' time she had become a wife and mother, and in the end, she had to return home to Georgia, home to her real roots, and deposit her newborn son to his great-grandparents. Why? Because her husband had walked away from his wife and their child. He had falsely accused her of a vile wretched act that he knew was a lie. She could never return to the life of that innocent fifteen year-old girl who walked off that train, no matter how much our Aunt may have desired her to. She had survived her maiden voyage from adolescence to womanhood. Now she was ready for all of the tomorrows that would surely come. She was starting over.

Once settled back in at her Aunt's place further down Warren Street near Haines Park, Mom and Aunt Tee talked about the changes she saw and heard about while back in Manchester, Georgia, and how everyone just fell in love with Baby David. Great-granddaddy was a tall strong man, well over six feet. He was the "Black EF Hutton" of our family. When he spoke, everyone would listen and adhere to his decisions. It was clear Daddy made the decision for Kenny to be left behind while Mom returned North. Even if everyone else had vehemently disagreed with Kenny staying, which no one did, it would have had little, if any, effect on Daddy's decision. He was truly the "king of his castle." Aunt Tee knew her Daddy well.

My Aunt knew Mom needed a job badly, but not bad enough for her to submit to being on her hands and knees for the rest of her life in some Jewish woman's kitchen, being disrespected by her children. No, that would not be the fate of her niece, not if she had a say in it. Even though I gave up Boston for New York many years ago, I still love the community I grew up in and its diverse population. Roxbury, down by

Dudley Station, still is the place to be, especially if you are a connoisseur of beautiful women, in an array of colors and styles, as I am.

Along the upper part of Warren Street in the direction of Grove Hall, there remain many of the original old homes from my Mother's era still standing tall and in good condition. Many of the connecting streets that link into Warren Street possess most of those vintage homes from that well-known era. Streets like Savin, Quincy, Dale, Rockland, Waumbeck, Wyoming and Hoborone. Bower is gone forever and so are parts of Sherman and Monroe Streets. But when my Mom was young, many of the streets along Elm Hill were still occupied by Jewish families, especially those dead end streets near "the old Puritan Plaza."

As the Black Middle Class (Black Bourgeoisie) began to buy property within Roxbury, the White flight slowly began to take shape. A few doors down from the church known as "Charles Street Church" on Warren Street stands a building now known as "Sky Cap Lounge," but many years ago it was a Jewish Social Center called "Puritan Plaza." Back when I was a kid, it had a long maroon canopy extending from the steps of the building to the sidewalk curb. Today, I believe, it is owned by a group of Black Transit Workers who are part of, or better yet, members of, the "Masonic Order." The Plaza, as it was known, was a place where many Jewish functions were held. One such function that stands out in my mind is called a "bar mitzvah," which was considered a very important event.

Under Jewish tradition, or Jewish jurisprudence, when a male child reaches the age of thirteen, a bar mitzvah is held to honor his passage into manhood. There is a somewhat similar tradition held for young Jewish girls (in the less religious circles) called a bat mitzvah, which commemorates the female coming of age ceremony. Jewish weddings and receptions, as well as other functions, were held there during the old days. Blacks throughout Roxbury were employed there. They worked on the back loading dock, unloading trucks of food transported from Brooklyn, New York, and other places that processed and sold kosher food products.

Many Blacks learned firsthand how to properly prepare many of the Jewish dishes by working alongside the Jewish cooks and top bakers. Some brothers even earned their food handling licenses while employed at the Plaza. Some truckers, only a few were Black, were Irish or Italian from Charlestown or the North End. Waiters were basically well trained Blacks who knew how to properly smile like a "Chess-A Cat" ("Cheshire Cat") – translation, "a nigga-who-can't-stop-smiling-no-matter-what" is going on! Many Black children went to bed with a full stomach due to the food their parents slipped out the doors, my brother and I included.

During that time period Aunt Tee was employed by a Jewish family who lived on a short dead end street that ran perpendicular to the main entrance of the Plaza. It is still intact to this very day.

Aunt Tee approached a particular prominent Jewish family on her niece's behalf. You know, she ran down the whole sordid story, leaving out absolutely nothing. She couldn't help but humble herself, beyond the limits of belief, to any white person. She may have even pledged/promised to do extra work free of cost if they would/could help get Mom a job at the Plaza. I'm in no way making a mockery of my dear sweet Aunt. She did what she felt had to be done to get the job done. And in the end, Mom was hired.

The same family had a lot of influence within the Jewish synagogues located along Elm Hill Avenue. One was at the beginning of Elm Hill close to Waumback and Warren Streets. The other was at the top of Elm Hill Avenue and Seaver Street. After remaining closed for many years, it was finally purchased by a Black community leader and strong supporter of the Arts. Her name was Ms. Elma Lewis. This strong willed woman had awareness and a vision for the community and Black Art and Culture. She created a safe haven within Franklin Park, a place where young Black minds could express themselves artistically on a real stage overlooking their families and community supporters. Free concerts were the norm.

Duke Ellington and many others gave freely to our community back when I was a teen. After Ms. Lewis' death, the old synagogue on top of Seaver Street became the property of "The United House of Prayer"

(Daddy Grace's House of Prayer). They do some down home cooking, especially the one located opposite the Magic Johnson Theatre on 124th Street and 8th Avenue in New York City. And the other one is located on M Street, NW in Washington, DC.

Mom got the job and was now working again. This time it was at the Plaza on Warren Street right in the neighborhood. This was around April or May of 1949. Her job was food prepping, dish washing, table setting and house cleaning. One day, Mr. Abraham stopped Mom with an offer. How would she like to run the coatroom? She said yes. She had no idea of the dissention taking that position would cause her amongst the other female employees. The job paid the same as what she was already earning. There were some things that would be different, though. She was expected to dress differently. And, she would be totally responsible for women's expensive fur coats along with the safety of the men's coats as well. Because of skin complexion, her height, age and being pretty with a Southern twang, gratuity came with this position.

Mom's other qualities are what got her chosen over the other darker skinned girls. No matter what, back then and even now, still White folks would draw on the Willie Lynch philosophy and keep us at odds with each other when it was advantageous to them. Why the media got upset with Johnny Cochran is beyond me. All he did was reverse the Willie Lynch Syndrome, at least a portion of it. Old Willie might have chuckled to himself on Johnny's move. The reality was real. Mom would now have a big advantage over those waiting on tables or cleaning them off. This was no regular restaurant; no tips could be expected from those being served for dinner. The money was made if you took care of their coats, helped them "old biddies" put on their coats, or if you helped them in or out of a taxi. Mom would tell us that them old "nigga bitches" would have daggers in their eyes but she had a Georgia Blue Steel Razor Blade, (a single edge with tape on the end so she didn't hurt herself) neatly tucked in her bra.

Many times while we were youngsters, Kenny and I would overhear our mother telling Aunt Sue and others how on several occasions she actually had to lay "Blue Steel" up close and personal against their "jug'lar veins." Before her death in 2001, Mom could be found sharing many of those same stories with her beloved granddaughters. In spite of her granddaughters hearing her share parts of her past with them when she was in her early twenties, still they found it hard to believe this mild mannered Christian woman sitting before them with her cane on her lap and walker nearby could actually be their Grandmother. Wow.

Had those "old biddies" known that Earline's new position gave her extra money to help support her young son down South, no doubt those women would have been more friendly and less hostile toward her. Mom's options may have been few in number, but her desire for total independence reached far beyond her limited options. She was a fighter and a survivor, not a quitter.

These are Mom's words. "One day while on my break out back, I saw this nice looking light complexioned older man smiling at me, so I smiled back. That went on for several days." Not having seen him before, she began to ask a couple of her friends about this handsome older man. Questions like, what's his name, how old is he, is he married. Questions women ask as well as men when they see someone they admire. She learned his name was William Gibbs. Everyone called him Gibby and that name stuck with him until his death in 1970.

Within days, this young mother of twenty-one was formally introduced by friends to this older man. It was apparently clear from the onset that this man was much older than she. Yet that made no difference to Earline. What was somewhat comical about the two of them was their height. Mom was five feet ten and a half inches tall, and Dad was about five foot six inches tall. A classic Mutt and Jeff match.

As things go, they began to see each other outside of work. She would ask him questions about his past and family. She would learn he was still legally married yet separated with two daughters. Mom knew once her family found out she was seeing a married man with two children, much disappointment would be voiced. Especially from my Aunt Tee. In spite of all the uproar, Mom would remain with this man until his last day. Why he never divorced his wife, or why Mom never divorced her husband is a question that neither Kenny nor I ever asked either of them.

Sometimes Mom and Dad would ask, "Are either of you hungry? Do you have clothes, a warm place to sleep?" What they were saying was "don't we as parents provide for you!" To this day, I still must say they did do just that, "provide" the basic necessities for both of us. Some of their methods I may not have been in agreement with all the time, but they provided for us.

Because of the nineteen-year difference in age between them, many (his friends and some of his family) felt that he was going through some sort of midlife phase and that it would soon pass. Mom's family and peers thought she was crazy to be dating a man old enough to be her father. The differences only seemed to draw them even closer together as a couple. At first he had thought once she found out he had two children and a wife that she would step back, but she proved him wrong.

My Mom was only six years older than my oldest sister. My youngest sister was only six years older than myself. Dad and his wife had been separated for quite some time before my mother came into the picture. He never slighted his financial obligations to his daughters; this was stated to us many times by my Mom. And to this date, I've never heard anything different from anyone.

My eldest sister Claire was very attached to our father. Many times when her parents would argue about his drinking and obnoxious behavior, my sister would defend him against her mother. When her mom would tell him to leave the house, my sister would weep. My father would never have a solid relationship with my sister Rose. How do you not love someone who is a part of you through blood? People, in fact, do it, but I'm not one who can, or even desires to, do anything like that. I know first hand through two of my daughters, "my two youngest."

It took my Aunt quite a while to warm up to this grown man who was seeing her niece. My Aunt never involved herself physically with any man after her marriage to Uncle Josh ended. She'd say, Jesus, God's son, was her man, and was all she needed. To her, Mom should be of the exact same mindset.

My family may not have had a lot in terms of material wealth, yet her family held firm to the morality of the era. Alcohol consumption was just as bad as adultery or fornication. My southern Roots were people baptized in water (and filled with the Holy Ghost) according to them. They believed that speaking in tongues meant you were literally communicating with Christ-Jesus (God) the Son of God (according to them). Prior to Mom coming North as they say in the South, she was sanctified and filled with the Holy Ghost. Now that she was smoking cigarettes, listening to secular music and keeping company with a married man, she now was a full-backslider-doomed-to-the-Hell-Fire!

Dad's family didn't go the fire and brimstone route. They may not have been as strong as Mom's family was "cloth-wise." No, their disdain was far worse than what Mom experienced. Dad's family's dislike was based solely on class. Being from the South, or newly arrived from there, was deeply frowned upon by Dad's family, as well as many other Black Bostonians of that era. Sad to say, "I strongly feel his family, my Dad's, led the charge…"

Some of my Dad's actions and personal remarks were fruits from that same poisonous tree of bigotry and racism. Black Bostonians who came up during my Dad's time and even up to when I was born, 1950, were very snobbish, clannish, along with being a bit color struck, to a degree. When I was a kid, we'd call a light complexioned person "Puss Colored." Nowadays, it's vogue to be called a White Nigga, Black Nigga, and even a Spanish Nigga. But let me tell you something, when one of them "Red Neck-tobacco chewing-Spitune Spitting-in-the-can White folks calls you a Niiigggaaaa, it's got a whole different twang to its sound, as well as its meaning, when it hits the airwaves. So, don't just get upset with "Joe Red Neck," get mad with yourself also. Shit is still shit, no matter what you put on it.

So, please, don't get it twisted, you don't have a right to passage based on your light complexion. Some Black people seriously have issues about not wanting to be Black -- (look at the King of Pop, MJ) – or appearing too Black at the wrong time.

24

My Dad's people had many of those same issues and some still do, to this very day. I guess they got the names mixed up. Blacks, People of Color, did not book passage on any one of those ships, the ones that left Europe from Spain, that Columbus and his crew of pirates sailed on along with his lunatic brother. True, many of his navigational crew were Black seafaring men. Still, we cannot claim lineage to them because their names are not listed on the ship's manifest. No actual names are, in fact, known to us.

Perhaps they are distant relatives to those so-called "Blue Bloods" who came on the Mayflower. Not likely. We as a people didn't even book passage on the Good Ship Jesus for that matter. Our arrival was predicated by brute force and intimidation. My father's family's moral compass is so far off that they seem to forget they are descendants of those who were forced into the belly of those slave ships.

ᜒ

Chapter 6 ~ Dad's Family

My father had three sisters. Barbara, Fanny, and I can't remember the name of the one who did the Kamikaze act from that building on the corner of Laurel Street and Humboldt Avenue before I was born.

My Aunt Barbara never once said a kind word to me or about me. She passed in 2004, I believe. She was 98 years old. I never knew her married name. She was the eldest of my father's siblings. Dad was born July 1st, 1909. I once got my Aunt Barbara's number from her son-in-law, Lawson Riley. I had hoped she might have softened up with age. All I wanted was to talk to her about my Dad and their family, and thought perhaps she might have some old family photographs I could pass on to my children. She went off on me in true Gibbs style. If she had been a much younger woman, I would have cursed my aunt out real bad, "Belim Style." But she was old so I gave her a pass.

Aunt Barbara had one child, a daughter named Romaine. She and Lawson Riley had two children, a boy and a girl. Their son was a Junior named after Lawson. Their son died as a young teenager from meningitis around 1961. His Dad took it very hard. (Riley's Funeral Home is still in its original location on Humboldt Avenue.) Dad used to take me there as a child. I recall going to visit once on Halloween. On most of those trips he was full of Fleischmann's gin.

As a youngster I was aware my father had a drinking problem. He was a functioning alcoholic back then. His alcohol addiction preceded my birth. I was born on December 19th, 1950, a few months after my parents moved in together. I do not carry the Gibbs name. I have the name belonging to a man I've never laid eyes upon, nor he on me. Mom was still legally married to my brother's father, David Belim. Mom didn't want her sons having different last names, so she gave me his. Dad was also still legally married to my sister's mother. At the time of my birth, they lived in the South End.

My Aunt Fanny was married to a nice guy named "Zeek," a cool laid-back brother. He used to work at the OIC, Opportunity Industrialization

Center, on Dudley Street, which provided education, job training and some job placement. Its inception was in the mid-1960s by a visionary Black Minister from North Philadelphia. Many inner cities throughout the country used his program as a model to start other such programs.

Zeek and Aunt Fanny had three sons and two daughters, if I recall correctly. I do remember one daughter in particular. In fact, we met recently at one of my niece's husband's funerals at St. Marks Church on Townsend Street in Roxbury in 2005. She was in awe of meeting her uncle's son after so many years. I was in awe of her, as well. I had much to ask this cousin. We even agreed to meet one day for lunch. Wouldn't you know, but she never called. Perhaps I, too, had a bit of that Georgia-Alabama dust on my shoes. My Aunt's children, to the best of my recollection, were Bobby, Richard, Raymond, Joan, and those are the ones I can remember from my childhood. Dad and Fanny were very close. Her married name was "Walden."

Dad was again his obnoxious self, even at his sister's home. I was never totally at ease with him while he was drinking. Also, I felt he tried too hard to force his side of the family to accept me. Never once was any overnight stay extended to me, nor birthday cards, Christmas cards or get-well cards when I was hospitalized as a child. Nothing. Not even from my own sisters. In their eyes, I was the epitome of the bastard child. But people in glass domains should not hurl stones. To this day, my sister has yet to offer me a cool glass of tap water. Perhaps I should be grateful "they have most assuredly embraced one of my daughters."

My cousin Raymond was closer in age to Kenny and myself, though older than me by perhaps three years. He played on the Pony League Baseball Team and Kenny played little league ball at Franklin Park when we were all young. Talk was going around that Raymond was good enough to play professionally. He went on to attend North Eastern University and became a child psychologist. He works at Children's Hospital in Boston. As for my other two male cousins, their lives would become entangled in drug use, and the other would OD in Harlem, New York.

Kids are naturally inquisitive about many things. So it's only natural that we would try to listen in on our parents' conversations. Yes, I was a nosy kid. On one of my many scouting missions, I overheard my parents discussing a rather delicate and bizarre incident that transpired in our home at 83 Bower Street in 1960. The story goes like this: Kenny and I are outside playing when my cousin Richard comes by. It wasn't unusual to see either Richard or Bobby at our home. Mom was out somewhere. Richard goes up the stairs to our place. Next thing we know, Richard is damn near running in the direction of Humboldt Avenue. Our thoughts were, "Dad didn't want to be bothered with Cousin Richard," so he ran him out the house. Little did we know, from my spying, I found out Dad was sleeping when Richard entered my parent's bedroom. Dad told Mom that when he woke up, "Richard had his dick in his hand and was about to go down on him!" My father went berserk upon waking up to that crazy scene and chased Richard out of the house. Shortly thereafter, Richard was institutionalized at Mattapan State Hospital in Mattapan, Massachusetts.

Now, as to how my dear cousin Richard came to have those issues is based on an incident that occurred at the Boston YMCA on Hunnington Avenue. His older brother Bobby was staying at the "Y" at the time. While Richard was there visiting him, according to my family's version, Richard mistakenly took a pill that he thought to be an aspirin. Again, according to family, that pill is supposed to be the source behind Richard's going crazy.

I don't personally buy that story. I honestly think my cousin Richard had a mental meltdown, and the pill story was my Dad's family's way of explaining away Richard's bizarre behavior. Richard's attempt to give his uncle, my Dad, some "head" was some lunatic stuff. Richard wasn't the only family member on my Dad's side to do some strange shit. Even when my Dad's sister's death would come up in conversation, in our house Dad would say she died from a broken heart, whatever that was supposed to have meant.

Mom would tell a much different story. Mom said Dad's sister actually committed an act of Kamikaze suicide by jumping thru a damn skylight. Her death was the result of her being jilted by an ex-lover. I never got the opportunity to meet my Aunt, her death occurred prior to my birth. Families back in the day would do everything in their power to hide away any unpleasantness concerning a family member's disturbing demise. Richard's actions, along with my Aunt's suicide, were taboo subjects in the Gibbs and Walden family. Do I think my family has issues? Hell, yeah. As for Cousin Bobby, he allegedly, along with two others, robbed the drugstore at the corner of Monroe and Warren Streets back in the early 1960s.

Oh, did I mention that his whole damn family lived around the corner from the drug store at the corner of Monroe and Hazen Streets? I keep telling my kids that their craziness is genetic and tied to their Gibbs bloodline. I'm blessed. I'm a Crawford-Steed-Belim. Yes, poor Cousin Richard had to be institutionalized at Mattapan State Hospital in Boston, Mass.

In spite of Cousin Richard's lunacy, my Mom liked Richard and Bobby. On many weekends, my Mom would catch the bus on Warren Street and ride it to Seaver and Blue Hill Avenue, walk the remaining couple of blocks to the hospital to visit my Dad's nephew, that's the type of person she was. Mom's last visit to Cousin Richard went as follows:

Shortly after arriving to visit Richard, Mom excused herself so she could use the Ladies' room. Mind you, this has always been a co-ed hospital. It wasn't odd to see a female patient moving about the hospital. Mom said many of the toilet stall doors were missing safety locks on the inside of the doors. Her stall was minus such a lock. In spite of Mom's uncomfortability at having to use such a toilet, she went ahead and entered one of the empty stalls. Within seconds of her sitting down on the cold porcelain toilet, the door to her stall flung open. Towering over her in the small stall doorway stood a giant of a woman, barefoot and wearing a faded pale blue Johnny that barely covered her scarred knees. Before Mom could regain her "Steed composure," the giant bug-eyed white woman standing before Mom calmly said "hello" as she attempted to hike up her Johnny and sit on top of my Mom. As the female Cyclops began to inch closer, my mother abruptly yelled out, "Bitch, get back or I'll cut your ass too short to shit!"

Earline never went too far from home without "Big Butch," her butcher's knife, or a "Georgia Blue Steel" razor blade neatly tucked in her bra. With that Georgia Blue Steel in one hand and burning fire in her eyes, she ran that Cyclops clean out the bathroom. Mom abruptly left the cuckoo's nest, that Mattapan State Hospital, without saying goodbye to Cousin Richard. No, she never returned to visit Richard again. As for my cousin Bobby, in 1968 Dad would receive word from Aunt Fanny that Bobby was found dead in a "Harlem Shooting Gallery of an apparent heroin overdose."

಩

Chapter 7 ~ The Tin Man

The majority of my personal life as a kid centered around hospitalization. During my mother's pregnancy with me, she had a very bad fall down some steps. No one at that time truly realized the exact extent of the injury done to the child she was carrying, until my birth. Shortly thereafter, it became apparent that I had developed some sort of birth defects as a result of her fall. The most obvious were my eyes being crossed. In addition, I was diagnosed with "cerebral palsy" because of the condition of my right arm. Strange words like "nerve damage" and "cerebral palsy" were used much when describing my condition.

From what I can recall, some of the doctors at the Polio Clinic at the Boston City Hospital felt very optimistic about the possibility of me outgrowing the condition. How they could ever come to that conclusion is still beyond me, even now in 2008. Yet, they were totally indifferent to those other opinions. Many cuckoo type tests would be performed on me during my childhood. Those damn nurses would put this glue-like gel on my scalp. Then one would attach these wires to the gel. The other ends were connected to some type of machine.

Up to this point, I was cool. I was given my choice of colored lollypops. Then I hear, "don't move, sit very still." Shit! I just instantly knew I was being electrocuted. I started to rise up to get off that damn examining table – and fast! I just could not figure out why my mother was also helping these crazy people hold me down to be electrocuted. After much restraint and threats of ass whippings and the promise of two more lollypops, I finally submitted to being electrocuted. "I just didn't die!"

The terms I remember as a child that were associated with the condition of my eyes were "stigma" of some sort and "weakness of the muscle." To a young child who just wants to play and be a regular kid, those medical terms were totally Greek.

My first major surgery as a youngster was done on my eyes, which were severely crossed since birth. Some kids are able to outgrow the problem I had, but I was not one of those fortunate young children. Any hope of correction had to come by way of surgery. To the very best of my recollection, my first eye surgery was done just as I was beginning the first grade.

To be perfectly honest, the operation was a welcome relief. Being "cross-eyed" as a kid ain't nothing nice, let me tell ya. Children, even some adults, can be extremely cruel and obnoxiously offensive. Children have their own vernacular and means of self-expression. The term kids used back then to describe my eye condition was "cock-eyed." "Look at the cock-eyed MF," they'd say.

I couldn't wait for that surgery to hurry and make me un-cock-eyed like the rest of the normal kids on my block. The surgery, for the most part, was a success. I mean, my eyes no longer appeared crossed, but there were still some "buts" that the surgery could not completely correct on its own. In order to prevent the weaker eye from becoming crossed/cock-eyed again, I had to wear an eye patch over the less weaker eye to strengthen the less weaker muscle in the weak eye. All this may seem generic and even somewhat simplistic, but what about those "buts" I previously mentioned?

Please be reminded that the era of designer frames had not yet reached Roxbury in 1956-57. Marc Jacobs, Sean John, Christian Dior, Gazelle and Cartier were still light years away from Roxbury, and myself, for that matter. And let's not forget the term "progressive lenses."

My "back in the day" appearance was very spooky. You see, not only were one of my eyes covered with a big black pirate patch, I also had to wear a pair of boogieman type eyeglasses to strengthen the less weaker eye and prevent it from becoming, once again, crossed as well. The damn lenses on those glasses were as large and thick as the bottom portion of the family size bottle of Pepsi Cola that was sold at Blair's Foodland Super Market in my old hood. Talk about being humiliated, that's an understatement, to say the least. Shit just kept covering this poor kid. Skin complexion and hair was a crimson color, now add a bad case of eczema to the equation.

My right arm and shoulder are both very small to this very day, and the muscle is still weak and I cannot hold it up over my head. The support of my left hand is needed to hold up the right for any extended period of time.

The second operation was to correct the defect relating to my right arm. Due to the birth defect, the bone in my right arm was not properly aligned or connected to my elbow. The surgeon's job was to reattach the bone to the elbow with hopes of strengthening the muscle. That first surgery basically was a success, though the muscle part was never accomplished.

How I appeared after the surgery was again crazy. In order for the bone to properly fuse, I was placed in a half-body cast from neck to waist. My right arm was in a one-piece cast to ensure that the arm stayed extended outward and the arm in-cast portion did not break. A stick was in-cast and it extended from the inside of the elbow to the side of the cast itself. On my fingers was this half-finger glove with spring-like connecting wire that was to give me strength when I opened and closed my fist. Its real job was to strengthen the upper arm muscle.

Man, all that medical jargon sounded cool in theory, but I had to return home. Knowing how I looked terrified me and I knew how I must have appeared to others in my neighborhood. Why my parents could not see my plight I don't know, or perhaps they did but just didn't know how to express it.

Coming home from the hospital was not a good feeling for me. I felt safer around others who were sick or recovering from surgery. I would have endured ten more operations if it meant not having to face those gawking kids on my block. I looked like the damn Tin Man from the Wizard of Oz except in place of "tin" I was encased in a suit of plaster.

Now you know you are screwed when those you look to for support start to clown you. The outside world and the people in it are far more critical of their assessment of you as a person. You know you are the brunt of their jokes and snickers. Still, you reach down to the very core of your soul for strength, the strength to force that smile on your face. Simply because you want to fit in and be accepted by your peers, at times it is far easier to say than to accomplish. Outwardly you smile, but internally you withdraw. You run away to a dark corner inside of yourself. Sometimes you find a safe haven and other times you're aloof. How does a child of seven or eight really run away from himself? You begin to do silly shit just to be accepted.

I've never liked being anybody's clown. Attention getting was accomplished through thievery and deception at a very young age. I'd steal change if I saw it lying around. To cover my tracks, I'd put the blame on anyone, even my brother, as long as I got the beef off me. Kenny had stayed down South for several years before I saw him, so he was a stranger to me, an enemy. Somehow, he understood my motives and would accept the blame. Doing so drew us closer as brothers.

After the first cast was removed, my arm was healing very well. It would never be 100% due to the lack of muscle strength. I even had a visiting nurse from the Savin Street Health Center come by. She would show me all these different types of exercises, but stopped coming when she realized I was not into doing them.

There was a very popular TV series called "The Rifle Men." It starred Chuck Connors. The show was about his rifle and his ability to use it fast if he had to. My brother and I finally got one each for Christmas from Mr. Beck's Five and Dime on Warren Street directly across from Warren Gardens. A liquor store now occupies the space where Mr. Beck's store once was.

Now that my first cast was off, I was hyped for trouble, and I found it. I did one of cousin Bobby's moves. Kenny, Chucky Snow and myself, "the leader," took our Rifleman guns and cap pistols. I had Kenny post up outside of "Blind Man Joe and Ida's Store" and tell anyone the store wasn't open yet. Kenny kept asking me why I wanted him to stand outside. I just said it was a surprise. Chucky and I went in and announced it was a stick up and we pulled out our toy guns, me with my Rifleman gun. Joe and Ida were both shaking like Don Knots.

Ida kept saying in her Jewish dialect, "Take vat you vant. Please don't kill us!"

"We only want the Hollywood Bars, the Three Cent Bars and Coconut Cookies in the big jar," I said.

We left with loot in tow. Kenny and Chucky got sick from eating too much candy and cookies and told on themselves. Their confessions put me in the mix as well. We all were doomed to get caught. We lived across from the store while Chucky lived down the street from the store. I can still feel the sting from that extension cord even now when I reflect back to that ass whipping.

That next summer we learned about a place called Franklyn Park near the old golf course. Franklyn Park is to Boston and its surrounding communities what Central Park is to Manhattanites and New Yorkers on the whole. Philadelphians have Fairmont Park, Washingtonians have Rock Creek Park, and Bostonians have our Franklyn Park with its lush green rolling hills and curving roadways for bicycle riders and joggers alike. Franklyn Park is one of those rare parks when it comes to the many things it offers, the diverse communities of greater Boston and the surrounding areas. From eight to eighty the park has something for all to see and do. For the athletically young at heart, the park has two ball diamonds, one for softball and the other for Little League Baseball enthusiasts.

One of the main attractions the park offers the city of Boston is the children's zoo. Many of the animals consist of exotic birds from Africa and other foreign countries. The zoo also has an array of other animals, large cats, elephants, zebras and tropical snakes. The zoo itself offers something of interest for the entire family.

During my childhood and early teens my family would bring my brother and I to the park on warm summer days. Not only is there a children's zoo along with the regular zoo within Franklyn Park, the park also has an outdoor stadium that many of the city high schools utilized to hold track and field events, as well as football games throughout the school year.

Richard Pryor, the famed comedian, once performed at an outdoor concert at White Stadium.

When I was a youngster, Franklyn Park served a multitude of purposes, not just for Roxbury, and the Black community of Boston, but for the entire city as a whole. For inner city families who couldn't afford a pricey barbeque grill, or those families who lived in one of the densely populated housing projects scattered throughout the city where barbeque grill accommodations were non-existent, Franklyn Park provided such grills for poor folks like my family. Several yards south of the manicured golf course overlooking Franklyn Park and the little concrete bridge leading to a contained area, several permanently placed barbeque grills were located. A few feet away from those grills were five long concrete slab style benches. While living on Sherman Street as a young boy I can recall other multicultural families using those community grills on the Fourth of July.

Another memorable feature within Franklyn Park was "Play House in the Park," a stage where there once stood some old concrete buildings that were cleared to make way for an amphitheatre. A feisty visionary Black woman names Ms. Elma Lewis was the main architect behind that project becoming a reality, not only for the community of Roxbury, but for the entire city of Boston. The Play House served as a venue for young talent throughout the city, offering a platform to showcase their individual talents before their peers and the community at large, including local talent such as Larry Woo and the Ambitions, and Tracy and the Play Mates.

Thinking back on our many fishing expeditions at Franklyn Pond, one particular memory stands out. On this occasion, rather than go directly to the old fishing pond as we'd normally do, we took a detour. For some reason, Dennis' brother Douglas suggested we "take a shortcut" through the dirt road that runs next to the Roubard Field near Dead Man's Curve. But instead of Douglas' so-called shortcut taking us to our fishing hole, it took us to a hill overlooking the ninth hole of the neatly manicured golf course. Someone from the group then suggested we all line our balloon bike tires up and ride off the hill like "The Lone Ranger" rides off to the wild in the old hit TV series of the same name. We all started hooting and hollering and getting really hyped up for the ride of our lives.

The agreement was we would go ride off on the count of three. Douglas shouted "three." Those balloon tires started rolling in the dirt and kicking up so much dust, it looked like a dust storm was brewing, while we were yelling and hollering like crazy people. By the time we were about two car lengths from the edge, bikes began slowing down. Not so for Kenny and myself and a couple of others. We continued on.

At about half a car length from the edge, it seemed everyone stopped but me. Only a few feet from the edge I could hear my brother yelling at me to stop. But it was too late. I went flying off into the air like a bird on my bike. I thought if I peddled faster and harder that I would stay up longer and go further in distance. Never once did I consider I could have killed or seriously injured myself. It seemed as if the ground reached up and snatched, rather slammed, me into it. That's exactly how fast I hit the damn ground. When I woke up, I was in a police car on my way back to my second home – the Boston City Hospital.

This time, the bone in my right arm would be completely damaged beyond repair and again there was talk of nerve as well as muscle damage. Back to being electrocuted. This time around they couldn't fool me with that lollypop trick. Again, I was going to be filleted as soon as my parents arrived at the hospital to sign consent forms. This time the operation would take much longer.

After some debate and X-rays, it was determined that the bone in my upper right arm was just too mangled to repair, so it was completely removed. A steel plate/rod was put in its place. I have four screws that can be seen with X-rays in my arm. The plate itself doesn't bend, so I cannot fully extend my arm. Two of the four screws are attached to my elbow and the other two are connected to my shoulder. Muscle strength is severely limited to this very day and it is still difficult to brush my teeth or comb my hair using my right hand.

Having the plate made my arm feel like it weighed a damn ton. Oh, yeah. I went back into my "Tin Man" outfit again, the cast, for several months. Because of those three major surgeries, I was hospitalized and out of regular school for about two years in total. Sure, I had a tutor, but I paid little attention because of all the things I had gone through after each operation, like trying to fit in and just be accepted as a regular kid, which just simply eluded me. Being mischievous provided a way out of dealing with the emotional pains of the "why-me" syndrome.

Now I ask you, how does a child of seven or eight years old explain that his emotional state of mind is in disarray? Can you answer that $64,000 question for this man? I didn't even know I had an emotional state of mind at age eight, let alone be able to explain its condition.

ଔ

Chapter 8 ~ The Tin Man Returns

Upon returning to the Julia Ward Howell Elementary School on Sherman and Dale Streets, I found myself repeating the second and third grades. All those eye patches, Pepsi Cola bottle thick lenses, skin issues, hair color and Tin Man outfits, those issues made school impossible for me. If I didn't have my brother's support and love, I would have no doubt been in a bed beside my cousin Richard up at Mattapan State Hospital.

While I was bent on deliberately sabotaging my education at that point in time, my brother would stand strong and fight all my physical battles. We bonded together and remained close until his death in June of 1971, in Detroit, Michigan. Now, I find myself searching for all the why's and how-comes regarding my education back then. Everyone thought I was slow, or stupid, etc. Academically, it wasn't an academic problem. It was a self-esteem issue. Why no one saw the signs still baffles me to this day.

A child's self-esteem can be easily bruised to the point that it can take many years to repair the damage, especially if and when drugs and crime are factored into the equation. All those bottled up emotions would create a mushroom effect that would transcend from early school days to adulthood, and crimes committed in the years that followed, along with fractured relationships, and one that ended tragically in 2000, as well as infidelity in my first marriage.

School was a place where I could truly act out on all of my aggression. I was a terror, constantly being sent to Mr. Wood's room. He was the school disciplinarian. He'd do one of two things: "run the murder game down, or whip ass." I learned to play the health issue, just as strong as Johnny Cochran played the race card in OJ Simpson's case. He and I had a real good understanding about me being physically disciplined. He would run down his murder game, then I would write on the blackboard 100 times, "I will not talk in class, or say bad words to the teacher."

Now Mrs. Catherine McDonna, the hard-faced Irish woman, had a face as rough looking as Mike Tyson's. She was the school principal and she'd kick ass and take names. You know, I had to try her also. I told her the doctors said I had nerve damage. She asked where was it? I said in my arms and hands, so she tried to spank me. I ran out of her office hollering like I had been beat down, "scared that white woman to death."

None of that worked on Earline or big hand William Gibbs. They did not talk the murder game, they put the murder game on your ass. We didn't have a phone back then, so whenever a report on my behavior had to be hand-delivered to my parents, for some reason it would jump out of my jacket or pants pocket, unbeknownst to me, of course.

So, my brother became the mail carrier and the same strange thing would happen. Naturally, we both would come under close scrutiny. One day, our plan came to an abrupt end. Upon walking in from school, my teacher, Mom and father all stood before us as we opened our apartment door.

No murder game was run down by our parents, they just put the whip ass game into fast motion. Mom was a big woman at 5 feet 10.5 inches, size 10 shoe and about 180 lbs. who loved to fight men, women, children, even the police for that matter. Mom would be talking to you very calmly in one breath, and in the next breath she would be all over you, knocking you in the head, hitting you with whatever was within arm's reach.

I've always felt Mom's mean streak came from our great-grandmother. We would be like, "Hey, lady, I'm your kid." Our great-grandmother was half Indian and Black, and very pretty with red skin and long flowing white hair down her back. Very statuesque, but she had a mean, short temper, even at age eighty. She'd say stuff language-wise we kids didn't understand. She spoke an Indian dialect, no doubt. I guess it's safe to say Mom got her mean streak from both her "Mom and Grandmother."

Those notes that got lost on the way home indicated I had broken a steady family rule. Talking under a woman's dress. In layman's terms essentially what that meant was I had made certain remarks about "kicking a grown woman's, my teacher's, ass."

Whenever a man, any man, said that to a Steed woman, or any woman, he had committed high treason, punishable by receiving a real Georgia ass whipping. Both my Aunt Tee and Mom stood by that until the end of their lives. My daughters Katina and Shera Zee are so much like those ladies. They have that same intense fire in them, as the matriarch's generations before them.

ഗ

Chapter 9 ~ Lunch Thief

One of my favorite schoolyard activities was stealing all the "goodies" out of other kids' lunch bags, or Tony the Tiger, The Three Musketeers, or Walt Disney lunch boxes. Even though my Dad worked two jobs, one construction and the other would be whatever second job he could find for himself, it seemed as though we always had to do some sort of penny pinching. Dad worked at a place called the "foundry" which was located near the South Bay Shopping Mall. Mom worked there every now and then, too.

Mom was very frugal when it came to buying food. Rather than buy pre-sliced "lonee-ne-meat" (our nickname for bologna), Mom would buy a whole uncut loaf, the kind that you needed a real keen eye to slice. My mother possessed neither the keen eye nor the sturdy hand that was needed to get an even cut. Once Mom got that Black-handle-Butcher's Knife in her hand, she would instantly become "cock-eyed" when it came to slicing the "lonee-ne-meat." One end would be nice and thin while the other end would be thick as two slices of Wonder Bread. To add insult to injury, Mom used enough mayonnaise to wallpaper a four-room apartment. The meat would sometimes just slide out from between the bread like riding a sled on snow in the winter.

In our house aluminum foil was used for two purposes only. Sunday cooking and blocking holes in walls with broken glass in it so the rats couldn't get at us at night. Rats are known to eat through anything. However, when it came to that glass wrapped up in that aluminum foil, them rats had no wins, the crushed glass would cut their asses up.

Mom said the kitchen had to be spotless because the rats had a good sense of smell. We used waxed paper to wrap our school lunches and we always had a piece of fruit. Now, if waxed paper was scarce, Mom would use an empty Wonder Bread bag she had stored away in the breadbox that was kept in the refrigerator all night. Whenever we would have real snacks like Hostess cupcakes we would eat them up on our way to school.

Each morning before school started, all the kids would line their pretty lunch boxes in a row next to the fence. While the boys played jacks and marbles, the girls played double Dutch. No one paid any attention to Kenny or myself. Kenny stood like a shield. I, in turn, would get behind him and go in all the pretty lunch boxes, switching our Wonder Bread wrapped sandwiches for those that were packaged neatly in aluminum foil or those clear plastic sandwich bags. If they had real good snacks like Devil Dogs, Chocolate or the yellow Hostess Cupcakes with the white zigzag frosting cutting across the top, "they too was a-goner!" I'd also take everyone's 3-cent milk money.

No kids had milk that day if they left their money in those lunch bags or boxes by the fence. I made sure Kenny and I ate well every day. That was the Belim Boys come up every day. We never did put anyone down on our come up, not did we ever get caught. I admit, it was not the right thing to do to those kids, but in the long run it sure made my brother and I nice and full each lunch period. That was my only concern at that time. There were two people I would make sure I got daily. Ralph and Linda Monterio who lived in the building next to the store at the corner of Dale and Sherman Streets directly opposite where McDonald's now stands.

I thought Linda Monterio was the prettiest red girl in the world next to Paulette Biggs who lived next door to us on Sherman. Ms. Monterio was in my class and when Valentine's Day came I truly wanted her to be my special Valentine. Not knowing how to put those feelings into words, I took their goodies daily.

June 14th was a day of much excitement in our school and the entire community. It was officially known as Flag Day, a day our school celebrated the American Flag and the state flag. To know and truly appreciate the day's events, you surely had to have been raised up in Boston during the mid 1950s and early 1960s. All year the boys from the Drum and Bugle Corp. had practiced long and hard for that day. Like synchronized swimmers, those kids, my brother included, did their thing all in step. They all had on white shirts, black ties, and khaki pants with black shoes.

The program itself was always held outside in the large yard in front of the school's main entrance as students, faculty and families looked on as those kids marched and played to the "Stars and Stripes of the American Flag." They were real patriotic.

My brother was the sharpest dressed and played his bugle the best. Mothers and fathers and all those in attendance cheered along as the kids played and marched. I don't know whatever happened to those photographs from those events. School would be closing in a few days for summer vacation after Flag Day. We kids looked forward to that day because we knew there would be all types of games to be played in the large school yard daily.

A few of the teachers were part of the Summer School Yard Program. One such teacher had a twin sister who was also a teacher, and both had an exotic appearance. There was another very light complexioned teacher, Mrs. Douglas, who for some reason took a particular interest in my brother. I mean to the point she came to our house to speak with our parents about the possibility of my parents giving my brother to her. That lady almost got her ass kicked for just thinking my Mom would even consider that. I told Kenny I would have come and stolen him back and together we would run away back down South.

Those summer games in the schoolyard included Chinese checkers, Old Maid, Jacks, Marbles, Ball, Tag, and cigarettes. The girls would play many of those games with us, but their games were Double Dutch and Hop Scotch along with making things out of Gimp. The big event was the "showers" or "sprinklers." The school had a sprinkler system they would turn on so we could play in it like a swimming pool. The girls had on those one-piece great grandma bathing suits, and us boys had on swimming trunks.

This one girl named O-Lee from Savin Street was black as "Midnight's Brother." Her lips were like teacups, but she had huge breasts and a big butt. Many of the kids in grade 4-6 wanted a chance to rub up on her ass. One day she decided to change her bathing suit right out in the schoolyard by the steps in a corner. A couple of the girls agreed to hold up towels while she changed. Some of the guys got together, ran by them and snatched away the towel. That was my very first time seeing a naked female. I was like WOW-WOW-WOW !!! Years later, she wasn't bad to look at. One of my brother's friends, Rosco Thomas, used to go with her.

Does anyone of you know what overnight female piss smells like? Brother, it ain't nothing nice. It has a rather wild aroma to it, like tiger or monkey piss. Let me tell you about this sister I went to school with I'll call "Deborah." She was a tall knock-kneed "Olive Oyl" type, reddish-brown hair, with a nice matching complexion. Her only issue was her bad memory. She pissed in the night and forgot to stop by the bathroom before leaving her house for school. She had a read bad habit of moving about in an enclosed area like a classroom. Stale piss and warm air truly don't mix well. The teacher would pull her off to the side and send her downstairs with a note to Mrs. Logan, the school nurse. Mondays were her worst days. "It was weekend piss!"

One day back in 1979, I was on Massachusetts Avenue near New York Pizza, dressed sharp and smelling like Halston Z14. All of a sudden I heard this voice calling my full name out loud, "Charlie Belim!" Now, to my knowledge, only two types of people holler out a man's whole name in a crowded street at high noon, "the sheriff, or someone from your past." In this case, it wasn't the "Po-Po." As I turned in the direction of the voice, I immediately saw this tall, at least 6-foot, flaming red-haired statuesque sister standing wide-legged wearing a bright red leather mini skirt, stockings, and spike heels. I'm thinking *do I know this woman?* I'm searching her face but still drawing a total blank.

All of a sudden she reaches down, pulls up her skirt, exposing her black lace panties with a bright red heart just below her neatly trimmed hairline, and says, "I don't smell like day old piss now!" Instantly, it all came together exactly who this woman was. *"Deborah" from grade school,* I thought in disbelief. Several times I called to her as she abruptly walked off shaking those two "turd cutters." Several months later I ran into "Deborah" at Leviticus, a popular nightclub in New York City. Only this time she didn't pull up her skirt or walk off shaking her sexy ass at me. Over several drinks, I apologized for having been mean to her, as she put it, when we were in grade school. It's safe to say we parted without any bad feelings between us.

When you're young and growing up in "Anyhood," USA, you see many strange things. One day a group of us guys were on our way to do some thievery, so we decide to take a shortcut through someone's backyard. While we are trodding through this yard, we see this much younger child standing on a first floor back porch facing us. The kid was crying like a crazy person, and looked to be about four or five years old, still in diapers, a strange sight.

Looking closer at the kid I realized I was seeing something odd. I thought I was looking at a young girl, mind you, but then again I wasn't sure. There was something protruding from the child's stomach. I told everyone to look, I was so in awe at what I saw. A boy or girl, I thought to myself. Please understand I had, up to that point, never seen a person with their navel protruding out from their stomach like that. So, naturally, I thought it was a dick.

After seeing several other kids, boys and girls, throughout the hood like that, I went to my Mom for an explanation. I wondered why Kenny and I didn't look like those other kids. Mom's response was, those children's parents didn't place a "Bow dollar" (silver dollar) over their child's navel with tape over it to hold it in place after birth. No doubt, there are plenty of males and females in the age range of 50 to 60 years old walking around Boston to this very day like that, because their moms didn't use that damn Bow dollar on their poor babies. Damn shame!

The other strange thing I saw was all these boys wearing stocking caps all day, even in school. I noticed how the teachers wouldn't get too close to these boys when they spoke with them. So, this time, Kenny and I went to our father for an answer. Pop used words like germs, bad hygiene and dirt to explain. Those kids had ringworm, simply put. He made sure our heads were washed, greased and cut. He would take us to Mr. Mitchell's Shop on Warren Street near Haines Park, across from Woodbine Street. We got our hair cut every week. That's the ritual I follow to this very day, even under incarceration, as I am in federal custody right now. We may have been short on cash, but never on being properly groomed.

When we were kids Roxbury had no real YMCA of its own. We had this tiny little office on Warren Street; that was the real "Y." It was right off the corner of Moreland and Warren Streets by the Warren Statue. Today, that space is occupied by a much-needed group in my old community, Narcotics Anonymous. The Muslim brother who sometimes chairs the NA meetings there is Brother Earl Keys. He and I and the rest of his sisters and brothers grew up together in the building at 60 Sherman Street. My mom and his mother, Grace Keys, were friends right up until her untimely death at a young age from cancer.

Back when I was young it was considered important for parents to know who their children were associating with, especially when it came to boys and girls and "courtship." So, it wasn't at all strange when young Amanda Houston's parents showed up at our home to meet my parents and ask if it was okay with my parents if Kenny could accompany their daughter to the neighborhood movie theatre on Warren Street.

Both kids were honor roll classmates who had a crush on each other. Naturally, their movie debut would be chaperoned. As for me being on the honor roll, not at all likely. Far too many surgeries, eye patches, and last but not least those Tin Man suits and half body casts. Me getting A's and B's was passé. Years later I would also meet a young female whose mother had the exact same values as Ms. Houston's family.

ॐ

Chapter 10 ~ Acting Grown and Selling Kool-Aid

My first try at "getting some" was a total disaster, plus I seriously think I got tricked! I had a serious crush on this girl named Denise R. She too wore glasses, so you know she was called a "cock-eyed female MF." Cock-eyed MF-ers seem to have a strong gravitational pull toward one another. She and I had made plans to sneak down this dark cellar across from her house, but first I had to let her brother ride my bike while we were in the cellar.

The closest I got to "getting some" was a damn sloppy kiss and a half ass feel on her flat paper thin chest, plus our glasses kept scratching together each time we attempted to kiss. Next thing I know her big nappy-headed brother is calling her name near the cellar door entrance. She gets scared and runs up the cellar steps leaving my ass in the cellar.

Years later I saw her down in the Zone, "the Combat Zone", as in La Graine Street. That was a notorious hoe stroll up to the mid 1970's in Boston, Massachusetts. When I saw her and called her name, she turned, realized who I was, and ran off. I really had to laugh at that. La Grain Street was live and jumping with hoes and tricks that particular day.

My first business venture was a Kool-Aid stand my brother and I made out of milk crates stacked on top of each other. We opened business directly in front of our building on 60 Sherman Street. I must have been no more than seven years old. We sold 5-cent and 10-cent cups of grape, orange and lime Kool-Aid. We did that so we would have our own money to spend on rides at Revere Beach. That July 4th was our day for Revere Beach. My entire family went, even my Aunt.

Everyone around our area supported that Kool-Aid stand. There was a group of guys in my neighborhood in their late twenties-early thirties who used to buy our Kool-Aid daily. They would say things like, "kid, this shit is real sweet," and "dope fiend sweet like we like it." At that time we had no knowledge of what "dope fiend sweet" was or meant. Not until one day we overheard that the two nice older guys had OD-ed (overdosed) on heroin.

Earlier that day, Bo-Peep and George Kelly had purchased two 10-cent cups along with a friend. Bo-Peep lived, and the others died. It's safe to say, on that day, we found out exactly what "dope fiend sweet" meant, as well as "OD-ing." At first we thought we killed them with the too-sweet Kool-Aid. We felt so bad, we shut down our stand and didn't drink Kool-Aid for years.

My next big job and my favorite to this day wasn't a job per se, but rather the effects of the whole environment itself. It affected a character change in this man that would shape and reshape his mind and actions for years to come. Those effects are felt now, even as I write this book. Now, as I sit in this jail cell awaiting my fate in US District Court in the Southern District of Maryland at Greenbelt, I know a positive change has emerged within this man, myself. Allah (God) truly does answer prayers.

ॐ

Chapter 11 ~ The North End ... and My Hood

The summer of my tenth birthday, I got the chance through a family friend named JB to work in a shine parlor in the notorious North End of Boston. Talk about being excited, I was light years beyond excitement. My Great-Grandparents had put some fear in the heart of Kenny about whites that would change in a few years. I had no such fears.

To get an opportunity to get out of Roxbury was like taking the A Train Express to heaven. Providence had Raymond Petrearcka, Sr. and Boston had the Five Angulou Brothers, the most noted was Jerry Angulou, Jerry being the patriarch. Although in certain circles, Raymond Senior was considered the head of the whole New England Mob at one point. In years to come, I would come to meet Raymond's son Junior and his crew in Federal Prison.

Many Blacks who hung out in a joint in my old hood called "Packie's" on Blue Hill Avenue would really be surprised if they knew who truly owned Packie's. Many things in life are only a façade for something else. The same can be said for people as well.

I was actually shocked my parents allowed me to venture that far from the neighborhood back then and at the age I was. I was happy they did, even now when I think about it.

The owner of the Shoe Shine Parlor was Italian. We will call him "Tony S." Back in the early 1960's all those Italians walked loud and puffed on big fat cigars. Every other word that came out of his mouth was a curse word. When we met, he introduced himself by extending his right hand. Pop had already schooled us that men always introduced themselves that way as they look you directly in the eye. Dad always said, "Never be fearful to look a man straight on."

Many times in life Dad would say, "You only get just one opportunity to impress." He had a saying called "talking without actually saying a word to the other person." The eyes and body language tell much about a person and their character.

After Tony and I went through the introductions, he told me he owned the bakery that stood across the street from the shine parlor on Hanover Street in the North End. I already knew how to shine by doing Pop's dress shoes and our church shoes. So when I was questioned I knew how to respond.

The next question was, did I know anything about the policy game. I almost yelled out "YES" because my Dad played daily. He asked where in Roxbury, when I said where, he just smiled to JB and his friend. Dad and many of his friends played the policy game; "the numbers" as we call them in NY even now. His pet number became 2155 and I still carry it myself. Today, it has been upgraded to a more respectable level and the name has been changed, not to protect the innocent, but the guilty. Now squares can play and not feel guilty? Bullshit. We are guilty of breaking the law one way or the other.

My job was to shine and look out for the Po-Po, the police. If they came and I saw them, I was to say, here comes Patty, reason being simple. They took bets over the three phones in the backroom of the shine parlor. They did sports, pros and college basketball, football, baseball, hockey, the dogs, the horses and the numbers. It was a real good trade off. I got to keep all the shine money on Fridays. I got to take home a big bag of fresh baked bread, and a bag of all types of meats, fresh, too. You know, we had ham in the bag, too.

I knew nothing of Islam back then, nor of the word swine or what it meant. I just know we ate like kings during that summer. All my customers paid a buck a shine, some even two bucks. At least, once a week some guy would win big and I would get a "fin" -- five bucks just because they felt good.

I was never once called out by name by anyone. Never called boy, spook or nigga. Always only just Charlie, or the kid, because that was who, and what, I was – a kid shining shoes in a shine parlor in the North End of Boston.

One day I was on my way home, going to North Station to get the Orange line, less than a half a block ahead of me is a group of boys about fir or six of them, all teenagers. Slicked back shiny black hair, Banlon knit sweaters half open showing those white wife beater T-shirts. I knew I couldn't outrun them all due to their size and numbers, so I kept on ahead.

When I reached them, no one moved aside at first; one kid about seventeen says, "You know, you're the first one to come down here, so you'd better watch out!" Sure, I was a bit "shook" (scared), but I had to hold it together; showing real fear might have caused them to rob my ass, taking my $20 in shine money which was in my shoes. I would have fought for that money, bread and meat Mr. Tony had given me.

Next day at work, Mr. Tony sends for me to come to the bakery. As I entered, he says, "Let's talk, Charlie. What happened yesterday on your way to North Station?" I told him about the boys stopping me, and what was said. He said, "You are safe down here, and no one will ever bother you again." And no one did. Then he went on to tell me something that has stuck with me for almost fifty years. "Charlie, remember this. Many times a man is much safer in a neighborhood where he looks different than the people in it. When you look like everyone else, it is a lot easier for someone to harm you because your guard is down. Never forget that Charlie."

Mr. Tony's favorite subject was loyalty and honor amongst men, and love of family. Without ever knowing or realizing it, Tony was preparing me for my induction into the streets. A few weeks later his spot got hit right after I left for home one Friday in late August. When I came to work the next day, he sat me down in the back office of the bakery and told me what had happened the day before after I had left for home.

He looked at me real hard in the face and said, "Charlie, I hope you learned a few good things from myself and all the men you met down here, things that will help shape you into being a man." He gave me an envelope, a big bag of bread and meats. I was to come see him to let him know how I was doing as time passed.

I went to see my old boss three times; once at age 14, once in 1972 and finally in 2000. At my last visit, he looked at me like he did that day we parted, and said, "I can see that both of your feet are now firmly planted in the street, my young friend. Be careful of the traffic." I never went back. However, in November of 2007 while in Boston, I heard he was very sick. I was busted on November 28, 2007 in New York.

Back in my own neighborhood there was an area known as North Hampton Street Station. A person could get a train or bus going in many different directions in the city. I was hungry for more excitement. So, I went to see Dad to ask if I could start shining shoes down North Hampton. His response was "Yes!" Mom's response was far different. She didn't want me down there. She and Dad came to an agreement. If Kenny went, I could go. It was a done deal. I found out that real shine boys didn't buy ready made shine boxes from any store, no! They built theirs. So, we set out to do just that.

We had to find the right wood needed. Once we found the wood, we went to Mr. Jonesy's store and record shop, who not only sold the latest 45's, but damn near whatever else a person might need to buy, nails, wood stain, sandpaper. Jones was located on Humboldt Avenue between Bower and Monroe Streets.

Kenny was real good at making things with wood and sheet metal. Me, I knew what we needed and where to get it at, even if it meant a bit of pilfering now and then. I was a true team player at a young age. I helped sand wood, stain it, saw wood when it was needed. Our project was a team effort by two brothers working for a common goal.

The project took us a whole week to complete. Kenny put latches on our boxes. Yes, we swung "stole" the tiny hooks from Ashmont supply when it was still on Blue Hill Avenue near Creston Street.

Upon completion, to celebrate, Kenny and I turned our piggy banks upside down and shook out a dollar in change from each one. We walked over to Blue Hill Avenue to a place called "Little Kitchen." It was a tiny hole in the wall Chinese joint next to the drugstore at the corner of Blue Hill Avenue and Quincy Street. They sold some of the best and greatest French fries in the town. The prices were 10-cents, 25-cents and 50-cents. You could get fries, Nee-High soda, along with an egg roll, all out of a dollar, and still have change left over for penny candy at "Blind Man Joe's" or the Arabian Market at the corner of Bower and Warren Streets. The owner and the "Sadberry family" were the first Muslims I knew at that point in my life.

Since Little Kitchen, Roxbury has only had one Chinese fast food joint. Since then, it was opposite Nubian Nation's on Warren Street. And please don't even consider Simmon's either. Simmon's is a fish market that sells cooked fish and chicken livers and gizzards to poor black folks in Orchard Gardens and dope fiends and alcoholics. They also sell Rot-Gut-Beer and wine, etc. The biggest hustle is the dreams they sell to the poor and downtrodden, by way of these BS one and two dollar scratch-off tickets, along with the state lottery game. All they are doing is taking that money out of Roxbury.

The people of Roxbury have never benefited in any way from Simmon's but misery and death from that "Rot-Gut Liquor and fried food!" Aside from that, those people come from Vietnam, not China." Those Black Bourgeoisie's elected officials of Roxbury, etc. should shut that eyesore down or at least make them give something tangible back to the community besides a dream with a bad ulcer and a hangover.

Blacks will never be allowed to go into any Asian Community in America and start selling them folks no "Egg Fu Yung, Egg Drop soup, cocaine and heroin. But we welcome them with open arms when they come into our communities selling us false hopes of instant windfall, lottery or scratch off tickets, cheap liquor, and unhealthy foods. Dope is poison, and poison can come in many forms. Wake up, Black folks!

Now that our shine boxes had been completed, it was almost time to become Shoe Shine Enterprisers. However, one main ingredient was still missing, and that was our supplies. You can't run a business without supplies. The most cost efficient way for us to acquire our inventory was to pilfer it. Going to Mr. Jonesy's store was out of the question. Rumor had it he shot a kid in the ass for stealing Red Penny Money Candy. As for his partner, Jonsey hit him in the head with the butt of his Nickel-plated Colt 45 just because he was with the other kid. Our options were really few.

Decco Supply was another possibility. It sold cheap beauty supplies to the poor black folks of Roxbury. The store sold everything for young up and coming shine entrepreneurs. It was located in the heart of the black ghetto shopping area near Blair's Food Market on Washington Street. Being a black managed store in the hood, you know every pair of roving and shifty hands were closely scrutinized by store personnel. After Kenny and I had checked out a few more stores, Blair's included, around the Dudley Station area, we started walking down Washington Street in the direction of North Hampton Transit Station.

Nearing Lennox Street, I suddenly remembered this really nice men's shoe store that sold Saratoga Stetson shoes, the ones with the white stitching. Every time I'd pass that store I would stand in front of the window, eyes tightly closed to the point I could actually see myself all grown up and wearing a pair of them "tan Saratoga's with the white stitching."

Two doors from the shoe store was a smaller version of Decco Supply. They also sold that "hoochie mama" hair kit product along with Jay Bar in the blue jar, a lye product used by brothers who was into taking a short cut to getting a process.

The store was at the corner of Lexon and Washington Streets, and around the corner was an old industrial laundry near the corner of Lexon and Shawmut Avenue. That store sold everything we needed for our shine venture to get started.

It took us three trips of thievery to get all our supplies, but we did it. Two black and brown horsehair brushes, one soft, one hard, black and brown sole dressing, saddle soap for cleaning shoes with stitching, black and brown shoe cleaner, and two secret tricks. One was used to clean off the salt from snow or water. It was a tall Alka Seltzer bottle full of water and baking soda. Next, a jar each of "seven day deodorant pads" for a spit shine. And the best quality shine rags we could steal. On our last trip, I think Kenny paid for the polish.

Not knowing exactly what to charge for a good shine, we decided to go down North Hampton the next day, minus our boxes, to see things and who was down there. First thing we learned, "if you had a ready made box" you got run off by the whole group. You'd have to work downtown by the bus station, etc. or even worse, at the Hill Bill Ranch Bar by Trailways Bus station.

The second thing Kenny and I learned on that first day down North Hampton was how things worked when it came to customers and shine boys. Taking, or even making an attempt to take, another shine boy's customer was not tolerated by the shine crew as a whole. Just like in the hand-to-hand dope game that's played out daily on any street, etc. in the USA. Taking a man's customer could, and in most cases would, cause a beef.

Being strong, or at least being willing to fight to hold down your spot on the block, was a must, no exceptions. For those, however, who couldn't hold down their spot on the wall, they got shook for their shine box and loot, in addition to being run off and never allowed to return.

Our spot on the block, as we called it, was actually the gray brick wall beneath the large flashing neon sign that flashed the words "Shanty's Lounge." Shine prices varied, regular shines were 25-cents, 50-cents for spit shines, 75-cents if we used shoe cleaner. Now, a one-dollar to a two-dollar shine got your shoes cleaned, polished (shined) and sole dressing added.

That very next Saturday, Kenny and I went back down North Hampton before noon with our handmade shine boxes. I made sure we had our butcher's knives, "one from our house and one from my Aunt's knife drawer." I really wanted us to have two each, but Kenny said "No" to my suggestion.

During my entire time shining shoes down North Hampton, I only had to use my knife once, and that was to scare off "Wild Man Steve's" fat ass bully son. Wild Man Steve was once a popular black radio DJ for a black radio station, the only black radio station in the city of Boston during the 1960's, called W.I.L.D. A.M. Allow me please to give you a window view of North Hampton Street.

ଔ

Chapter 12 ~ North Hampton

North Hampton and Washington Street was the pulse of the community in terms of a person letting their hair down, so to speak. Even now, I can close my eyes and see and hear the hustle and bustle of the people as they moved in and out of the many bars along that strip of Washington Street. Men rushing quickly to get up those rickety steps to Baby Tiger's Gym above Shanty's Lounge to place a bet on their favorite horse or lucky number.

Looking directly across from Shanty's, the Dudley bound bus would be just pulling in under the elevated train tracks, high above in the air. People rushing off one bus to transfer to yet another bus to take them home to south Boston, D Street Projects and Old Colony, home to many of the cities' poor white, Blacks and many others in route to Columbia Point, which sits on tops of the old city dump.

Today, the word "dump" has been changed to "landfill." I wonder why? Poverty is colorblind, but people are not. Perhaps, now that we have a multicolored and multi-ethnic person waiting to step up to the helm come January 20th, 2009, I pray the new changing of the guard will cause many perceptions about black and white to change, but who knows.

Perhaps, now the tilted-up-end of the Playing Field will now even itself out. May Allah continue to bless Mr. Barack Obama.

As I continue my reflection, I can see myself as I search through the maze of the crowd with my eyes. I quickly see the familiar smile on my brother's face as he steps away from Joe Nemo's hotdog and coffee joint to enter the street with our hotdogs and sodas along with chips in a box.

Next to Dirt John's hotdog joint downtown, Joe Nemo had the second best dogs in the city. At the intersection of North Hampton and Washington Streets four bars sat, plus Folsom's Market. On one corner you had Big Jim Shanty's, two doors down from where there was Mullan's Café. They had a mixed working class of Blacks and Whites.

Directly across the street was the then famous Louie's Lounge. On the east corner was the Eastside Tavern, another racially mixed spot as well as the large bar at the corner of South Hampton and Harrison Avenue. Directly opposite the Harrison Avenue Pharmacy stood Blanchard's Liquor. Jack's Men's Shop was in between Mullan's Café and Baby Tiger's Gym. Jack's was still standing a few years back.

On the Eastside of Washington Street, right next to the Eastside Tavern, was Jack Shepard's Record Shop. Down the block from Jack was Skippy White's Record Shop. Word was Skippy's family had a big bank but due to his passion for that forbidden fruit called "dark meat," you know, jungle fever, fried chicken, jungle music, the family cut him off financially. With all those temptations, a white man's resistance is bound to get weak. He still maintained a thriving business in Central Square, Cambridge, MA. Also, he's big in Gospel Music and has a Gospel Show on Sunday mornings on W.I.L.D. radio. Still dipping into that forbidden fruit basket, it is said.

Next to Skippy's first shop on Washington Street at the end of a dead-end alley was the 1824 Lounge and Basin Street South "the mob joint" was a few blocks down the street. Also along that strip were a couple of bucket-of-blood spots. Even though we had our butcher knives in our boxes, we knew it might be a death play going in or coming out of one of those bucket-of-blood spots.

Man, them people hated kids as bad as WC Fields did. A shine boy might get robbed by anyone of them cut-face Negroes from Jackson or Meridian, Mississippi if they disliked the shine. Spitting on their shoes for spit shine purposes got you robbed for sure, and a size 12 shoe in the crack of your ass on the way out the door.

Kenny and I always had our hand on our knives going by those spots. All the men and women had the "red eyes" from drinking too much. One of the joints was Don's Den, and another bar was The Party Café (not the one on Warren Street near Nubian Motions, although Tucker owned both places). The original was on North Hampton Street between Washington and Shawmut Avenue. The music was real southern "Rufus Thomas, BB King, Alert King, Ike and Tina, Joe Tex, etc. Not knowing any better, we called it "homie music" as kids. We even called those who listened to it "homies." You see, that Bostonian nonsense had got on my shoes a bit also.

That spot was a wild and funny place. Just ask people from age 55 and up who used to live in the area. Many of the women and men who hung out there had them nasty razor cuts on their faces as well as on their necks. The women wore some real short tight Go-Go skirts, white Hoe boots.

Why do dark sisters like them wild colors like Fire Truck Red, Canary Yellow and Bright Orange? You know, my sister had on her fishnet stockings with the black line up the back, four (4) pairs for $2.99 on sale at Dutton's, and last but not least, a ten-dollar wig from Wigs and Things.

My brothers had on them skin tight bell bottoms or high water double knit polyester pants with the cowboy slash pockets, red shirt and long pointy-toed shoes, and a hairdo half fried with a hot comb or a jar of Jabar Hair Relaxer.

The next spot was the Sheik Lounge. It was straight Alabama-Georgia-Mississippi-Florida. The doors swung just like those on a saloon from a cowboy movie. The people who managed the place got tired of mopping up blood, so sawdust was used on the floor throughout the place, easier to clean. It was located on Tremount Street up by Station # 10, the Po-Po house. The Rainbow Lounge wasn't as deadly. It was also located on Tremount. During those days, the old Tremount Trolley cars used to ride by the Rainbow, then turn into a lot-like yard near Estelle's Lounge. They were actually called Street Cars. You could see them along Warren Street, Blue Hill and Humboldt Avenues.

Mom and Aunt Sue used to hang out at the Rainbow Lounge when I was a young kid. During this time period, it wasn't uncommon to see Black Sailors moving throughout my community of Roxbury. This was due, in part, to the Quincy Ship Yard and Charlestown Navy Yard.

When it came time for socializing, those Black swabbies in their Navy dress blues could be seen in all the local Black bars along Washington and Tremount Streets. Many young Black women in the early 1950s and 60s managed to marry many of those young sailors who frequented those Black clubs. "Aunt" Sue was one of the young fortunate Black sisters to marry one such brother in uniform named Frank back in the early 1950s.

Frank was like many other brothers back then, "sharp and debonair in his Navy dress blues." That debonair look not only caught the attention of Aunt Sue, but also a certain sister named "Ann" and the inevitable happened. "Frank and Ann" became intimate. Intimate to the point that Ann became pregnant by Ol' Frank. Ann soon gave birth to a son by Frank.

I would come to know Ann and Frank's son well, along with his sister Patricia. Naturally, tension and tempers would rise high whenever those two women would encounter each other in one of the neighborhood watering holes.

On one such occasion, Aunt Sue and Mom had had two drinks over their limit when out of nowhere, up pops Ann at the Rainbow Lounge. Words are exchanged between Sue and Ann. Sue being a down home Georgia girl like Earline, it was not unusual for her to have her own "Blue Steel Single Edge Razor Blade," wrapped with tape on the safety end, neatly tucked in her bosom.

Alcohol and a bad attitude has sent many a damn fool to two places -- "the penitentiary and Mt. Hope Cemetery." Blue Steel missed its intended mark – Ann's jugular vein, but not the side of her face. Somehow, Blue Steel was never found by the Po-Po, nor was any of Ann's blood found on Sue or Earline. That took place well over fifty years ago. That whole crew are all deceased, Ms. Ann, Aunt Sue, Laura, Vivian, and my dear mother as well.

Each time Kenny or I would have a customer in Louie's Lounge, this short, brown complexioned woman who waited tables would speak to us. Sometimes she'd even slip us a buck or two from her tips. After telling our parents about her, we found out she was married to my Dad's first cousin "Sonny Lovelace, Sr."

Sonny Lovelace, Sr. and Dad were two sisters' kids. Sonny used to come visit us all the time on Sherman Street. Sonny died a few months prior to my Dad's death. Sonny has a son who is also named Sonny Lovelace. In the street, it is said that he was once a pimp. His claim to fame was when Diana Ross and The Supremes first came to Boston and did their show at Basis Street South. I know that to be a fact because I used to walk by the club and I remember the lights and the advertisement in the window of the club.

Sonny Jr. was a regular at the club. He got an opportunity to get down on Ms. Ross. She was young and naïve to the point that he charged her for being all up in his face. That pimp talk, it's rumored that she gave him some money. "I guess she enjoyed his conversation."

To this day, I've never met Sonny, Jr. personally, even though we moved in the same circles, somewhat, years later. Perhaps time and circumstances will not rob us of the opportunity of finally meeting. Perhaps he has old photos, along with stories of our fathers that he might care to share with his cousin.

Kenny and I usually made between fifteen to twenty dollars each on good days. I really didn't care about making shine money. I was in total awe of the different characters we saw and met. On slow days, all the guys would pick up their shine boxes and go over to Jack Sheppard's Record Shop to listen to the latest sounds coming out of Motown. One of the hot new artists was a kid our age they called "Stevie Wonder," and he was blind. His first hit was recorded live. It was titled "Fingertips, Part I and II."

Another popular tune was "The Twist" by Chubby Checker. Some say Hank Blard recorded it first, but who knows. There was even a dance called The Twist. He had all them prissy white teenage girls shaking their posteriors. American Bandstand was coming out of Philadelphia back then. A movie was made called "Twist Around the Clock."

Whenever Jack saw us kids coming, he knew our business was down. So he would immediately put one of his huge speakers outside his shop so we could listen and try out some steps. Like I said, he was our age (Stevie Wonder). Someone we could really respect, plus he could sing really well. All the young girls loved Stevie Wonder. People were going around saying he was Ray Charles's son. It seemed possible to us, what did we really know about Little Stevie Wonder at that point?

One day while things were a bit slow, a bunch of us had gathered outside Jack's shop. Jack did his usual with the speaker and put on one of James Brown's records for us. All of a sudden, this kid comes up dressed nice, hair processed, perhaps a year or two older than us, not more than that. He introduces himself as Junior Barrett from Lenox Street Projects. Someone in the crowd said they heard of that name and asked, "Do you dance?" His reply was, "Yes. Yes, I do dance!" We asked Jack to play Fingertips, Part I and II. Boy, could he dance. He did all the James Brown splits and some stuff we had never seen before.

As a crowd began to gather, people began to throw loose change. Some even put down a dollar. Others got shines and some even bought a record or two from Jack. All of us shine boys were in total awe of this kid called Junior Barrett. One day while he and Kenny were in Joe Nemo's, he said his real name was Douglas Barrett and he dreamed of becoming a famous dancer like Sammy Davis Jr. or the famous Mills Brothers. Sammy used to be in Boston quite a bit back in the late 1950s early 1960s.

Barrett wasn't the only kid I knew who aspired to be a great entertainer. Phillip "Silvertooth" Gibson who lived in building 250 on Ruggles Street in the Mission Hill Projects could sing and dance. He moved to the West coast back in 1969 or 1970. We never heard anything on him after that. Then there were my two schoolmates, "Gilbert White and Larry Woo."

The most colorful brother who I came up around who also aspired to be a great entertainer was Charlie "Satin-top" Johnson. His family also came from OP as my family did during my mid teens and early twenties. Bobby Brown's family also came from the bricks (OP). Charlie "Satin-

63

top" Johnson, deceased, was cut down by a crazed out of his mind young brother in Dudley Station, winter 2003.

Guns are truly dangerous in the hands of a fool. Charlie, and some other guys his age, formed a dance group. They also had dreams of fame and fortune. The group called themselves "The Shufflers," to the best of my recollection. The members are as follows: Charlie, Clyde Bacon, Lamount Brewer. If I've left anyone out, I apologize and stand to be corrected at a later date. Those brothers could dance. I mean for real. I've seen Charlie and Clyde in action. Charlie was the most colorful of the trio.

Charlie could also dress along with some other brothers like Reggie Budd, June Mitchell, Butchie Brown, Gus Smalls, Frankie Clarke, Harry Collins, Mitchell Davis. Those brothers would have made them GQ Boys sit down and take serious notes. Those brothers were truly a class act to see. Especially Charlie Johnson. Big knives weren't the only things we shined, boys carried in our boxes, we also carried "Whisk brooms." If and when we could trick a drunk guy into getting a shoe shine.

Myself and Kenny, or whoever was doing the shining, would pull out our whisk broom. That was the unspoken signal for everyone to gather around the guy. If it was my shine, I'd start brushing him off with my whisk broom in front, then Kenny would ease up in front. I'd get behind him and together we would brush him down, while I would be slipping my small hand in his pocket, front first) to get a few bills.

Many times the guy would bust us and we would have to run, yet many times we got away with his money. The most we ever got at once was a hundred dollars and that's because I "whole hogged it," meaning I stuck my whole hand in the pocket. Man, I had a death grip on that money, and came up with it all. The money slipped out of my grip just as I was breaking it off, because he turned.

A pack of bills hit the ground. Kenny grabbed it and started to run. So did I, leaving our boxes behind. Victor White and Lester Mayo were also with us when we ran. Victor gave me his big knife and Kenny and I went back to get our boxes. He was so damn drunk he didn't know who we were. In years to come I would put up my "whisk broom, and really master the Pickpocket Game."

Down North Hampton we always had to be on the lookout for "Black Stewart," the cop from Station #4 in the South End. He was known as a mean Black Police. Rumor has it he locked up his own mother. He knew we Shine Boys were playing the "Shake Game," as we learned to call it back then. Stewart would kick you in your ass and throw your damn Shine Box in the street if he caught you doing wrong. Everyone down there knew him. Big Jim the Winter Hill Crew who ran "Basin Street South" all gave his black ass a few kibbles and bits to keep his damn mouth shut. So, why press us kids?

Many of the socially acceptable from my community could be seen on any Friday or Saturday night slipping in and out the side entrance of Louie's Lounge on North Hampton Street, not wanting to be seen. Talk about being hypocritical. Also, word was Stewart used to have rank in the department and got busted down from riding in the police car with the white boys to being a "Buck-Private-beat-cop." I guess if I was a lame like him, I'd be frustrated to the point I'd be kicking little rug-rat kids in the ass, too.

The same ones who'd slip in the side entrance at Louie's Lounge come Sunday, their Lord's day, how easily they'd slide into those cushioned seats at all those well established churches throughout Roxbury, Dorchester, and the South End, tapping their feet and acting as if they were so self-righteous and above reproach. Those were a lot of the types who slipped in and out the side door of Louie's Lounge, too fearful to walk in through the front door. I once heard a man say, "A coward dies a thousand deaths, a man dies only once."

Perhaps now that this great country has elected its first African-American president, hopefully those who have chosen to die a thousand deaths will now find the courage to claw through those self-imposed graves of fear and ignorance and live and enjoy themselves. Louie's Lounge not only had live bands doing shows in the back. For adults, the management came up with the concept "Sunday Afternoon Coke Sips" for the under twenty-one set. The idea was to teach pre-adults good social skills in a semi-adult setting. No alcoholic beverages were served or allowed at those Sunday afternoon events. Still, I'm sure many of them young sisters had their purses stuffed with a small brown bag of spirits.

Because of our youth, we could just daydream about being there. We went down to see the fly-brothers in their fly outfits and processed hairstyles and gawk at the pretty sisters.

Long before "Mop City Barber Shop" came along, the shop for young and up and coming pimps to get their hair done (processed) was Playboy's Barber Shop on Washington Street, across from Kornfield's Pharmacy, or "Buster's Barber Shop" at the corner of Stanwood Street and Blue Hill Avenue. The best barber Buster had was Tony Briggs. I knew of the two guys who used to wash our heads in Playboy's. "Black Bumbo" from Lennox Street Projects and "Big Socks." And even Billy Bo. For my money, "La Car" was the best barber at Playboy's.

Terry Yancy, who used to go to Reverend Adam's storefront church with us on Shawmut, had a brother who did, or attempted, a little pimping, used to be at Playboy's. At one point, Yancy became a Bail Bondsman for Jimmy Gilford, who also owned a barbershop by that same name on Tremont Street. Back in the day, Yancy had bailed out my man "Fat Eddie Newsom." Word is Eddie jumped the bond (didn't go to court) and Yancy tried to collect the money. Bad idea -- and bad decision for Brother Yancy. No blood was ever shed. Eddie just thought the brother should be keenly aware that he, Eddie, was playing for keeps. A man must always know his limitations. I think brother Yancy realized his after that confrontation it's fair to say.

Black entertainers who came to town during the 1950s and 60s who needed their hair done usually went to Mr. Gilford's or the New Frontier Shop that was around the corner from Shanty's on North Hampton Street. That shop is still in existence in the South End. One day I was coming out a store near it and noticed the name on the sign. So I went in and kicked it with the owner. It was the daughter of the original owner. Nice looking sister about my age, too old for me, though.

"Basin Street South" was another place that held Sunday Coke Sips back then. Junior Barrett could be seen sitting up in there even though he wasn't legal yet. The joint was a mob owned spot, and we all knew it. A few years down the line, some of those same men Barrett was sitting drinking with would come to play an intricate part in his death. It's all a matter of common knowledge to date, but for many years, the Barrett family never truly had closure on Douglas Barrett, Jr.'s death. Not until a turncoat informant went bad in 2003 in a federal case.

Let me be very clear now, please. It is not my intention of kicking mud on anyone who I may speak of. Nor would I ever put anyone in harms way. I am simply telling my story through the eyes that Allah gave me.

Many names have been, and will be, changed, not to protect the innocent, but to shield the not so innocent among us. As for the dead, they should never be forgotten. They are part of our past. Yes, I still owe an allegiance – loyalty, if you will -- to the "underworld" that helped shape me into the man and Muslim that I am today.

Although, my biological Dad wasn't my brother Kenny's biological father, you couldn't tell them that. My brother was far more close to Pop than he was to our mother. Much had to do with those years Kenny spent in Manchester, Georgia.

We as humans are emotionally and physically capable of many exciting things. Yet, when it comes to changing the past or the last moment that just passed, we are in total awe, because it's an impossibility. So, how does a mother replace, or replant, herself in the life of her child? Yesterday is gone, today is undoubtedly only the now, and tomorrow has still yet to come. The reasons behind the decisions she made are gone forever. Today is all we have.

Kenny and Mom never quite learned how to just live in the now moment with one another. To him, Great-Grandma was Mom, and Mom was "Sis" -- Mom-the-stranger. When she would be whipping him it was like she really wanted to harm him. To add insult to injury, many times he'd show no emotion, no tears whatsoever.

Many women, only generally speaking, mind you, take many feelings of frustration, hurt, anger, betrayal, their sense of low or no self worth, out on that male child, who looks so much like the man who walked out. That is not to say there is ever justification for abandonment. I mean, how do you one day say to your wife, *"Hey, Honey, I got the claps (gonorrhea) and you gave it to me."* But, you know, it's all bull. Okay, so you want out. But, Brother Man, not like that! Not once did you reach out to your son.

Not William Gibb's son, David Belim's son. You have a grandson and a granddaughter as well as three great-grandchildren. I pray to Allah that you're not deceased and still living in Florida, Tallahassee, or Pennsicola, and that one of your family members confronts you on what you did to my mother and your son. They may no longer be with us, but their memories live on in the hearts and minds of those they left behind who also carry the Belim name.

Most of the shine boys we knew got the opportunity to stay out late enough to work the "Big M" or "Wally's" on Massachusetts Avenue. Those two bars had a long history. One was known for being a pimp and ho's haven where whores sat at one side of the bar, scantily clothed in prostitute attire, while tricks gawked and licked their lips. The other bar was known for good jazz played by local jazz bands, as well as those that came from other cities just to play at Wally's on Mass. Avenue. We shine boys knew about the stories of how some shine boys actually got five dollars and up to ten dollars just for wiping a clean shine rag across the toe of a pimp's shoe.

Rumor had it that some in-town shine boy once got a brand new crisp twenty dollar bill for shining a whore's red ho boots. Pimps like Wilbur K. Skippy House, Foots, Big Lee, Nate Robinson, Billy Poison, Lance and his pimp partner "Touch," who was white," and can't forget my good friend Clark Ross out of Seattle, Washington who had a fetish for exotic women and exotic cars. "Stutz Black Hawk" and the "Stutz Bear Cat." The Four-Eleven Lounge and Frankie O'Day's were two other late nightspots we shine boys wanted to hustle at night. Upon becoming a young adult, I would finally claim my rightfully earned seat at many of those same bars while enjoying Remy Martin VSOP.

Many would come and go in the years yet to come. But, none but two would be truly able to carry the torch of the past when it came to charging a whore. One of those pimps, perhaps "Macks" better describes them, is an old schoolmate of mine who came off Wyoming Street. His name is "Chapman." As of the Summer of 2008, he was down for his in Vegas. I got real cool with a young fly pimp while awaiting federal transfer from New York to Maryland. He had been in the recent company of both men. The other Brother I only knew from a distance. His name is "Comfort." They met on South Beach in Florida.

Some Saturdays, when business was slow, our crew would slip into the train station at North Hampton and ride two stops to the Famous Combat Zone to have pizza and sodas at the King of Pizza. We'd hustle down there 'til it was time to go home.

When I was a kid and up to my early twenties, that part of downtown was known as the "Combat Zone," a red light district for real. I believe it was the first publicized red light district outside of Vegas. If a kid could stay out until ten or eleven pm, he could get fifty dollars, easy. Still, I loved North Hampton. You'd see guys like Whitey Bulger, the Rifle Man Fleming, and Frank "Cadillac" Salemme.

Many friendships were made at that four-corner intersection of Washington and North Hampton Street. In the early morning hours you could find hustlers eating breakfast at Bickford's on Massachusetts Avenue, near "Cye Stacy's" clothing store for men. The other slick store was "Sandy's" on Columbus Avenue. Those stores died simultaneously along with Martin L. King on April 4th, 1968. Part of America died that night, as well.

Working as a shine boy in the Old North End and down in the hood would directly and indirectly expose me to things far beyond my imagination. Those experiences have shaped and reshaped my way of thinking beyond belief. The people I met from the North End down to those on the Four Corners of Washington and North Hampton Streets that summer would become my true role models.

69

My Dad, whom I loved dearly, only instilled what not to do, never fully explaining the bigger picture, the why's behind not doing a negative thing. Perhaps, he was astutely aware of that instinctive nature that exists within a man that says if too much is exposed too early a man-child just might be lost. But in reality, the decision was truly never his. For, as they say in the game, "every tub must stand on its own bottom…" You are only responsible for your own actions and decisions, and Charlie for his own. Perhaps he just assumed too much.

Just having love for a child, or a person, isn't truly enough. Remember what Tina said in that song? "What's love got to do with it" doesn't safeguard that child from the ills of the world beyond the confines of his or her parents' home. Is it not true what they say, that it "takes a whole village to raise a child?" It should also say, "It takes those of a positive mindset to assist in the development of a child."

The North End, along with North Hampton, should be included within the context of that "village." Especially, a male child, be he Black or White is truly not relevant in the true science of things. Do we honestly, willfully, exclude those men and women of the North End and North Hampton Street from being a legitimate part of the village? Their only desire was to give a kid some tools for survival. For, they knew "the playing field that lay ahead would not be level."

It is now fifty years later from when I first met those men of influence and the playing field isn't as level as United States Supreme Court Justice "Clarence Thomas" thinks it is. Like they sometimes say, "Justice is a bit blind at times," and so was Brother Thomas when he took his position of levelness.

My father lacked depth, and above all "vision," beyond his own personal childhood. This, I firmly believe to this very day, at this moment, November 9th, 2008.

Some parents placed much more emphasis on being a buddy or a friend to their child or children, losing that child's respect in the end. We have the innate right to pick and choose our friends and lovers. That chain of luxury doesn't extend to choosing parents or children.

Parents and children are for life. Friends, associates, lovers, come into our lives for "reasons, seasons, but few last a lifetime." Consequently, it is extremely imperative that parents, myself included, become far more proactive in the lives of those we bring into this world, by Allah's decree. Fathers are especially needed to take a more healthy and active role in their male children's lives. Physical presence alone doesn't equal active participation.

Stop! Men! Stop with that excuse about not getting along with the child's mother, or getting an attitude because she's no longer willing to do you sexually, so you don't do anything for the child. And Women need to cease – STOP – using the child as a pawn, a chess piece between father and child because your man decided he's got to move on with his life. Don't stunt your child's growth and development because you can't have your cake and eat it, too. Every project requires a specific set of tools. Otherwise, the project is in jeopardy of failure.

I became a failed, incomplete, project, and to add insult to injury, that attitude has affected the growth and development of my own children. True, none has been on the count (penitentiary), or are smoking crack, or sniffing dope Yet, they are functionally dysfunctional. They are not dysfunctional by choice.

No child who is a clearly thinking rational fourteen-year old sits down and says, "I'm going to get pregnant and have a baby," and then does so, unless that child is in pain. No female child should have to suffer the indignation of being touched and threatened by a male church member in his house, and with his wife and children there. A young eleven-year old girl should not have to endure that.

Another young girl child should not have to be brutally raped by her Mom's half-brother from a second marriage from the age of five to thirteen. Two older sisters shouldn't constantly be going through men like General Grant went through Richmond during the Civil War. And, another girl child shouldn't be without her father's last name.

When parents fail, as I have failed, failed to step up to the plate of fatherhood, all types of things happen and take on a life of their own in one's family. Please, please! Remember, this is only my story, not anyone else's. If what I've shared doesn't apply, then let it fly. But, again, is it not true that it "takes a whole village to raise a child?"

That last summer I spent shining shoes, was the summer my Mom and Dad got into it big time. They had a fight on the back porch of our house. How or what it started over is unclear to me. This is what I do know.

My parents had been drinking. Someone got accused of something. Mom comes up with a Coca-Cola bottle and hits Pop, either directly or indirectly, in the eye. The end result is, he's minus one eye.

That incident was the straw that broke the camel's back, for it cut deep within my Dad's family, in the way his sisters and others would come to treat my Mom after what went down.

I've never directly, nor Kenny, been privy to what was said between Dad and his two sisters, or my sisters. There is one particular incident I do recall.

I had gone by my Aunt Fanny's house because I was out playing ball near her home, and I was hungry. After ringing her doorbell and announcing myself, she allowed me to come up all those damn stairs so she could say the following.

First, she demanded to know exactly what I wanted. As I started to say her name, "Aunt Fanny, I'm hungry," rather than hearing a positive response, what I heard was a piercing voice saying, "Don't call me Aunt! I'm not your damn Aunt!! And, don't ever come to my door again!" Her anger was based solely on what had happened between my parents. I cried all the way down Humboldt Avenue.

Once home, I found everyone in the kitchen. Immediately, my Aunt ran to me asking what was wrong. All I could say was, "You're my Aunt...you're my Aunt." Her response was a "yes" several times over. After everyone heard what had happened, it was "Regulators mount up time!" I had never seen my Aunt angry or heard her curse until that day. Dad immediately went to his sister's house.

Good thing he did go, or he might have gotten jumped on and had his other eye knocked out! Mom was ready to get that big handled butcher's knife from under her bed. She was ready to call out the troops, Aunt Sue, Aunt Laura.

Them three Georgia women was serious trouble once they got them knives and razors in their hands. Aunt Tee had to call Uncle Albert from his house next door to calm Mom down. Mom and her crew would have cut Dad's whole family up that day, even down to the damn kids, along with the cats and dogs.

I have five beautiful daughters, all adults. Katina is by far the meanest. Charlene is all mouth and a coward by herself. But when she's with Shera and Chanel she's with the killing. Melanie isn't going for too much talk either.

That incident took place around 1961 or 1962. The next time I saw my Aunt Fanny, minus my sisters, was in Riley Funeral Home in January of 1970 at my father's funeral. They just stared. Not one of his family members spoke directly to me or even put a hand on me to offer any form of condolence. Not even my sisters.

Why my parents chose to stay together after all the shit they went through is beyond me, especially after that bottle incident. If I would have been either of the two, I certainly would have gotten far away from the other.

Down South, there's an expression, "If you play with a dog long enough, he will lick you in the mouth one day." Now, you must keep in mind that that's the same tongue he licks his own ass with. And the asses of other dogs, both male and female. Now, I don't know about you folks, but I ain't got that kind of freak in me.

Now, just who was the damn masochist and who was the sadist is still a jump ball on my court. Next time I visit their graves, I'm asking them that damn question.

My thing is this, if a man, woman, dog, or cat, says, "Hey MF, I'm going to cut-shoot-bite-scratch you," I take that shit very serious. Same for the police callers. If you say you'll do it, in fact, you probably already have done it to somebody. Tina made it ever so crystal clear, when she sang, *"What's love got to do with it?"* Not a damn thing, when you got me looking like the "one-eyed-Jack" on a deck of playing cards.

On my way out of BCH (Boston City Hospital) I would have been humming Tina's tune minus one eye. If I'd been Mom, I would have been gone long before Pop reached BCH with kids in tow. Remember, "many a hidden feeling is expressed when a person is, so called, playing or acting angry with another."

So, be a real good listener next time you find yourself in a confrontation. I'm not going to allow you to make me the brunt of your jokes amongst family or friends. *See how I had to fuck that nigga up, or see how I put it on that bitch's ass last night? Man, I almost killed that bitch!*

I would rather be alone, with both eyes and in search of Ms. Right, as opposed to staying in that same relationship and risk losing that damn eye. The thought of walking around with a damn seeing-eye dog on a damn chain toting a red, white and blue stick, talking about, "Oh, she still loves me," or "he still loves me." Not acceptable. At all.

My sister, Claire, held much resentment against my mother, and perhaps so did her mother, Rose. I doubt if she cared one way or the other. There would be another situation that would again show Claire's resentment, forty years later. It had nothing to do with our father. But, rather, her son-in-law, my daughter, and myself, along with a threat my mother made.

I've learned over the years that we can't change people. All we can do is change how we deal with them. You simply cannot let everything they say or do affect you. I call it "Renting Space in Your Head." I'm sitting there stuck on stupid, while they have moved on to doing some other source of Tomfoolery toward someone else.

I'm by far a pacifist. I'd rather choose my fights and when. It's always about winning with me. Do we really cheer the loser in a fight, or do we rally around the winner's circle? Why, of course, it's the one in the winner's circle who gets all the cheers. Don't get it twisted. I love my sister dearly. She's just a square who's from a different era of time. I'm from the streets. My family isn't.

As the summer was slowly coming to an end, I knew my days of shining shoes down North Hampton and the North End were over. I instinctively knew I'd never again pick up a Shine Box to earn another quarter -- not for any reason. Shoe Shine Boy had put his box down.

ଔ

Chapter 13 ~ Setting Down My Shine Box

Nineteen-sixty-one was an exciting year.

JFK had just taken office, winning the election the previous November. He would be the then youngest President Elect in the history of this great country. Also, he would be the first Irish elected president and a local hometown boy.

My Dad did his civic duty, working on the polls as they called it back then. I can still close my eyes and see this little man standing by the Humboldt and Bower Street bus stop. Behind him stood the real estate office with that big green clock in the window. He would be handing out voting instructions and leaflets on who to vote for.

"John F. Kennedy, who else," he'd shout out. Then, he would move on down to the Elliott Church, opposite the Lewis Jr. High School. Regardless of his many character flaws, I loved this man.

Is it not the defects and character flaws, idiosyncrasies, that also define who we are? Surely those are some of the things that add up to the sum total of who we are individually. Could I ever measure up to the man within the man? Not the one who drank "Rot-Gut-Fleischman's Gin," but rather, the one who worked two jobs for the eighteen years I knew him and called him "Dad," "Daddy," "Pop!" I undoubtedly fell short of my mark.

Now that it was almost time for school to start, what would I do with my free time after school? Shining shoes was out of the question. I didn't miss the act itself, I missed the action, the excitement of the moment, the people, Black and White. The North End mob guys, the Irish mob down at Baby Tigers Gym and Basin Street South, the gamblers, the black pimps, the sexy whores of the Combat Zone and Massachusetts Avenue. Those are the real true reasons why I would get back to those people.

But, as young as I was, I knew deep within, that one day I would be a part of that life.

Before I could figure out a way to get back to that environment, another crazy reality would manifest itself for all to see and know within our family. I am, forty-six years after the reality, and seeing myself reveal this is almost like reliving it. Dad was hard at work, as usual. True, they had been going at it, as usual. No big deal. Everybody's Mom and Pop have beefed about something back then.

In walks Bill the TV man. And, there, I've put my family's dirty laundry out there for all to see. As I sit here in this jail cell, alone, writing, I could easily change things with the stroke of the pen. For, it is true what they say, "the pen is mightier than the sword." When you've been crooked all your life, sometimes you even get a moment of clarity about yourself.

Bill the TV Man is the only handle Kenny and I knew him by. Bill the TV Man was a white man. That's right. You read correctly. To this day, I still don't know where or how he met my mother. I just know, one day I came home and he was fixing the TV. At least, from all outward appearances it seemed that way.

First meeting, I took him just as he appeared, no more, no less. It would be much later that the ugly truth of that encounter would come to light. In reality, he was my Mom's (in today's terms) maintenance man...or was she the maintenance woman? Death has robbed them both from being able to honestly answer that question.

Kenny, on the other hand, knew something wasn't right from the start. They, he and Mom, would clash much more after that, never saying directly what was behind what he knew or felt it was about. It became an unspoken understanding between them. Kenny wore his emotions on his sleeve and his disdain would show at times.

Our mother and grandma were very wild and mean women at times. They thought nothing, and I mean nothing, of splitting your head "to the white meat," and then taking your ass to the hospital. Mom would hit you in a minute with whatever was within arms reach.

Kenny kept telling me he didn't like Bill the TV Man. I'd say, "He's just the TV Man, Boy." One day, that belief was shattered.

Mom (women are real slick with their shit and Mom had her own down pat) says, "I'm taking Charles with me by Catherine's house." We called her Aunt Cat. She lived at 3 Maywood Terrace. Her Mom owned the entire building, and her Grandma owned a few on Harrison Avenue down by Blanchard's Liquor Outlet.

So, anyway, Mom and I are walking along, just talking. Never once does Mom mention Bill the TV Man. Nothing. When we get there, to Aunt Cat's house, I'm told to go watch TV with Crystal, Aunt Catherine's daughter. So, I do as I am told.

After a while, I say to Aunt Cat, "Where is my mother?" I didn't see her, so I started to look in other rooms. As I'm about to open a particular door to a room, Aunt Cat screams, "NO! Don't go in there!" I'm like, "Why?!?" She replies, "Your Mom is busy in there."

A while later, I see my mother emerge from that room. I look behind her and see Bill the TV Man. Instantly I knew my brother Kenny was right in what he'd been thinking. I was told by my mother and Aunt Cat not to say anything to anyone, "especially not your father!!" And, I didn't, but not for fear of a whipping. I knew if I had told my Dad, it would cause a serious fight and I didn't want my parents to fight again.

My mother's decision to take me with her that warm sunny day would trouble me for many years to come. To make me a party to her tryst by remaining silent created a lot of pain for me. I wanted to know all the "why's" and "how comes." But, who could I ask? Certainly not my Mother or Dad. Not even my dear Aunt Tee or Uncle Albert.

So I went to my brother. He kept saying, "She's not my mother! Your Momma is nasty!" That statement would cut deep into the heart and soul of Charles. I began to think how safe and secure I had felt in the hospital. And, now, I longed for that same safety. Still, too young to run away, although kids did it regularly in our neighborhood, where would I go if I ran away?

One day, I went to Kenny and asked, "Is the TV man going to be our father?" Kenny looked at me like I had two damn heads. He told me, "I have a Daddy already, one in Georgia and one in Boston...Great Granddaddy and William Gibbs. That White Man "Bill the TV Man" ain't our daddy."

One day I found the courage to ask my Mother the question, "Do you like the TV Man better than my Daddy?" Her look really scared me. Years later, I would come to know it wasn't anger I saw in her face, but a need being fulfilled that she could not explain to a child. Mom's only response was to tell me that one day I would understand better. Before that day of understanding came, hate would enter the picture first and I would express it. Before my Mom's death, she and I would have many long conversations about her life and past needs. In the end, I loved my Mom just as much as my Dad.

You know, a fly in a bowl of buttermilk will always come to the top of the milk for you to see it. Now, was my Dad astute enough to see the fly, or was the fly camouflaged due to his drinking? I can't say. Sometimes, just sometimes mind you, the thickness of the milk will provide cover for the fly.

Consequently, I can't say with certainty that he did feel some shit. I know our family knew. Aunt Tee knew, Uncle Albert and even Brother Adams knew. My mom and Aunt Tee would have many beefs on the subject of Mom's ways. My Aunt would always say, "Earline, you are going to bust Hell wide open one day!" Mom had no defense for those statements.

We may not have seen Bill daily or weekly, but you knew he was still around. True, my Pops drank and cut the fool, as they say, but he never cheated. We never heard anyone say they ever saw him with another woman. No one in our neighborhood ever said anything out of line to us in any way, but you feel things, even if you don't see or hear it.

My brother had no problem showing his disdain for Bill the TV Man. Kenny would accept nothing from him. I, on the other hand, was like, *Okay, so you want to give me a buck...cool. Got anymore? Need a shine? Allow me to use my whiskbroom on your ass, also!* For eighteen years I lived under my parents roof, before my Dad's death. I only saw Dad leave twice, and each time, he would return.

I've often wondered, was Dad's leaving related to Bill the TV Man? This man actually wanted to marry my mother and move us all to Arizona. He remained a fixture in my mother's life until the early 1990s, still asking her to come to Arizona. His daughter was even all for it.

Kenny and I would not have gone. We would have stayed with drunk-assed William Gibbs first! Mom would always say, she only had love for two men, "Kenny and Charles..."

Years later I would be sitting on the balcony of the twenty-first floor, next to Theresa Mack, on Kulkulkan Boulevard in CanCun, Mexico, in 1998, overlooking the Caribbean Sea. Theresa and I were talking about our families and their personal, as well as collective, struggles.

Instantly, I began to think of my mother, the past, and how it related to my Mom, Dad, and Brother. Right there, in all that splendor and warmth, I began to have a much clearer picture of who and what they were, as well as their personal struggles.

In 1948, the year my brother was born, she was truly this young innocent woman, married, in love, and with child. Then one day her dreams were shattered. Even her faith in a Higher Power was on shaky ground, due to what she experienced at Brother Adams' house. Not having had a relationship with her father also damaged her emotionally. I began to factor these things along with my Dad's issues of alcohol and his thinking he was better because he was raised up North into the equation I call "my Mother's life." The hypothesis is this. Mom became damaged goods long before Bill the TV Man and my Dad came into the picture.

Upon my return from Mexico, she and I would really talk about all those things, finally. All my Grandparents would pass, even my Dad, Brother, and even Theresa. I would go on to the Henry L. Higginson and the Ellis Schools. Kenny would go to the James P. Timothy Jr. High School. We were then living at 60 Holworthy Street. My shine-box had been long put away and it was not 1963. JFK would be assassinated. And a new singing group would emerge from Liverpool, England to take the world by storm. They were called The Beatles.

One day, my Dad was on our porch, and as he leaned over to look down, he happened to see a cardboard box with a four-digit number on it in dark print. He had me go down there and write the four-digit number down on paper. The number turned out to be 2155. Back during those days, the local newspaper, *The Record*, used to publish the daily number.

When I was a kid, Boston was the only town to have a four-digit and three-digit number at the same time that you could get down on (bet on in the street). It was called the "top and bottom track." The number 2155 was hit many times by my Dad when we were young. Kenny and I used to put his numbers in down on Washington Street, directly across from the graveyard, near Kornfield's Pharmacy. I would work there at age fifteen.

The kids in the neighborhood, especially those on our block, would know that our Dad had hit the number because Kenny and I would have plenty of bags from Filene's Basement. Filene's Basement was famous all over the country. They sold top shelf clothing from the best upscale stores at discount prices. After an item didn't sell within a certain amount of days it would automatically go down in price. They sold all types of minks for men and women, in all those exotic colors. And, I'm talking about back in the sixties, right up until they closed in the 2000s.

We called the basement "the hole." It was deep in the basement. They even had a "sub-basement." They sold imported skins, like alligator, crocodile, lizard, sharkskin, turtle, snake, ostrich, suede, and you could get them, the skins, mixed and in colors right out of the rainbow. People can say what they want about New York being a fashion city; it's true. They may have designed it there. But, Boston Blacks and Italians sure knew how to put it together and they still out-dressed the average Brother in any hood in the Big Apple. Don't get it twisted. New York is my town for sure. It takes a licking and keeps on ticking.

Massachusetts was the shoe industry state for many years with Stetson, Joan and David, French Shriners, Taymores, etc. In my teen years, we'd catch the bus from Ashmont Street in Dorchester and ride out to South Waymouth, to the Stetson Shoe Factory. They even sold "Rainbow Alligators" back in 1967. My homie, Kevin Copeland, had a pair from there and a pair from Leighton's in New York. Like I was saying, you knew when Pop had a bank, because his two boys was *sharp*!

When we moved to Holworthy Street we no longer got our haircuts at Mr. Mitchell's shop on Warren Street. All the neighborhood guys went to the barber school down on Dover Street. Now it's called East Burkley Street. When we were young, the Orange Line would stop there between North Hampton and the Essex Street stop in town. The barber school only charge 35-cents per cut back then. Only problem was they were student barbers, and many times our "crow-vartis cuts" were way off.

We'd then walk to Dover and Washington Street. We'd put on our pie faces and beg people for change to catch the bus. After an hour of begging, we'd slip under the turnstiles and get the train downtown to buy pizza at the King of Pizza. It was a big place and took up a lot of space on Washington and Essex Streets. Now, it's a Chinese Cultural Center of some sort.

Back then, we'd get two whole pizzas and sodas or tonics and sit in the big booths by the big picture windows and wave at all the pretty working girls who had the day shift. Some would even wave back. If they didn't we would give them the finger. Many of us had imaginary girls. We would say they were working for us, and that's why they are not talking whenever we would wave. Many of the working girls I knew from when Kenny and I, and others, would be in town that last summer of my shoe shine career. Guys would fight each other if you'd say his girl was your girl.

I remember shining Edmond Paradie's shoes one day. He was an African pimp. He lived in my hood when he first came to the States, and was older than we were. I knew his brother and sister. He said, "Pimps never fight over women." Not real pimps. "We just accept the knock, and keep it moving." So every time I saw my friends fight over a whore that wasn't even theirs I would think back to what Edmond said. Once our pizzas were done, we would hang outside daydreaming and lying.

Being in town was real therapy for me, and Kenny knew it. He would say, "You like this action," and I would just smile and say, "Yes, big brother." I just knew I was going to be a part of it, I just didn't know when or how. I just knew I was seeing myself in those cars and clothes Edmond and Pretty Eddie and Billy Muscles and Billy Poison all had.

In sixth grade I met two kids, one was Gilbert White and the other was Jessey Anderson. Those two was so cool and smooth, ya know, fast-talking. I hadn't met anyone like them before. Little did I know that Gilbert's dad and Jessey's uncle both were doing a little pimping themselves. Years later I would meet Gilbert's dad on 118th St. and 7th Avenue. By then, I was all the way down in the town (crewed up and getting C-notes daily). Skip Gilbert's dad had just come from Cali' with an "All American White Woman" – Italian – named "Joe" (short for Josephine), and she was dropping that "pack real good." Playing the con game, that is. To this very day Gilbert, his Dad, and I are still friends.

Jessey was senselessly killed in 1969 at the corner of Lawrence and Blue Hill Avenues. He was coming out of McAndrews Restaurant when he lost his young life. Those they say were involved are also deceased. Fate and the twist and turns of life have their own way to even things out for all concerned parties. A shout out is in order here: *Hey, Ms. J. Gates, with your fine self!* That was Jessey's girl.

One day, I came home and my youngest daughter, Chanel, introduced me to this young man in his twenties, to find out it was Gilbert's oldest son. He was living down the hall from me at 140 Humboldt Avenue with his Mom, who I was also in the sixth grade with. Gilbert's son is now a minister. Now, we are all fat and many of us are also a bit gray. Not so with Gilbert. He still has a youthful appearance after more than forty years. ❧

Chapter 14 ~ Government Cheese & Powdered Milk

One day our mother tells us we have to go deep up in Jamaica Plains, (Deep white folks country back then), to where the old factory outlet store used to be, past Green Street train station on Washington Street. Back then, damn near every Black family had a block of hard long cheese, if you lived in my hood. Don't forget the powdered milk, peanut butter (and it wasn't Skippy's either) in the can with them big black letters saying, "Not to be sold" all over that silver can. And that damn rice in the bag that had so much starch in it you could use it as mortar to put a building together. And, let's not forget that canned beef.

We make a joke about all that now, but for real, if Barack Obama can't get this country back up and running, many who missed the first cheese wave surely won't miss the next cheese line of 2009 and beyond. So, again, please don't laugh. You may be at the head of one of those lines. All those who think they are Similac Babies or Wic Babies just might truly be "Powdered Milk Babies," courtesy of your government, after all.

My brother and I go all the way up to Jamaica Plains. I guess we must have had some type of voucher that said the Belim Family was certifiably depleted-poor-destitute. Yet, at home, we had an entire deep freezer full of all types of meats from chicken, steaks, beef, fish, even down to the damn "oink of the hog." Mom was always angling for something. That 'something' also meant moving to the projects.

When Kenny and I get to the place, we give the people our paperwork. Two guys loaded us down with two shopping bags full of everything, cheese, milk, canned beef, powdered eggs, X-brand oatmeal, rice, etc. Rather than just walk right back to Green Street train station and ride the train one stop to Egilston station and the bus up to Humboldt Avenue and change buses and come down Humboldt to Holworthy Street, my brother comes up with an idea.

Kenny says, "Let's buy sodas and cupcakes and beg for change." After eating and drinking we started walking. Next thing I know we hear, "Hey Niggas! What are you doing outside of your cage in Roxbury?

And what do you have in those shopping bags?" We knew we weren't that far from Egilston Station, in fact we could see the cab stand in the distance. There were too many to stand and fight, plus we had them damn heavy bags of cheese and canned food. On the count of three we started to run. The cans in my double bag started to get very heavy and were banging against each other. Kenny yells, "Don't slow down or stop, Charlie, they gaining on us!"

All of a sudden one of Kenny's bags springs a damn leak and out slides a long block of "Government cheese." *BOOM!* It sounded like the whole sidewalk broke in half when that block hit the ground. Then my bag with the canned beef in it starts to feel lighter and lighter. On the ground, rolling to the curb are three large gray cans of grade-A-government beef.

At the next corner, footsteps became faint, looking over our shoulders, we discovers our pursuers have stopped. Half a block or so behind us, we could faintly hear their cheers and loud laughter as they waved cans of beef and blocks of cheese at us. I actually thought I heard one fat red-haired boy say, "Come back and get your dinner, Niggars!"

By the time we got back home, we were exhausted, hungry and sweaty. As for the provisions, we got home with one block of cheese, a box of powdered milk, and a bag of rice. After explaining to Mom, she playfully said we had to go back and get a new issue. We all burst out in laughter. Mom made us two large glasses of Hershey's chocolate with the powdered milk and two grilled cheese sandwiches from the lone block of cheese we got home, after we took baths. We never went back up there again. We found a safe pickup spot in the hood.

 og

Chapter 15 ~ Playing the Welfare Game

Back when I was a child, whether your real Daddy, Play-Daddy, Uncle "Scuby-Doo" was around or not, when it came time to get what folks called "free money" in your hand, none of those above titles or the actually men existed. You see, you couldn't get a check on the first and fifteenth of each month, if you had a man, husband, cat or dog as a support system. Your reliance had to be totally and solely on an AFDC (Aide for Dependant Children). Essentially, whomever Mom had as a mate had to get "ghost" when them folks (welfare/caseworkers) were due to come around playing "Ms. Snoopy."

Them folks would actually look through your whole damn house for any signs of a man. That meant hiding our Dad's clothes, shoes especially, based on size. My Dad wore a size six and a half to seven. So his shoes always stayed put in our closet. Sometimes people would damn near get caught by the Irish caseworkers. Their Dads, Mom's man (Play Uncle Willie) would hide in our house for an hour 'til Sue O'Toole left.

Those workers were real slick, too. They'd see you in a new pair of jeans or Chuck Taylor's (Converse high tops with two-tone strings) and they'd say, "Those are very nice, where'd you buy them at? Paul's Army and Navy? Did Mommy get them for you?" That was the sixty-four thousand dollar question; who bought them.

Some kids got caught out there, but never us. We knew what and when to say anything to the caseworker. We kept our long deep freezer (purchased from one of Dad's number hits) out on our porch for two reasons. The main reason, you might have guessed, the caseworker.

People who were on AFDC were supposed to be destitute and totally dependent on those two monthly stipends on the first and fifteenth. On any check day you'd see all Dads and gunslingers (dick sellers) hanging around mailboxes, especially the green one that has no lip opening for mail. That green box was where they kept the next days mail that included those checks.

In my hood, check day was called "Father's Day." And it still may be that way. I'm not saying there wasn't widespread abuse of the program. Perhaps, if the playing field for hiring would have been level and the "Louise Day Hicks" of that era had really and truly been about seeing poor white and poor black folks get a proper education, then perhaps they wouldn't have been a need or demand for AFDC agencies and caseworkers doubling as "German Gestapo agents from WWII."

Talk about embargoes! There should have been an embargo against the AFDC and the Boston School Department, along with Cuba during that same time period. Oh, and the other reason, we hid our deep freezer on the porch was -- you guessed it – nosey black folks. They are worse than flies on manure. When they think you got two bits more then them, they will get mad and put them folks on your ass. We kept ours covered with an old raggedy quilt. We told people it was an old trunk we played cards on. We even kept the cord covered that ran through the small crack in the open window. Whenever them snoopy caseworkers came, we'd just unplug it until they were gone.

One day, I got caught stealing "Hostess Cupcakes" for me and Kenny out of the big grocery store on Harold and Hollander Streets. I was mad as hell. So I waited a couple of days, called the store, and said a bomb was in the store. Boy, them damn Jews went crazy. They called every police and fire station in Roxbury. Them people turned that store upside down, walked over everything looking for a damn ghost. Now, I'm vindicated. I've been big on getting even, but I like winning most of all.

I had a childhood friend named "Pinky" who was light skinned and lived directly across the street from us on 60 Holworthy Street. His Mom was a real nice lady. She had some type of thyroid problem that caused one of her legs and one of her feet to be extremely large. Her ability to move about was limited because of her illness. In spite of her situation, she was always extremely nice to all of us kids on the block.

Pinky's older sister, Maria, who lived on Blue Hill Avenue near Intervale Street, ran an after-hours spot called The Green Door. Her apartment was on the top floor facing Blue Hill Avenue. The spot got its name from the color of the door of the building itself. The Green Door was my first exposure to bootleg liquor and a gambling spot.

My first time there with Pinky was an exciting experience, the music playing, and how people interacted with one another while drinking and gambling. I was in total awe of what my young eyes were seeing for the very first time. Many times after that first visit to Pinky's sister's spot I would tell him, "Let's go over on the avenue." He knew I was trying to get him to go by his sister's place.

Since my early teens, I've been close with a group of guys from Blue Hill Avenue. One of those guys, we'll just call him "Blindy" for now, I met his Mom and Dad several years before he and I met. His Dad "Jim" and I met at Pinky's sister's place, The Green Door. That group of guys are Mike Collins, Earnest Manigault, Bryant Green, Ricardo Wilson, Danny Davis, Clyde Bacon, Ronnie Manterio, and Errol Crawford. All are deceased but two, including myself.

Another popular bootleg and gambling joint (skin hole/Georgia Skin) was on Normandy Street around the corner and was a popular numbers spot owned by Mr. Gates. The owner who had the skin hole on Normandy Street had two sons, his oldest being very good friends with an ex-NBA ball player, Earl "the Pearl" Monroe, who played for the New York Knicks.

The possibility of living in one of the many public housing developments (the projects) scattered throughout Boston, was the dream of many families in my community. When I was a youngster, our family was one of those families who dreamt and prayed nightly for that same miracle.

Under Franklin Delano Roosevelt's terms as president, from 1933 to 1945, seeking emergency powers proclaimed the "New Deal," he put into effect a vast number of administrative changes. Foremost was the use of public funds for relief and public works. Under Public Works is how what we in the hood called "the bricks" -- the projects -- came about. It is fair to say that FDR is the architect of public housing, as we know it today.

Before you start applauding, chill a minute, sister. The architect didn't have your grinning ass in mind when he and his cronies drew up that plan. Those bricks were built for white blue-collar workers. They were built to give each blue-collar worker an opportunity to save enough money to purchase a piece of the "American Dream" of owning their own home.

Many of those workers did in fact save enough money while living in those dwellings to buy that dream house. By the time poor whites and disenfranchised blacks got to the bricks, their dreams of home ownership, owning a piece of the American Dream, they were oblivious, it was gone from their conscious minds. In short, those dwellings had long seen their better days long before the disenfranchised moved in.

As for saving money -- what money? They had none to save for their piece of the pie. Who was going to give a single black or white woman, unskilled, with three or four children, a loan (down payment) on a home? Talk about investing in her, or her children's future, they had no future. Realistically, how could either woman come up, legitimately, with the five percent, let alone the 20 percent, that is required in today's market across the board?

When people like my mother finally got in the projects, the American Dream, and owning a fraction of that pie, or of my Mother or Dad ever reaching that plateau, became unreachable and unattainable for them, collectively and individually.

The reality is this: poor Whites, as well as poor Blacks, only got half the dream, if that much. They made it to the projects, but they never got to the promised land of owning the home that Roosevelt supposedly had in mind for all people.

True, at least we did get to the projects, "Orchard Park Housing Projects, 8 Adams Street, Apartment 497."

CS

Chapter 16 ~ Meeting Reverend Ike

Prior to the projects, my Aunt Tee would hear about this young curly haired minister named Frederick Eikerenkoetter. The Reverend Ike was rumored to have the power of Jesus, in terms of his ability to heal the sick, just by laying his hands on them physically.

My Aunt was an all in all poor sister. She would have given that man her life savings, had he requested it. I truly do concur that faith is based on the things not seen with the physical eyes, but rather with the eyes of the heart and soul. Just exactly what eyes my Aunt was seeing his healing powers through is still a blur, even after forty-eight years.

Our house was in an uproar. Mom was calling people, my Aunt called Georgia and Alabama to tell them she was going to take me to the weeklong nightly revival. She would tell people how he was going to lay the hand of God, Jesus, on my "right arm" and it would be healed.

Mom even called her Play Sister and confidant, Aunt Sue. She told Aunt Sue she was calling Catherine, perhaps Reverend Ike could talk to "Pissy Mary" and help her from falling out when she gets drunk and pisses on herself. She smelled like tiger piss, strong and stifling. I was like, "Yes, let her go in my place, save her ass. I'm cool."

Even though at this point Mom wasn't attending church any longer, she still held onto beliefs, and one of those beliefs was that this man could fix my arm. Poor people, historically Black and White back in those days, didn't have a lot of options when it came to health care and big time hospitals, or the money to pay for those exorbitant surgical fees. In many cases, even today, they were locked into poor health care providers at understaffed hospitals in the inner cities of our country.

When talk began to spread about a Miracle Man laying hands on the infirm, people flocked to him, for he was thought of as their savior. Let me just say this now. I am Sunni Muslim. I've been that for twenty years, even though I was raised up in what is known as the "Church of God and Christ." I was never "saved," nor was I "dipped" (baptized) in any tub, lake or river. However, my brother did go that route before he accepted Islam and became Sunni Muslim in 1969.

Even as a kid, I never felt complete with Christianity. It just did nothing, absolutely nothing, for me spiritually, emotionally and physically. And, the subject matter of the Trinity along with the belief that Jesus died on the cross for my sins is just silly to me and other Muslims as well.

Webster's II Pocket Dictionary, revised for our 21st Century, defines the word "trinity" as "The three person Godhead of Orthodox Christian belief."

Now, answer this if you can. If God (Allah) is One, and he surely is "One," then who are those other two "Godheads?" His bodyguards? I couldn't figure that question out then, nor can I now. And no one else has been able to explain to me who the other two folks are that were hanging out with God like they are Gods. Or, are they Gods for the daytime people and another for the nighttime people when the big God is chilling and maxing-relaxing on one of the Heavenly clouds?

I realize that some will say, "He is making jest of Christianity, no?" Not at all, I am only saying it makes no sense to me as a logical thinking man. It is said, "Opinions are like a—holes, each of us has one..." and I was expressing mine.

My Dad's take was, "I'm from Missouri. Don't talk about it, (healing his son's arm) – do it!" A true pragmatist, all the way. My honest opinion? All bullshit.

The night of the revival, I had to take a bath in olive oil and hot water only. Don't ask me why. I just did as my Aunt instructed. I even had on all new clothes. My Aunt and I would be the only ones going. Everyone gave us a hug but Dad. He just looked at me, smiled and winked.

The small storefront church was located on Shawmut Avenue, about a block from Ma Dickson's Restaurant, (her first location). Upon arriving by cab, you could hear the sounds of voices singing the song, "I'm a soldier in the Army of the Lord," feet stomping banging against hands and knees.

As we stepped in, two ushers dressed in all white greeted us by saying, "Hallelujah! Praise God." My Aunt and myself were immediately directed to two empty folding chairs in the third room. Due to the brightness of the fluorescent overhead lighting inside the small church, it took several minutes for my eyes to adjust to my surroundings.

From the size of the church crowd, it was obvious many people had come for this first night of the week long healing revival. The words "miracle extravaganza," and "a God sent healer of the people," were heard from the lips of those seated.

Many of those present that first night were young children on crutches in leg braces, while others were in wheelchairs, and some others were blind. For a brief minute, I thought I was back in Boston City Hospital waiting to be seen by the doctors.

Moving my eyes to the front of the church's podium area, I immediately saw several men sitting in chairs while tapping their feet to the sounds of a popular spiritual being sung by many of the church goers that evening. It was obvious this was one of those "pew-jumping, Bible-thumping, tambourine-waving non-fornicating churches." On both sides of the men who occupied the podium that first night, stood a woman in all white. My first thought was those women were nurses from the city hospital holding a fan while they swayed to the sounds of singing voices. Of the three men seated up high on the makeshift platform, one of the men stood out from the other two.

Rev. Ike lacked any signs of graying hair, and he wasn't balding like the others. I had seen many pimps while shining shoes with different types of processes. Never had I seen a black man, (was he truly 100% black?) with hair like his, so curly and jet black. He even had the "Ron Isley" look, a curl dangling between his eyes for all to see. His complexion was "reddish orange." The brother looked like he had just stepped off one of those Apache Reservations. The brother wore an embroidered robe of maroon and black. Under his robe he was dressed in a gray hounds tooth suit, white shirt, tie and gray alligator shoes.

As the singing music slowed to a stop, one of the older balding men got up and slowly approached the podium with his black zipped up Bible. He slowly opened it to a marked place and began a short sermon on the miracle of Jesus' birth and the subsequent miracles he performed during his short life on Earth. Now that he had done his thing to prep the congregation, it was now "Showtime at the Apollo."

Reverend Ike stepped up to the podium and introduced himself and announced to the congregation that the prayer revival was about to begin. "All those desiring the Hand of Jesus (God) upon them, please come to the front seats."

That was my Aunt's cue. She takes me by the hand and leads me up to the front. The brother comes down to where we are all seated, going from one to the other, laying his hand, (the Healing Hand of Jesus), on all of us. The blind man says, "I can see Jesus and feel Jesus laying His hand over my eyes…Yes, Lord Jesus, I now can see!"

Now, he's jumping up and down, speaking in 'tongues' to whom, I still don't know after 46 years. The congregation goes wild behind the blind man who has been blind since birth, saying he can now see. A young woman on crutches drops them to the floor as she suddenly begins to walk for the first time. Seeing this miracle unfold before her eyes causes an older woman to leap up from her seat and begin speaking in tongues.

The ushers rush to her and hold on to her before she gets a murder charge by knocking someone down. Then, there's twelve-year old Charlie. Reverend Ike puts his hand on my shoulder and starts calling, "Oh, Jesus…heal this child's body…"

To this day, I'm still waiting for his Jesus (God) to take this damn plate out of my arm and replace it with a brand new bone. As to why Charlie and the others didn't get healed was, as he and my Aunt put it, "… all a matter of faith" and His, Jesus,' timetable. "Keep praying," they both said. "Jesus got something in store for you."

As I stood outside that church that night, I could swear one of two of them not yet healed folks eased off while puffing on a cigarette, and minus their cane. That was one hell of an experience for me. For, it caused me to have many doubts about religion for years, until Allah put Islam in my life and heart.

Everyone was sad at home, all except Dad. He just smiled and winked again. I knew from that night on I'd never be a true born again Christian filled with the Holy Ghost. In fact, I didn't want to be one, either.

They say you should never kill a man's hopes, for to do so is to kill him. Those people were already dead before they entered the church that night, thinking that he (Rev. Ike) had a direct line to Jesus and he could heal you. Oppression of any form is worse than slavery. People who go around playing the 'healing game' are truly oppressing people and taking advantage of them spiritually, emotionally, financially, and in many cases, sexually. Remember "Jim Jones?" Remember "Waco, Texas?" The list goes on.

Now, allow me to give you a history lesson on Brother Ike. And, let me also ask you a question. First off, we are blessed today to be a lot more intelligent than those Brothers and Sisters of yesteryear. Today, we know we have options. We don't just accept a thing because someone said we should. If it don't sound right or look right, it's usually not right. Back then, we were the blind leading the blind. Not now, thank God.

Back to Ike. Reverend Ike truly started his ministry in Boston. In fact, his mailing address used to be Boston, Mass. for over thirty years. It may still be that way. A childhood friend of my Mom's boyfriend used to be the person who wrote Reverend Ike's one-hundred-dollar prayer cloth blessing. In short, Ike was (and is) still charging people for God's so called money blessing. You receive a small red square cloth, along with some mumbo jumbo Bible verse, all for just one-hundred-dollars. Now, you tell me that ain't crazy!

If you had only ten-dollars you got a ten-dollar cloth, and a ten-dollar prayer. You were to pin the cloth onto your clothes and not take it off. Many a Black man or woman, and even some foolish-ass whites, all went to their graves with them rags pinned to their clothes. Even in death, they are still waiting on their financial windfall blessing. Now, you know something ain't right. And it's like Ike and his BS. His radio pitch was, "Money ain't the root of all evil, *not* having any money is the root of all evil!" W.I.L.D.-A.M. Radio Boston used to announce his mailing address for donations and this wasn't that long ago. His first church was in Boston. It was still standing in 2007 in the South End. Word was an after-hours club was under it at night.

For many years now he has been doing his thing out of an old movie house up on Broadway in Manhattan. I believe it's the old Leow's 175th Street Theater, known as "The Palace Cathedral." Word also is that he has put a lot of money into fixing it up.

Back in 2007 was my first time seeing him in many years. What he's done now is tap into the Hispanic community. They are very religious people. He's got a Hispanic minister that he has groomed well out front now. I've seen them both together on several occasions. Reverend Ike's ministry has now gone global, without a doubt. He's like old "Jimmy Swaggart." Remember him? That's Jerry Lee Lewis' first cousin. Remember how Jimmy would cry on TV for cash for those kids in Guatemala and El Salvador on Sundays? Then come Friday and Saturday nights, he's down on Bourbon and Canal Streets buying sexual favors from the 'working girls.' The money spent was the same money he begged up on Sunday for those kids in Central America.

All those types of people are suspect, selling false hope and begging people for their money to be used in un-Christian like ways. Acceptance of Islam has given me a better understanding of man's purpose on this Earth. I guess you know I've never gone back to another revival healing meeting since that night with my Aunt.

NEWS FLASH : Reverend Frederick Eikerekoette died in 2010.

C3

Chapter 17 ~ Becoming a Teenager

Becoming a teenager on December 19th, 1963 was a huge thing for me. It soon meant I'd be stepping into the shoes of a man even though that would be a few years to come. Still, the thought of it really excited me. To me, being a teenager meant I was supposed to act and think much differently. JFK's death would also make me have a different perspective about life.

Many people, Blacks especially, felt all hope of ever being treated equally and justly had died with him that November day in Dallas, Texas. I learned that one cannot put all hope for a better future, a better world, on the shoulders of one man. Rather, it should be a collective effort from everyone concerned. One cannot be the crossing guard and the person seeking to cross the street at the same time. Otherwise, who is truly watching out for you, or impeding the oncoming traffic? Life is a collective endeavor that involves all of us pulling in the same direction.

Growing up in the hood, as opposed to growing up in Scarsdale, is truly a lesson learned. It's Basic Training 101 Hood style. Turning thirteen meant basic training time had begun. And we all know there are those who never make it through basic training camp. Some are ill equipped for change and some become casualties of friendly fire. In any hood there are children who are emotionally unprepared for life because of things done to them by family members or family "friends." Some have trust issues based on what they have heard, seen, and/or experienced, at a young age. And, some, maybe many, are cut down simply because he was driving a car up a street with his friends in it and the car was nice. Or, his life was cut short because they couldn't get his cousin. So, his life was taken as he sat at a traffic light on Washington Street in Dorchester, Massachusetts in 2001. His name was Dwayne Taylor.

So, now you see how much goes into becoming a thirteen-year old in any hood, in any town. That cliché is so very, very true. It does take the conscious collective effort of the entire village to nurture a child.

A system of checks and balances are essential necessities in any endeavor, be it a child's development, the running of a country, or a

Fortune 500 company. However, when that system is no longer balance checking, those in charge of running that country or guiding that child's development, then we or they have failed the country, and the children within it.

Turning thirteen, I knew the system of checks and balances was unbalanced for me. If society and family wanted a far different finished product, "then someone should have properly applied the system of checks and balances…"

❧

Chapter 18 ~ First Party

I attended my first real party at age thirteen. I mean, where the "Black Light" was in full effect and the punch had real whiskey in it. The guys were grinding on the girls as they slow dragged (danced) with them and the girls quickly responded by grinding back. Man, I thought I had died and gone to heaven. Truth be told, I didn't have permission to even be there.

Normally, on Friday nights Kenny and I would either carry our gym clothes with us or have them on under our clothes before going down to the gym at Lewis Jr. High School. I had long decided that upon turning thirteen, I was not going to wait to get the okay to go to a real party. I had heard two weeks in advance about these twins. Not the girl set from Holworthy Street. Many people actually thought we were related because we all were skinny and wore glasses.

This particular set of twins lived on Blue Hill Avenue near Glennway Street. I knew one of the twin's brothers. In fact, I heard he had a daughter by a girl we grew up with from Sherman Street where I used to live. So I knew I could get in. Getting there was my dilemma. So I had to come up with a plan, especially because Kenny had changed his mind about going to the gym that night.

All day I thought and thought in school about how I could still get to go to the party if Kenny wasn't going to go to the gym as he usually did. On my way home, I saw my friend Glenn Mosley who lived around the corner on Harold Street by that store I got caught stealing goodies from. He also wanted to go to that damn party. He said Natalie Dotson and her girlfriends were going.

Natalie lived up the street from me on Holworthy. She had a younger sister named Nunee and a brother named Bubbie. Now I knew I had to get there. She had all the fly girlfriends like Valerie Poindexter and Janice Lawrence from Townsend Street. So here was the plan.

Glenn would put his party clothes in a bag, drop them out his bedroom window and pick them up when he left like he was going to the gym.

Then he would cut through a yard and come up my back hallway and drop off his clothes. He then would go by my window and whistle for me that was the signal that he had put his clothes by our back door.

I already had my clothes in a bag. I'd yell out to my family, "I'm taking down the trash before Glenn comes to get me for gym." I learned a lot of covert sneaky shit down North Hampton shining shoes from them roguish South End thugs.

After leaving my bag in the hall. I went to my window and whistled for Glenn to ring our bell so I could let him into the building. Upon entering our apartment, he immediately greeted my family, "Hello Mrs. Belim and Kenny." Dad had stepped out to the corner store by this time as they sat watching Bonanza on the TV. Glenn was a familiar figure at our house. Seeing him that night wouldn't have aroused any suspicion whatsoever. I quickly grabbed my coat and hat and headed for the door, being mindful to say goodbye before clicking it closed behind me.

The adrenalin floodgates opened wide as Glenn and I raced down the winding steps, two at a time, scurrying quickly to get around the building to the back hallway where our party clothes awaited us. With our Chuck Taylor's Converse sneakers tied firmly onto our feet, our footsteps made little if any noise as we entered the darkened back hallway. Finding our clothes, we quickly dressed in silence and total darkness. Once dressed, we placed our clothes inside our gym bags.

Quietly, Glenn and I eased our way back down the steps to the landing leading to the boiler room and neatly stacked our gym bags in a corner. Like two thieves in the night we slipped cautiously out the back entrance of my building, quietly making our way in the darkness behind all the buildings leading to the opening of the empty lot between Holworthy and Hollander Streets.

Cautiously, we made our way to Hollander, then a short walk to Waumbeck in the direction of Warren Street. Knowing we had to pass my Uncle Albert's house at 23 Waumbeck Street was nerve wracking. Then all of a sudden from two houses away I see lights luminously glowing through his living room window. Even the damn front porch lights seemed to be glowing extra brightly. Fear of being seen, or worse, caught, filled my mouth with a foul bile taste. To ensure we were undetected, we had to stoop low to the ground using the parked cars on both sides of the street for cover as we crept past the house.

Nearing the intersection of Warren Street and Elm Hill Avenue allowed us to breathe a sigh of relief. We smiled and gave each other a quick pat on the back while walking the short distance to the bus stop in front of Puritan Plaza. Several minutes passed before our bus pulled into our stop to take us the rest of the way to the party. On the ride up Blue Hill Avenue we talked about all the fly girls, many older than us, whom we knew would be at the party. Our young faces glowed with excitement at the thought of actually slow dancing with a pretty girl.

Near the corner of Glennway Street we both looked eagerly out the side window facing Blue Hill Avenue at the large crowd of girls standing across the street. It was obvious that they were part of the partygoers. Minutes later, Glenn and I found ourselves walking across the avenue in the direction of Black beauty.

That night was my first time ever seeing a "Black Rainbow," a rainbow of beautiful black females in an array of beautiful blackness. Even to this very day, red complexioned, high yellow, beautiful blackness to jet midnight black women, standing five-nine to six feet tall, f---ed me up! Factor in them being one-hundred-thirty-five pounds to one-hundred-fifty, and I'm "stuck like Chuck!"

Glenn and I actually knew some of the girls from the Lewis Jr. High School who were in the group of girls along with some females from the Burke High School on Washington Street. Trying hard to be cool, we thought it best to speak, and surprisingly, they spoke back. Man, when I saw Valerie Poindexter and Janice Lawrence, I thought I had died and gone on to heaven. Those sisters were beyond fine looking. They both had hourglass figures and a sexy swagger to go along.

Several feet away from the girls, a group of older teenage guys were standing in a semicircle smoking Kool cigarettes while talking shit and smiling at the pretty passing females. As we made our way up the steep set of crumbling concrete steps leading to the party, Glenn and I heard a familiar sound coming from within the party. It was the sound of "Shot Gun," a popular tune of that era by a group called "Junior Walker and the Allstars."

Once inside the house we could hardly see each other because of the lighting. To actually be in a party where black lights were in effect was a first for us. Shit, being at a real party was the biggest treat of all for Glenn and myself.

People were in two rooms. Some were talking to each other over the electrifying sound of the music that was playing. Others were sipping from white styrofoam cups as they coolly swayed back and forth to the sounds of that same music. We've all heard it said many times, the expression "fake it 'til you make it.' Well, that's exactly what we found our thirteen-year old selves doing that very night.

Neither Glenn nor I had ever been to a real teenage party in our lives prior to that night. Shit, we didn't even know how to dance, not even the slow drag! Fate has its way of coming to the rescue, though. Someone handed us two cups of what we honestly thought was punch, but in reality was "spiked up bad." We drank three full cups before our bodies heated up like a furnace. Up to that point neither of us had ever had any alcohol before that night.

Instantly, our inhibitions vanished and we found ourselves mixing and mingling with all the fly girls. Much of what took place that night would be a blur the next day for both of us. We both would agree that we did in fact dance, not the best, but we did cut a few steps. As for that up and close two-steps, sad to say it didn't happen that particular night.

We had to get liquored up a few more times before we found the courage to ask a girl to "slow drag." Oh, boy! When I got the chance to get face to face with one of them fine red complexioned long legged sisters I held onto her tighter than a Johnson & Johnson bandaid sticking to dry skin. The best "very best" part of all was my dick was hard as Chinese Arithmetic! Talk about dying and going to heaven, I had surpassed levels one through six. I was in seventh heaven.

Had I bumped into the wrong person after that dance we would still be fighting right to this day, as hard as I was they would have thought I stuck a "357 pistol in their gut!" Many years later, and alcohol free, I would experience a very similar situation, in 1999 while slow dancing in a night spot called Slades of Boston with a certain sexy sister. Luther Vandross' song, "If Only For One Night" could be heard playing softly in the background.

Without warning, my "357" was once again pressing firmly up close and personal against the pelvic area of a very sexy seductive sensual woman. Upon her realizing my firmness, rather than pushing me away, the sister pulled me close and whispered slowly in my ear, "It's okay, baby," as she pulled me even closer. (And if she reads this passage, she is sure to recall that moment and the night in question. The sexy lady is "Christy M. Taylor," and I'm certain she won't mind me mentioning her by name.) Back to the party...

We didn't realize just how drunk we had actually gotten until our bus ride home. Why is it that things start to spin around very fast as if you are in the eye of a hurricane when you get drunk? I've never been able to figure that shit out.

As soon as we sat in our seats on the bus ride back home, "the whole damn bus started spinning like crazy," especially when it was moving down Warren Street. How we made it off that bus still baffles me.

By the time we made it to the back entrance of my building that night, both of us had thrown up at least four times. Both of us were just too damn drunk to even change out of our party clothes. Glenn kept talking stupid and burping as though he was going to throw up on my silly drunk ass. Shit, I got mad and said, "I'm going in the damn house. I don't give a shit if I get caught. You can sleep in the hallway, or take your drunk ass home." I left Glenn standing in the darkened hallway babbling to himself.

I must have fallen up the stairs, not down, but up, at least three times, before I made it to my apartment. As I eased my key in the locked door, my brother instantly "snatched open the door." I tried to smile as I drunkenly asked, "Is Ma or Daddy still up?" That Negro snatched me through the doorway like he was the MF police, and marched me straight to our room in the back. His first words were, "You stink, have you been drinking? I should go wake Ma and Daddy up." Unable to respond, I immediately sprinted to our bathroom to throw up again.

I'll never ever forget what it felt like being drunk at age thirteen. Kenny was fifteen at the time and saved and a born again Christian, sanctified filled with the Holy Ghost, I mean for real, with all that spooky shit in his head at that point in time. I knew with assuredness that my brother had the capacity to tell on me. So I had to do a lot of pleading with him. At one point I was ready to say, *'nigga, go and tell now, I'm tired of all the pleading,'* but he held up.

For a long time, though, I didn't trust my brother. I had learned many things in the North End of Boston from those gangsters as well as the old black and Irish guys down North Hampton, Shanty's about 'telling.' I believe to this very day if you play police games you'll call the MF folks on a person. In other words, if you tell me, Charles, I'll put the PoPo on you, it's a done deal. Just not executed, that's all. All that shit about being mad and caught up in the moment is bullshit.

Ever since that night with my brother, I've had a host of MF chump-suckers and last but not least, so called friends, along with their women, and let's not forget family members, put them folks on me. For him, Mike Spike, it was on Nov. 26, 2007 for his woman, Dawn, aka Silver Fox, it was on Nov. 18, 2007. Both incidents took place in New York City. In December of 1980 that same Rat, unbeknownst to me then, and I, along with Steve Brody, Muhammad Ali's man Blood and West Indian Joe, all fought side by side on the corner of 123rd Street and Seventh Avenue. Steve and I were both stabbed as a result of that incident.

Years later, 1998 to be exact, Glenn and I ran into each other in the ATL. You know I had to clown his ass about that night back in the day. Eventually, I didn't have to sneak whenever I wanted to attend a house party, nor did I have to be drunk in order to ask a female for a dance, "especially not a slow dance." Getting all soaked and wet from all that fast shit wasn't my style. I wanted to be up close and personal with a sister, and I'm still that way.

ଔ

Chapter 19 ~ Kenny Leaves Home

During this time, Kenny and my mother would clash a lot. Much of the clashing had to do with her sneaking around with Bill the TV Man. The other issue was Kenny had become very close to Brother Adams from my Aunt's church. Kenny being saved under his guidance was the ultimate slap in the face. Ma was right. My Aunt did play a significant role in my brother being 'saved.' But it was done without malice. My Mom was the daughter, the child she couldn't have, and my Mom knew that. Ma knew we knew nothing of what happened at Reverend Adams' house. But my Aunt knew, and that's what bothered her most.

The whole damn house was in a daily uproar it seemed, so my Aunt said to send Kenny to her for a while. At the beginning of 1964, Kenny went to live with our Great Aunt. That 90-day cooling off period was needed, and it was good for both sides all around. Bill never again showed his face at our home. Yet that didn't deter Mom and Bill from seeing each other away from our home. Sometimes, it's not what you do, but rather how you do it.

No child wants to see their mother with another man, especially when the biological father is still in the picture. The real pain and trauma is if that man is of a different ethnicity, be he black or white. And it has nothing to do with being racist, which I am not. The child may begin to look at his own self and say, "Is there something wrong with my white skin, or, is there something wrong with my blackness?" Or is it just my gender? How my brother and I would come to deal with women in general had a lot to do with my mother's behavior with my Dad and Bill the TV man.

Now that I've honestly looked at both of our behaviors, I must admit we possessed a great deal of repressed anger and hostility toward women in general. I'm talking about trust. I've always had surface trust but never total trust, around the corner type trust. Only twice did I honestly find the strength to go beyond that surface trust. The first woman is dead, she died in a New York hotel in 2000. The second died twice, neither was a physical death, on me, once in 2000, and again years later. She just doesn't have the strength to hang in there with a man. But, we have remained friends through it all.

My Brother's infidelity was fear based. Fear that his then wife would be a carbon copy of his mother, not being astute enough or trusting enough, even in himself, to share that fear. Consequently, he succumbed, like many men do, to stepping outside his marriage. Now there are those who will ask, how do you know this? We talked about it in 1970 while both of us were on the run in Chicago and sitting inside the Greyhound bus station on Randolph Street down the block from Pad's Steak House on a chilly Sunday afternoon. (Like I've said before, this is not a book based on fiction. If you want fiction, go read "The Cat in the Hat," or go play in traffic at rush hour.)

Kenny ran away from love because he hadn't had his lessons of love taught to him properly at home. All those years down South didn't help either. As for myself, just imagine you and your mother walking down any street USA laughing, talking and holding hands with the first woman in your life, Your Mother. Unknowingly to you, she is off to meet Mr. Vanilla Good Bar. Now, that's the ultimate betrayal of a child's love. Talk about being hoodwinked and bamboozled.

Some might think, "the author of Shoe Shine Boy" hates his Mom, even in death. Not so. What I hate is her own Dad not being the nurturing father he could have been to his Georgia Peach. So you couldn't deal with my grand Ma Grace. What I hate is my Brother's dad playing that BS game on my Mom and never reaching back at his handsome son or grandchildren. What I hate is a perverted-ass Reverend trying to rape a young woman, my mother, in his own house while his wife was downstairs. What I hate is my brother not knowing how to trust his wife enough to express his fears. What I hate isn't my Mom, but rather just the plain ignorance in people.

People in the position of power and influence do a lot of talking about doing positive things in my community of Roxbury, but in reality that is truly all it is at the end of many days. James Brown (the undisputed Godfather of Soul) truly had far reaching vision along with insight when he came up with these words to one of his many hit songs, "Just talking loud and saying nothing," during the era when the Black Panther party was very vocal throughout American, and especially so on the West Coast and Chicago there was a term circulating within the movement called "Arm Chair Revolutionary." Simply put, "Just talking from a position of up high" never ever getting out of the chair to do anything for the so-called cause.

Today, I see many of our political leaders Black and White fitting that same description as those armchair revolutionaries of the 1960s. Now that the people of America have elected not only an African American president, they have also elected a new mindset as well, this brother, and I say brother with deep conviction as well as respect for him and his lovely family. I pray Allah guides all of his decisions starting January 20, 2009, the day of his well earned and deserved inauguration.

In 1965, the federal government allocated money throughout the country in support of the many inner city programs. Boston along with Roxbury, and other surrounding communities received some of that money. One of the programs to benefit from that funding was the Summer Job Youth Program. This program provided many disenfranchised youth, "Blacks as well as Whites," with an opportunity to learn social skills and earn an honest dollar. The criterion was simple: no drugs or weapons, no fighting and above all, show a strong willingness to help clean up our community. Teens were paired in groups of twenty. They would all meet daily Monday through Friday at eight a.m. sharp at pre-designated locations throughout their neighborhoods.

Many times they'd meet at lots where old abandoned cars, refrigerators and other discarded debris were strewn about. For some strange and unexplainable reason, young children back then found much fascination with playing games inside those death traps we so casually refer to as refrigerators   Some lots would have several of those death traps laying all over the damn place while kids innocently played the old game of hide-and-go-seek. I'm certain even you, gentle reader, played it yourself as a child.

Many children were not properly taught about the do's and don't's of those safety hazards. Kids being kids, unfortunately some would seek out hiding spots inside those coffins to hide from their playmates, never once realizing once they got inside, getting back out by themselves would be an impossibility. Suffocation is an agonizing death for any person, but when it happens to an innocent child, the horror and trauma of the loss is unimaginable.

So with screwdrivers and crowbars in hand, those teenagers would dismantle the doors from every refrigerator they could find lying around those lots. That summer job program served a multitude of purposes, parents knew their kids were in a safe environment and they were doing something productive for their neighborhood. That's not saying all the social ills that plagued Roxbury were suddenly eradicated. By far, that was not the case at all.

The public school system, better yet, those in Roxbury, lacked educational balance as well as many others did across America in 1965. We must remember this country was only a decade away from the Landmark case "Brown vs. Board of Education" in Topeka, Kansas.

I hear people talking a lot about the leaps and bounds being made in cities across America. Boston is the crown prince when it comes to colleges and universities, even down to the second best hospital in the country behind John Hopkins in Baltimore, Maryland. All this talk about the Sylvan Learning Centers, Magnet Programs in Orchard Park Housing Projects (now called Orchard Gardens), or Mission Hill (now Mission Park); what about Lenox Street Projects and Cathedral Projects? Even though there's a huge cathedral one block away, it does very little for that community if you're not Catholic.

Those areas have one of the highest dropout rates, (plus a high mortality rate that isn't attributable to old age, either) in the city. Let's not forget old Colony-D Street and those other impoverished areas. Changing the names and applying a new façade doesn't fix the problem of unbalanced education in this country.

I can still remember holding my daughter's hand as we walked to a bus stop on Westland Avenue and waiting for her bus by a Laundromat. I couldn't help but think of myself when I would look at her with her patch on one eye and her glasses over it. I'd pray in silence that her life would not be subjected to the twists and turns that my life was subjected to. So, please be mindful the next time you decide to boast about Boston being the educational hub of America. As an added note, those walks that Charlene and her father took on those cold mornings to that bus stop were after Federal Judge Garrety had total control of the Boston Public School System.

Control is fine, but what about fixing what you have total control over? Like James Brown said, "talking loud and saying nothing," or doing nothing either.

Boston is still my hometown and most of my family is there, three of my five daughters live there, along with four of my ten grandchildren. But, for real, "the town is much too slow and small."

I'm a Harlemite 'til my eyes close.

ෞ

Chapter 20 ~ Becoming A Black Panther

As 1965 was slowly coming to an end, so was my brother being "sanctified and filled with the Holy Ghost." That was slowly running its course. He still did the church thing, even had a church sister for his girlfriend, a nice Christian girl named Darlene Miller from 2 Batten Court, Old OP. She had four sisters and two brothers.

All of us went to church together on Shawmut Avenue, opposite Lenox Street Projects where the flag used to hang years ago. After a time, all of us would leave Brother Adams' church and attend Reverend Henry Young's church on the corner of Massachusetts Avenue and Tremount Street. He also had a large family of girls. Doris, Theresa, Audrey, Rachelle and a son named Henry. They lived on Cabot Street in the Projects. Theresa was my very first girlfriend.

I met my brother after school one day by Paul's Army and Navy Store across form Joe Nemo's by Dudley Station. We had not seen each other in a couple of weeks. He'd been missing at Sunday School and church as well, so seeing him now made me happy. However, the closer I got to my brother, the more strange he began to look. It was his hair, no longer was he wearing a regular low haircut. He had an honest to goodness Afro. It wasn't a real big one yet, but it was on its way. He immediately wanted to know how I liked it. And to be honest, I was in awe of his look.

He said he had been attending these meetings at North Eastern and U. Mass. along with some Brothers from the local Panther Office on Blue Hill Avenue. He told me he had joined the local Black Panther Party. He told me about our people being slaves and being oppressed by the White Man. His term was a lot harsher than "White Man." He used the term "Pigs." All that shit he was talking sounded Greek to me, Pigs and Panthers. *Nigga, you really need to come on home for real. Ain't no damn pigs and Panthers in Roxbury.* I was serious and so was he.

He did come back home, but now he was all consumed with this Black Panther/Black Power thing. He had now taken on the personification of a real Black Panther in the flesh. I even went to a few of those meetings with him and his friends. Many times I contemplated following behind my big brother. I, too, had an Afro as many others did. Yes, I read "Soul On Ice" by Eldridge Cleaver, and I heard many of the taped speeches made by Malcolm X, etc.

I deeply respected all of what they were standing for. But I was not ready to commit my life to picking up anybody's shotgun, setting fires, etc. His response was, "A coward dies a thousand deaths, a man dies only once." Once I truly accepted Islam, I truly understood the depth of those profound words.

Back then my mind was only on the things I was exposed to in the North End and North Hampton along with the Zone in Town. If it wasn't about money, working girls, pimps and gangsters, I was not willing to listen for long. He went his way and I went down the road that had my name on it. The beauty is, in the end we both found what we truly wanted. Islam. What I've come to truly understand is this. We plan, but Allah is the very best of planners.

‫ω‬

Chapter 21 ~ Moving to OP

For many years, my Mom prayed for the day to come when we would get the letter saying she had to go before a Board to be approved for an apartment in the Projects. That letter finally arrived, and my mother went to the meeting. That's how things were done back then. They did a criminal history check. I believe that is how it is still done before you can get into certain public housing developments throughout the country. I haven't resided in public housing since I was a teenager.

My Mom was approved for occupancy within thirty days from that meeting and was allowed two choices. First choice was the Cathedral Projects in the South End. She wanted one of those apartments along Harrison Avenue. Many were double occupancy. No one over you, only one family beside you, plus it was near Blackstone Park. Many of her girlfriends lived in that development. Laura Boyd, and Vivian lived at 1462 Washington Street. Aunt Sue and Laura lived in the same building and there were others.

Her second choice was Mission Hill Projects because of her girlfriend Catherine and her daughter Crystal. Whenever I'm in Boston and riding past Simmons Liquor and Fish Joint, I always stop in and look for Crystal. She's like my baby sister even though she's over six feet tall. She lights up when she sees me. She gets to talkin' shit to her friends. "Don't be sweating my brother back the fuck up bitch;" "Brother, a bitch is doing bad, do something for me." I can't say no, that's why I got out my car, to hit her crazy ass off and keep it moving.

We didn't get the Cathedral or Mission Hill. We got Orchard Park. "OP" for short. My family was the (George) Jeffersons without the frills. We just didn't make the East Side, so we made OP. The way we acted, you would have thought someone had hit the damn numbers real big. Moving to the projects would mean good heat and cheap rent, that would even be a Godsend, especially in light of the day's economy. So, sometime in February of 1965 we moved to Orchard Park, 8 Adams Street, Apt. 497.

In 1965, OP still had white families living on the backside of the projects, right behind us along Hamdon Street, and even on Harrison Avenue. Many of the families had been there ten years or better when we moved in. The Green family I came to know very well. Ma Green's oldest son Butch and my brother played football together. Her son Bryant, whom we called Shorty, is to this day a very close friend of mine.

The Johnson family was another old family. Louise Johnson and my Mom knew each other as teenagers. Ms. Johnson had four children, two boys and two girls. Louise's Mom and sister were also well known throughout our community. Louise's Mom lived on Shawmut Avenue, and was one of those sisters who people went to when things wasn't going right with their man, etc. She'd do her "Root Work" on his ass and he'd be back in line come Monday morning. Mom said her whole house was in "Polka-Dot-Pink." Yes! Polka-Dot-Pink!

Long before Dennis Rodman ever picked up a basketball, or even dreamt of being a pro ball player, even longer still before he had the notion to do a rainbow coalition hair color, around the North Hampton Street area there was a lady about five feet five inches with red complexion. When I was a shine boy, I'd see her all the time down North Hampton. She'd have her hair in those rainbow colors. One day I mentioned it to my parents. They both laughed and said, that is so and so. She was Ms. Louise's sister. After that, we never made fun of her again. She was always nice to all the shine boys.

Many of the families in OP we knew from our days on Sherman and Bower Streets; Billy Baker's family, (he's now a minister); Philip Williams (aka Chilly); Garland and Tommy Sweeney. In many ways it was like old home week. Members of the New Edition Group also came from OP. Bobby's sister Bethy was very close to someone I was engaged to marry. Her name was Theresa Mack. While Theresa and I resided in Stone Mt. Georgia, we had a clothing business. Bethy used to come by often. In fact, the Brown family had Christmas dinner at our home on Christmas Day 1998. I have some photographs taken with Mr. Brown as I began to carve up a turkey in my dining room.

Theresa died in 2000 due to diabetes. Bethy died in 2002 from cancer. My wife of today, Jacqueline E. Jones-Belim is also very close to the Brown family.

Prior to Bobby's divorce, his dad and I had discussed starting a limousine business in Atlanta. I had the money, and he knew the stars through his sons Bobby and Tommy. Before we could get things off the ground, Mr. Brown moved to Jersey with Bobby and his still then wife Whitney Houston. Ms. Louise's son Charlie is who they say taught young Bobby how to dance. Charlie and Bethy are no longer with us, but their son and daughter are here to remind us of both of them. May their souls rest in peace.

Back in pre-project and project days, everybody's families knew one another. The kids knew each other, but that sense of camaraderie has now been fragmented and splintered beyond belief.

Now, in those same housing developments and outside neighborhoods, our kids, in the collective sense, are being brutally murdered for the most ludicrous of reasons. If I were president elect Obama on the day of my inauguration, January 20, 2009, part of my speech would be that immediately upon entering the White House my first signed bill would be that every able-bodied student would be encouraged to read the book entitled, "The Willie Lynch Letters" by William Lynch and Kashif Malik Hassan-el for junior high and high school. It should be part of the core curriculum and students should be required to write papers on it in order to pass the grade. This reading should be encouraged in all white schools as well.

How many stray small and large caliber bullets must miss its intended target and hit the unintended like it did that day on Humboldt Avenue? Remember Tiffany Moore? And what about that other stray one that caught that young child playing in that makeshift park on Quincy Street and Blue Hill Avenue? Remember the day those stray one went crazy at Dudley Station and killed a Roxbury legend named Charlie Johnson? Do we really care, or just say we care and keep it moving? What happens when that stray one hits your child or grandchild? What if, what if, if it's you it hits?

CHARLES H. BELIM

OP was much different back when I was a teen. I didn't have to worry about going to Ms. Green's apartment at 13 Woodrow Wilson Court for a slice of one of those good pies of hers. Back in 1965, they still employed white maintenance workers throughout the projects to keep the place spruced up.

 G

Chapter 22 ~ Mom Breaks the Silence

My Mom was a strange woman at times. Shortly after we moved into the projects, perhaps it was March or April of 1965, Mom had been out with my Aunt and they had had a beef about Kenny not being saved now that he was hanging around the Black Panther office on Blue Hill Avenue.

From what I'd been able to piece together along with Mom's "Johnny Walker Red Label" version, Brother Adams' name came up because he made a statement about Kenny no longer attending his church. He dropped a lug as if my Mom was behind us not going to his church any longer. Truth be told, all the fly sisters along with the Hollins family were now attending Reverend Henry Young's church on Massachusetts Avenue.

Reverend Adams' remarks to my Aunt about my brother attending his church created a big beef between my Mom and Aunt. Mom came home angrier than an MF. Kenny and Pop weren't there. After several minutes of mumbling to herself, Mom said, "Charlie, get your coat." Soon as I saw Mom ease 'Big Butch' out from under her mattress, I knew somebody's ass was in big trouble. Our destination was Reverend Adams' house.

All the way up there she is cursing between drags off her Chesterfield Kings. Just as we pull up to the house, I see Reverend Adams' car. Now I know where we are. Now I start asking, "Mom, what's wrong, what's wrong???" She kept saying over and over how she should have cut him up years ago for putting his dirty hands on her. When I said, "Who hurt you Mom?" she just looked at me and started crying.

After she paid the fare and got out the cab, Mom stormed up those steps with her knife out, ready to do work and she wasn't joking. After laying on that bell, Sister Adams came to the door. She saw us and was just about to open the screen door when she looked down and saw "Big Butch" in Mom's right hand. Sister Adams stepped back and yelled, "Josh, she got a big knife! HELP! JOSH! HELP!" As soon as Mom saw

Brother Adams appear at the door, she broke the whole glass window out and cut her hand doing it.

My mother was in a trance-like rage. I started saying, "Ma! MA! You're bleeding!" She's like, "Shut the hell up! You don't know what that bastard tried to do to me! Now he wants to talk about my son? NO, NO, NO!" Mom stuck that knife right through the screen and it almost struck Reverend Adams in the chest. Now he's yelling, "Earline, what's wrong? What's wrong, young sister?"

"What's wrong?" Mom said. "You dirty MF! You tried to rape me in my room!" And again, Big Butch went through the screen door at him. "No! NO! Earline! It won't dat way, you's wrong, you wrong!" Then, from somewhere within him, he said, "Earline, I sorry, I sorry I hurt you, please! PLEASE! I sorry!" At that moment, I finally understood Mom's dislike for Reverend Adams. His wife stood at the door saying, "He's sorry, Earline! He's sorry! Please don't hurt him!" Mom just continued to cut and cry at their door. I was traumatized, hurt and all confused at the same time.

With all the noise that was being made, somebody called the police. All I remember is them taking "Big Butch and Mom away," she in handcuffs and bloody. The police allowed Mom to hand me some crumpled up bloody bills to go home with. I just stood at the bottom of those steps for a long time, no longer crying, just totally numb.

Finally, Sister Adams' voice could be heard saying, "Do you want to come in?" I looked at her with such venom. She did not ask me twice, and I just walked away. I have not laid eyes on either of them ever since. Imagine. My Mother carrying that shit around inside her all those years.

Now that I'm a grown man, I can better express those feelings of anger toward Reverend Adams and his "Sanctimonious Co-Conspirator Wife." Whenever I play back the tape, and I've done it many times over the past 45 years, I still hear that voice of hers apologizing for him as if it were an unintentional act. But deep within her loins, she knew what he had done, and it was not his first time doing that to someone, I am sure. His apology will never be accepted by me.

I started walking until I saw an open store near Dorchester Court. I entered and purchased a ginger ale and washed Mom's blood off the bills and my hand, and caught the bus to Dudley. From there, I caught another bus down North Hampton. Going there always made me feel safe and good, like the hospital.

I saw a guy named Leon whose shoes I used to shine. I asked him for a cigarette. First time I ever smoked a whole one. I coughed like crazy, but wouldn't put it out. I asked, "How much does it cost to go to New York City by bus?"

Leon looked at me real hard for a moment, then said, "Something bad happen, Charlie?" I said, yes. He told me it would cost about ten dollars and asked if I had the money. Again, I said, yes. Then he put his hand in his pocket and took out a stack of bills and gave me a fifty-dollar bill. "Put this in the toe of your shoe for hard times."

He walked me to the North Hampton station, and instructed me to hang around the areas where all the working girls would be. I'd be safe, they'd look out for a youngster like me. I would find out all his suggestions were right on the money. Now here I am on a damn bus. And Leon was right about the fare (it was $9.85) to New York City. I just needed some breathing room. I felt Mom would be okay by morning, and I would be proven correct. However, it would be a few months before I would know that for sure.

The closer that bus got to New York the more my self confidence took leaps and bounds that I didn't understand or know how to express as a fourteen year old teen. Perhaps those feelings are best described in this way, as if it were the very day that the news began to spread that the "16th president of the United States had signed the Emancipation Proclamation freeing black folks." The feeling they felt upon hearing that news is what I felt. "Free at last, free at last," as if a great burden had been lifted off of me.

I had thirty-five dollars in my pants pocket, and a fifty-dollar bill Leon had given me wrapped in paper and stuck deep in the front of my right shoe. Prostitutes are not like square broads. They are nonjudgmental and they ask few personal questions. Soon enough I would learn firsthand that the women I would soon come in contact with were only concerned with what I wanted to be called.

Never once had I at that point wanted to be called anything but Charlie. Not Charles. (Years later a nickname would cause me much trouble by way of the Federal Government) and I've been Charlie ever since. From the days of feeling and looking like "Mr. Tin Man" from the Wizard of Oz, running away was something I truly harbored. The restraints of having endured two half body casts due to two major operations on my right arm, the eye operation followed by a series of eye patches under thick eyeglass lenses, red hair and an eczema problem, and last but not least, "Bill the TV Man." Now I could truly begin to exhale.

I knew how to steal already, and I knew how to talk to hoes on the stroll, as well as their pimps and other assorted hustlers. The North End and North Hampton Street had given me some survival tools, the only thing missing was "Big Butch," which the police had taken away when they hauled Mom off to jail in Boston.

೮ you3

Chapter 23 ~ New York

The Boston bus pulled into the Port Authority Bus Terminal at 2:30am. I hadn't slept the whole ride to New York. Excitement had overpowered any need for sleep. I was truly in a New York state of mind.

Stepping off that bus inside the Port Authority terminal was one hell of an experience for a fourteen-year old kid at 2:30 in the morning in 1965. The amount of people in that station at that hour blew my mind. Although I'd never been out that late in Boston, I knew nowhere in Boston could you find that amount of people at that hour. I mean, I was in total awe.

When I figured out which way was the front, I came out on the Eighth Avenue side where all the cabs were lined up taking people home, or wherever they wanted to go. For a split second, I wanted to get inside one of those big belly yellow taxis and say, "Take me home to 8 Adams Street, Roxbury." But I knew that was not possible. I was too far from home to take a taxi.

As I made my way through the maze of people traffic to the corner of 42nd Street and 8th Avenue, panic hit me hard. I just stood frozen in time and space until this woman asked me if I was lost. "Are you okay?" I just nodded my head to indicate that I was fine. It was the reality of my actions that had me frozen in time for a brief moment, running away from a warm and comfortable home even though its occupants were a bit "dysfunctional."

My daughter Shera's mother loves to use that word to describe my family. She says, "Your family is very dysfunctional and I guess you came over on the Mayflower." I would not encourage any fourteen-year old to up and run away. I was blessed I had some built in survival skills that kept me out of harm's way. Many times I had to draw upon them daily to survive.

As I crossed the street to begin my first walk ever on "the Deuce" (Forty-Second Street), I saw many strange looking and strangely dressed people.

Not having had much sleep except for a nod or two on the bus, I knew I had to find a place to rest. In New York back then the movie theaters on 42nd Street stayed open all night, but I knew that wasn't a good move for many reasons, including being mugged, the other reason as them strange looking people. I sure wished I had "Big Butch" tucked in my belt. I knew I had to get one tomorrow, for now I needed something to eat and some sleep.

On the South corner of 42nd Street was a huge all night restaurant that had several different sections where you could buy cheap beer, hot dogs with saurkraut, hamburgers, papaya and coconut juices. The place had a lot of booths to sit in. Many people were just sitting around talking over coffee and smoking cigarettes. I ordered two dogs, a burger, fries, and tasted papaya juice for the first time. It was good. After eating, I felt really tired. So, it was either an all night spooky movie house, or the bus station. I chose the bus station for my resting place.

On my way in, a black woman was struggling with her luggage and a small baby. Immediately, I offered some assistance, which she accepted. I walked with her to get her ticket to Alabama. Her bus was scheduled to leave at 7:30am. She said she left home early because she came from a place called "Bushwick" in Brooklyn. I had heard of Brooklyn, by way of the Brooklyn Dodgers, but Bushwick was Greek to this fourteen-year old. I told her my Aunt was coming in on the 7:30 bus from Georgia. "Do you mind if I sit with you?" I asked. "Please do," she said. She wanted some company, so we talked a while before we both fell asleep. My first night in New York, I slept in a chair alongside a young mother and her baby inside the Port Authority Bus Terminal.

At 7:10 am, I woke her up, watched her single luggage while she took her baby to the Ladies room to change her and freshen herself up. When she returned, I told her my Aunt's bus was late and I could help her to the bus gate, where we said our goodbyes before I went outside again. I remember that morning well. It was very cold, although it was September. I knew from stories back in Boston that working girls worked late to early morning around the bus station. So this time I found my way to the back of the bus station on the Ninth Avenue side. Immediately I found what I'd been searching for.

On the other side of the street where the men were loading trucks with beef on hooks at some kind of meat packing house, I saw a group of girls in them white Go-Go boots flagging down cars and laughing with the truckers. Rather than ask one where I could get some food for breakfast, I told one who looked to be a couple years older than myself, whose name I later learned was "Star Child," that I was hungry and had no money.

One of the older girls looked at me and said, "Go home, kid. What are you doing around here?" The one named Star Child said to leave me alone. "The boy is hungry, and got no money." She told me she was still working, but if I wanted to wait she'd treat me to breakfast with her friends. She said I could wait in a doorway or go back to wait at the station where there was warmer. I wanted to stay near her, but I was cold, so I went back over to the station to wait inside the doors facing the street.

I watched as Star Child and her friends stopped cars and some got in. Some cars only slowed down to just stare gawkily at the girls and quickly drive off. When Star would stop a car she'd motion for him to pull over so they could talk. If it was a go, she'd slip inside and immediately disappear from sight as the car pulled away. I saw her do the same thing several times before I realized what she was doing. As the guy drove away, she would immediately start on him. She'd be back in ten to fifteen minutes, depending on traffic. After about an hour, she motioned at me from the other side of 9th Avenue to come on out of the bus station as I stood looking out through the glass doors.

By now it was beginning to warm up a bit. Star Child with two of her friends and I poured ourselves into a big belly cab. Someone said, "Take us to the ham and eggs on 50th and 7th Avenue." It was really named "Ham and Eggs." Upon entering, I immediately had the sense I'd never be hungry as long as I stayed in New York. The place was full of pimps and working girls in all shades of color, old ones, young ones, and not so young. The place made me think of Bickford's on Massachusetts Avenue in Boston, MA. There were a few scattered Whites and Hispanics, and working people.

Everyone seemed to know one another, including the employees. As we sat down the waitress only gave one menu. I thought it was odd. Then Star started laughing and said she knows exactly what we'll eat. We don't use menus in here. Her friend with the wavy slicked back hair smiled and said, "They call me Butch. Just Butch." Then she turned in the direction of a girl about 19 or 20 years old and said, "This is my woman, Cinnamon Toast," and she kissed her full on the mouth. I had never seen women kiss like that in my young life. I was like in total shock. Star said, "Now, what do they call you?"

Everyone is called what they choose in this town. It wasn't about what's my name but rather who I wanted to be. I knew more about who I didn't want to be, and that was "Mr. Tin Man." All I ever wanted to be was just me, myself. So, I said they call me Charlie. Star began smiling, and laughing and so did everyone else at the table. Then Star got serious and explained that her Daddy was named "Charlie," he had died a year ago. Star then introduced herself as "Star Child." I had two helpings of everything that morning. No one asked at that table where I was from or why I was in the streets hungry.

Star's friends left first, kissing and hugging all the way out the door. Then Star looked over at me from the other side of the table to ask, "Where would you like to be dropped off at?" I didn't know how to respond because I only knew the bus station. Then she gently touched my hand and said, "You don't have any place to go to, do you?" I did nothing but nod in agreement, as the tears rolled down my face.

She held my hand tightly and said, you are safe and in good hands with Star Child. From that day to the day I left New York for home, I was her little brother, only for a minute. We sat there in the Ham and Eggs for a couple hours. I told her my story and she told me hers. Star was just 19 years old and from Hartford, Connecticut. Her Mother died while giving birth to her, her Daddy was a minister who had remarried a woman who was very light complexioned like her Dad. She, however, came out very dark like her mom. Her step-mom was very mean and abusive to her all her life. She used to call her "Midnight Black" and "Tar Baby." When she'd tell her Daddy, he'd say she's only playing. Once he was gone, she'd really get on her. Her Dad died of cancer, and right after he died, her step-mom threw her out the house into the streets. She came to New York, met a pimp at the bus station named "Ice" who pimped her 'til he started beating her for not making enough money. The more she made, the more he'd beat her up.

One morning she came home and he was high and started his shit. She ran to the dresser and grabbed a pair of scissors and stabbed him twice and ran out. He didn't die and he's never bothered her again. I told her about all my operations, my Mom and Bill and the fight, my Dad and his snobbish family. I just needed a strong shoulder to cry on. She even started to cry. That was our cue to get out of there and go home, as she put it.

Star Child lived in an apartment type hotel on 46th Street between 6th and 7th Avenues in midtown Manhattan. She had what was called a studio, her own bath inside, not in the hallway, and a small area where she could cook. She had an old refrigerator, a big oversized bed, a TV and a closet. I learned all about the pussy game from her and about the needs of men, especially white men. How they would call her dirty names while she sucked them off. "Nigga Bitch, suck it," was a favorite of theirs back then. She said she did very little fucking. She'd say she was on her period, so she'd give them "just head only." Some even wanted to do her, even assuming she was on her period. At those times, she said she wished she was really on it, so they could do it, just so she could see how nasty they truly were.

She would take time to explain many things to me about 'the life,' as she called it. She said, there's no game older or stronger than the Pussy-whore-hoe game. She said whores are real slick and tricky. "We fake like we are coming to get a trick off us," she'd say. Not all whores fuck, she'd tell me. Some suck dicks and slip their hands in a trick's pocket while they are making him cum. Some hoes will stop a car, one hoe on one side ups her skirt, sticks a finger inside herself, then in her mouth. The other girl is on the driver's side with one breast exposed so he can see and touch it while she's grabbing at his dick and the other hand is in his pocket or the other girl slips in on the other side and is all over him. He winds up getting beat and not even knowing it. Think hoes ain't slick? Fuck with one and you'll find out who's slicker than who.

I learned that hoes who were pimp-less (no pimp, not paying any pimp), were frowned upon by whores who had pimps and by pimps in general. A hoe without a pimp is called a "renegade whore" because she's not part of the flow of the game. Then you have Butch whores, they are holding a bitch down, whores who've been abused by their former pimp, or some man who sexually abused them at some point in their lives. Naturally, some girls just like women altogether, and they only deal with women, even though they are hoes. Butch chose that name because she's gay and only gets down with women. No doubt, she's also got a story to tell.

Star and I were both tired. We took turns using the shower. I washed my shorts, T-shirt, and socks and now I had nothing to sleep in. Star gave me a big beach towel to wrap myself in. I asked for a blanket and one pillow so I could sleep on the carpet by her big bed. She said, "Boy, you crazy! Get your ass in this bed!" We slept at separate ends of the bed, which was cool with me.

From our friendship, I learned much about hustling women, and hustling period. Star taught me how to survive in New York. She'd say you got to earn your keep and that's what I did. Whenever she or one of her girlfriends would get in a trick's car, I'd write down the tag (license plate) number, etc. That way, if the girls had problems with a Trick, the girls would tell the Trick their little brother had his tag number. Sometimes a Trick would even try to take back his money, or he might try to go where she felt unsafe. Some Tricks would try to force the girls to do acts they felt uncomfortable doing, or they just didn't want to do.

Once those Tricks heard someone had their tag information, they wouldn't get out of line, and it made the girls feel safer. Even the pimps had no problem with the girls giving me the five-dollars for my service. That is how I earned my keep. No one gave me any shit just because I was a kid. I was the "everything-kid," the "kid Friday." I'd get the girls hot chocolate off the truck along with cigarettes and beer from the bodega. Many times I would even hold their "weed."

One day, I told Star I needed to buy myself a "Big Butch." At first she didn't understand exactly what I meant 'til I pointed to the scissors that she kept in her bag. Star took me to an old pawn shop on Eighth Avenue and 44th Street where I purchased a nice "Baby Butch" for seven-dollars.

The only woman I'd ever been shopping with at that point in my life was my Mom. But all that would change. After a week of wearing two pair of Levi's, Star took me shopping. I had saved two-hundred-dollars and she also gave me two one-hundred-dollar bills. She explained that they called them "C" Notes, rather than just hundred-dollar bills. She also explained that people in the life, those who hustled, spoke a different language than squares. So I adopted that same term which I use it to this very day.

The weather was still mild enough for us to all go out to Coney Island. I had heard so much about the place and seen it in movies. Going there would be a real treat. All four of us went together, Star, myself, Butch and Cinnamon. My next big surprise would be the best. Star said, "Charlie, how would you like to go to the Apollo Theater?" That was one place I never thought I'd ever visit, and now I was being invited to go there.

"Sure I'd like to go!" But before I could go, I had to get a fresh cut and new clothes. Butch announced that we were going to her stores. Butch was 100% butch. She wore men's everything. Star said Butch even wore men's socks and under shorts.

The flyest men's store I had ever seen in my life was Leighton's at 47th Street and Broadway. Man, Leighton's had the best of the best in shoes of all the popular colors, and skins, hats, coats and slacks. Downstairs was their shoe department. From the moment we stepped through the doors we got the royal treatment and all because Butch was a valued customer in a big way.

Butch spent a lot of money in Leighton's on a regular basis. When I said I had some money on me to help pay for the clothes, everyone just laughed. Butch said, "Charlie, your money is counterfeit today!" Today, I was their "pimp," and they had planned on making me New York sharp. I selected two pair of slip-on one-hundred-percent lizard, one pair in dark blue, the other burgundy with suede toe-tips. In addition, I got matching socks, two one-hundred-percent Alpaca V–neck sweaters, one dark blue and white, the other burgundy and white, two short hair beaver hats, one Knox 44 the other Dobbs. Butch would later show me how to put baby oil on them to make them shine.

From Leighton's we went up Broadway to 49th Street to a store called Phil Kornfield's, another fly men's store where we were again treated like royalty, to buy matching leather jackets and slacks. To this day, I have no idea how much money those women actually spent on me in those two stores.

We all went uptown that Friday and Saturday night to the famous Apollo Theatre on 125th Street. We saw The Dells and The Impressions and Jerry Butler. Talk about being sharp. I was beyond sharp that night. And we took many photographs.

I've been five-feet-ten-and-a-half-inches tall since I was thirteen years old. That weekend I was six-feet tall or better. That Friday would be my first time ever having a drink, smoking weed, and experiencing sex.

When Star and I got home, she was real happy about the whole evening, and so was I. At one point, I excused myself to use the bathroom. Upon returning, Star had two paper cups with rum and Coke in each. In one hand she had a joint of weed. After looking at me long and hard, she finally said, "Charlie, from tonight on, you are going to be a man!" She handed me that drink, which I didn't refuse, patting the bed for me to sit down. I followed her lead, relighting her joint as the embers dulled. After two short inhales, Star took a long drag from the joint and held it for a while. Then she took my young face in between her soft hands and slowly blew all that smoke into my virgin mouth. She pressed her mouth tightly up against my own to keep the smoke from escaping. She repeated this twice more. Then the question was asked.

"Charlie, have you ever had sex?" Man, I shook like an earthquake had hit my young vulnerable ass, and responded with a resounding "NO." Star Child said to me, "Tonight, Charles, that is going to change. Tonight you will embrace your manhood through me." I wasn't quite sure what all those words meant, but I believed it meant we were going to do it, and I was all for that. Star guided me to undress her, starting with her stockings, which were hooked to her garter belt. I undid them one at a time. Next, she said to slide each stocking down slowly. So I knelt between her legs and slipped each stocking down her long smooth sexy legs. Star stood up wide legged as I unhooked her skirt and watched it fall easily to the floor. She ordered me to unbutton her blouse slowly. Again, I was shaking.

In a calm voice, Star reassured me, "It's okay, just take your time, Charlie." Slowly, I slipped off her blouse and gently laid it on the soft quilt on her bed. Her next request was once again soft and sensuous. "Remove my bra, Charlie." I let her bra fall away from her body, revealing two firm breasts. Slowly, Star whispered for me to please, please place one of her throbbing breasts in my mouth as if I were a young baby in need of milk from it's mother's breast. Small cries of joy could be heard from Star as my warm lips and tongue made contact with her dark brown nipples. Suddenly, she pleaded with me to cease. She now wanted to sit on the bed so she could now undress me as I had done her. I sat there totally immobile as I watched Star make us two more mixtures of rum and Coke over ice.

Trying hard to be cool, I offered to relight her joint. She responded, "No, baby. I'm going to light it for you, and I want you to do exactly as you saw me do. Now pull on the joint as I light it Charlie, not hard, slow even. Get as much smoke in your mouth as you can, hold, then slowly blow it in my mouth, Charlie." The combination of us doing that back and forth several times, along with the rum and Cokes, had me higher than a research monkey in an NYU lab.

Star slid seductively down to the floor so she could remove my shoes and socks, one by one. While in that kneeling position, she said to stand up and face her, as she slowly and cautiously opened my belt, unzipped my pants, causing them to drop silently to the carpeted floor. There I was, protruding and standing at attention as if I as about to salute the President of the United States! Star complimented my being circumcised, explaining that uncircumcised men are a turnoff to most women, especially when a woman wants to give back the same pleasure they may have just received (some explosively super good head) from their man.

Without a word being said, Star reached out with both hands and eagerly engulfed my manhood deep within her warm mouth. Building deep within my loins, the eruption that took place now, Three Mile Island could not even come close to. Star being the pro that she was sensed my imminent explosion and withdrew herself from me immediately. Without any hesitation, we both slipped out of our underwear and got into the shower together, taking turns washing each other playfully.

Rather than drying ourselves off, we ran and jumped into the bed, throwing the covers over our wet bodies. As our bodies began to slowly dry from the warmth of the quilt, Star reached for a bottle of baby oil that she had heating in a saucepan on a low flame. After pouring several drops of the hot oil into her right hand, Star motioned for me to lie on my back as she massaged the hot oil into my skin. When she reached my waist and pelvic area, she seized all of my firmness with both hands and slipped it deep in her bottomless throat and held me there suspended in space and time.

Now it was my opportunity to return the favor by putting the oil on her velvety smooth body as she lay before me on her stomach. When it came time to expose the front of her voluptuous body to me, I felt bolts upon bolts of electricity moving through me when I applied the oil to every curve of her body. The firmness of those curved breasts even now still remind me of two ripe coconuts that have recently fallen from a tree in the wild. Her eyes encouraged me to take her nipples one by one in my mouth, their taste was that of freshly squeezed mango. The very tips of her nipples brought a chill to my tongue suspended in time. I watched as drops of oil slowly disappeared into the dark mound of curly hair between her thighs. It reminds me, even now, of light summer rainfall cascading through trees.

I had never been that close or intimate with a woman in my life. The effects of that night, even though it has been many years, are so vividly clear now, as if it was night 45 years ago, so long ago. As I moved down to massage one of her legs, she opened them both very wide and reached to guide my head to her waiting mound of dark flesh. As her voice reached my ears, I heard her whisper, "Charles, please touch me down there," Star pointed to a little spot with her finger, "with your

129

tongue…Don't stop licking me there 'til you hear me scream and you taste my cream."

And it all happened in order. She began with a faint cry, urgently gripped my head, pressing it into her mound of deep darkness with both of her hands. Suddenly, she yelled out, "Yes-yes-yes, Charlie, right there, right there, don't stop, much harder with your tongue, pleeeeeeeease!" Then the rain of her cream was all on my tongue and face, hot and sticky. Star shook violently for a long time. Finally, she said, "Lay with me and just hold me close," I did just that.

After a bit of silence, she said, "Charlie, I want to go horseback riding without a saddle on my horse." How are we going to do that, I asked. Star just smiled and slowly mounted me. Then instantly, I knew what she meant. She rode her horse for about thirty minutes. She came, I went, I came, she went, then we both came and went directly to sleep.

When we awoke we had a real long man and woman talk. Star explained that what happened between us did not make us 'man and woman,' in other words 'a couple.' It was just something we both needed to give and accept from each other, without any attachments after the fact. She wanted to know if I was okay with what she had explained, and I responded by saying, yes. Looking long and hard into my eyes, Star finally said, "I do believe you, Charlie." What really blew me away was when Star said, "You have too much compassion and passion in what you did last night -- you allowed yourself to trust in a hoe. A woman for that matter -- to ever become a pimp, "unless a woman messes over your feelings. You're not my pimp, and you didn't turn a trick with me. (You didn't buy my sex last night, Charlie.) So don't ever feel like a hoe beat you out of anything."

She gave me five "C-notes" and a long kiss. Then, we did it again, except this time she extracted from me what I had extracted from her when she held my head tightly up against her mound at her moment of release. I now held her firmly in my grip, between my hands and legs, as my body erupted into spasm after spasm. It was as if hot lava flowed forth from me into depths deep within her throat. I shook and hollered as the last of my semen dripped into her tightly closed mouth.

We slept for what seemed like days, which in reality was but a few hours. We awoke, ate, relaxed, and did it again, except this time Star showed me how to come in what she called the "back door" without a key or a need to knock. She cracked the door and I slipped in, and found that spot that made her tremble, as she slipped my fingers into her mouth and sucked hard. There's a saying in New York, you get all your breaks on Broadway, that's not necessarily so. I got my break the morning I walked out the rear entrance of the Port Authority bus terminal onto 9th Avenue where I approached a woman who called herself "Star Child" and was only three years old than myself. All I said to her was that I was hungry, and got a New York hipping in a New York minute. I knew I was laying next to a full woman, a woman who brought the man from deep within the teenager all the way out.

No matter what may lay ahead for me in life, all innocence was forever gone, lost to oblivion. She also told me and showed me that I was okay just as I was. God she said gave me these eyes crossed, not man. God made my arm the way it was, also my eczema, and red hair, were all gifts, gifts from God. How could I ever seek more or want something better when I was truly better already?

In those four months, I would experience and learn much about life at a young age through her eyes, as well as my own personal experiences. Each day would bring new and exciting challenges to both of our lives. She would come to trust me and I would come to value her trust. Working girls as she loved to be called, sometimes got busted twice in one week, and she was no exception. I knew where her bank was, as she sometimes called it, or just her stash, or her bankroll (BR). Twice, I had to call a guy named Ray Robinson. He had a bail bonding office on Baxter Street, No. 77, behind "AP1." Court Rm. AP1 is the courtroom that's on the first floor in the back facing the park on Baxter Street at 100 Centre Street in lower Manhattan.

In years to come, 77 Baxter Street would become a fixture in my life and the lives of many of my friends. Ray the Bondsman would be sent to prison for doing drug business with some uptown people, "so they say." I, personally, take no position on any of those allegations. Seventy-seven Baxter Street became my attorney's office in the mid 1970s to 1985.

Whenever Star got busted, I knew exactly what to do, and she counted on me doing it to the letter.

One evening, Star got busted early, but she still didn't make Court until after 11:00pm, or more like after 12 midnight. I paid her fine and court costs on the first floor in Room 100. As they were releasing her, the Matron said, "Your man paid everything." The words, "your man" scared her bad. Immediately, she thought it was "Ice," she was scared to come out. Finally, she came out and saw me standing there with two cups of coffee in my hands. She ran and damn near knocked me down, she was crying and hugging me at the same time. On our way uptown, she told me the whole story about what the Matron has dais, as she slowly unzipped my fly, she said, "You are my man, Charlie..." She was a bit too preoccupied the rest of the cab ride to speak.

New York players have a language and swagger uniquely unto themselves. They have a saying called, "coming into your own." To some outsiders (squares, people not in the life) they would say that's some nigga hood shit. It means you have arrived, you got a big "A" on all your life skills exams, and now you're ready for underworld America, as well as square world America, and beyond. So, when a young player is told by an older player that you have finally come into your own, go ahead and pat yourself on the back because a lot of us don't make the GPA requirement – an "A+" in integrity. They miss some of their lessons along the road of life, males and females. In 1965, I was a strong "C+" student. Today, I'm, well, you make that judgment call.

I have a dear old friend whose name I'll omit because he's on that same wanted list I was on until my arrest on November 28th, 2007 in New York City. I'm not talking about being on that local Most Wanted list, either. I'm referring to being on the high Sheriff's most wanted list, "America's Most Wanted." We will call my old friend "Bemo," or "The Chief." One day, he, my homie Paul (White), and I were looking for someone to play. While riding, out of sheer boredom, Bemo says, "Man, I thought I was as slick as they come, 'til ..." (and he shared a story about a woman, without revealing too much) and he continued, "there are far too many ways to e a sucker, and we can't duck them all!" Keep that in mind when you're dealing with women.

My friend Star also told me something similar. She said, "Baby, a woman's moods change like the leaves on the trees. They can't beat you physically, but she will play you, if you don't stay the stronger of the two. Always stay the stronger of the two, no matter what the situation may be." Way back then, she used to talk a lot about owning her own real estate property. She said that the house her Dad had was his and her Mom's, and it couldn't legally go to her stepmother. It had to go to her directly upon their deaths. His new wife knew all of what she said was true. She told me one day she'd go back and do what she was supposed to do and what needs to be done. She told me that I would also someday go back and do what needed to be done, but that I'd always return to New York City, and that maybe she'd still be here.

The next day, Star revealed to me her true birth name and that of her parents, not the one the streets or the courts knew her as, but the one her parents gave her at birth, along with an address in Hartford, Connecticut. I told her my whole name as well, and gave her my family's address and phone number. The first week of January 1966, I would return home to my family in Boston.

The night before I departed, we made love, Star and I. We both cried. She held me tight and said, "I love you also, Charles. I know as you know you have to go. I know you would stay if I was to ask, but as bad as I may want to, in my heart, I can't. I don't have that right. It would not be fair to your family or you." She made me promise to come back and check on her. If I ever needed her for anything, I knew how to find her, just like I found her that morning back in September. Plus, I knew how to find "Butch and Cinnamon."

We parted, all of us, just as we met, on 9th Avenue behind the Port Authority Bus Terminal; but we all would reunite again.

Chapter 24 ~ Going Home

Going home felt strange and good at the same time. A thought comes to mind. How we see ourselves on paper is far more revealing of our vulnerabilities, and our idiosyncrasies show themselves, allowing us to see and know we are truly just human. That guy or that woman in the mirror is only who we tell ourselves we are, or who we try so hard to be. Many times that person in the mirror isn't truthful to the face we see.

Yes. Returning home did feel good and strange. Strange because of the strong gravitational pull I kept feeling, as the bus got closer to Boston. Now and only now am I equipped emotionally enough to explain my honest feelings at that moment -- anxiety, anxiousness, agitation best describe my feelings as I stepped off that bus. I stayed stuck inside the bus station for two hours before I finally decided to leave for home.

Home? What home? Whose home? That's how indecisive I felt. I was no longer that insecure wanna-be-crowd-pleaser that I was almost five months ago before I left. I no longer felt I had run away. "I just left" because I no longer liked what was happening to me, as well as what was happening within my family. That's the real reason I got the hell out of there. At age fourteen-fifteen I was bailing a woman, my woman, out of jail. Kids don't do that type of shit. They just don't have the savvy or self-discipline to follow through on that type of mission. Being a team player is at times far more stressful than the person that is giving out the commands.

You never know what position you may be forced to play out of plain necessity. I can lead well and I can fall back and let the other person shine and not feel less than. What I'm saying is I didn't feel fifteen any longer, and no, I don't want to shoot any damn hoops, either! I did want to make up the months I again missed from school. Walking out of the Bus Station I patted my pocket for two things, "Baby Butch" and my "BR." I already had my house keys in my other hand.

New England weather can be quite cold in January, but for some reason, it wasn't cold or windy. It was as if the weather stood still all around me.

Today everyone was on the stoop talking, including my whole family. Even my Aunt Tee was over our house. On that particular day it was as if they knew I was coming home.

As the cab eased to a stop at Number 8 Adams Street, everyone immediately started gawking. Project folks are known for that. They are real nosey. While paying the driver, my Mom and Aunt were breaking their necks to see who was in this cab, but the glare from the sun didn't help. Kenny, however, was in a far better position to see me. Before the cab door opened, Kenny was up and running to the car.

I can still hear that deep voice of his saying, "Ma! Ma! Ma, it's Charles! He's come home!" Now everyone on the stoop is up yelling and screaming like crazy. You'd have thought I was Moses coming to part the Red Sea.

Everyone was pushing and shoving to get at me, as if they were crazy. Mom and Dad made everyone give me room to get my suitcase out of the trunk of the cab. I had left empty handed and now I was home with a suitcase. "It seemed like everyone wanted to help," Dad said, as he looked over at me. Once upstairs, I was bombarded with a thousand and one questions. Dad stepped in and said, "Go talk to your Mother in private. She needs to say some things to you." So, I went to my parents' bedroom to listen.

Immediately. Mom said she was sorry for getting locked up, not for trying to cut up Brother Adams. She owed me no explanation for nothing, "Not even Bill the TV Man." But, I held back on saying that part until many years later. "Mom," I said, "I understand why you were always mad at him and Kenny. We never knew what he tried to do to you. Did he hurt you bad? Did he rape you?" She said, no, to not raping her, but he did hurt her.

Then she pointed to her heart, and I said, "I'm sorry." She said she loved and missed me. She wanted to know where I had been and where I got those nice looking clothes. She said I looked like a pimp. I had on my dark blue outfit and my coat was still in my hand. She said, "Did you come home to stay, or to say goodbye?" For a long time I said nothing because at that moment I wasn't sure what I wanted to do, or where I truly wanted to be.

Then finally, I hugged my mother and said, "I'm staying." Again, she wanted to know where I'd been and "with whom." To make a joke and take the edge off, I said, "I wasn't at Aunt Fanny's house." She laughed and so did I. Then I told her all about "Star." Some parts I left out, but I did say we had sex together. She just looked at me real hard and said, "I understand." I said, "I know you do! Also, Mom, please don't ever ask me again to lie to my Dad."

She said nothing, but we understood I had grown up in the past four and a half months. My Mom was always fearful of venereal diseases. "Let me see your thing." Immediately I said, "No, Ma! I'm not a little child anymore." She nodded with understanding. The next day, we had agreed I'd go with her to the clinic to get check out, and we did. I was fine.

My Dad and brother and myself all took a walk that night and I told them everything form A to Z, omitting nothing. Dad just smiled and said, "One hell of a gal!" Kenny kept saying, "So, when we going back to see them?" It felt good being with family again. When Kenny and I were alone, I told him I was going back to see her. Why'd you come back for, was his next question. I said because I missed him. Also, it wasn't the right time to leave Boston altogether. Now, as I write this, I know I'll only be back there for funerals and then my own.

Mom's girlfriend got me into summer school at the Old Teacher's College on Hunnington Avenue. I did well. Still, I missed my friend in New York. I knew we'd see each other again, but I could not say when.

For the rest of the summer I just hung out in OP meeting people and going down North Hampton or up on Blue Hill Avenue to Jewels Pool Room. Kenny and I were from the Hill, so going up to Blue Hill Ave and Jewel's wasn't a problem. Plus, Kenny was busy doing his Panther thing. I got the opportunity to meet some real slick brothers and sisters hanging out at Jewel's Pool Room. Guys like La La, Rico Wilson, Gary Stevenson, Pedro Nunez, James Spear, Earl Crawford, Clyde "Pee Wee"

Bacon, Greg Robinson (who's been down since 1974), L. Roberts, Ernie Manigault and his slick talking sister Sam, sexy Michelle Collins and her sis Debbie, Dee Dee, Janet Blair, Dale Kilgore, Ronnie Montero, and the list goes on.

There was a commonality that each one had with the other. They all had been "Cannons" at some point, and many had worked together. Out of all those men mentioned, only two are still living. As for those fly sisters, all are living but two. In less than two years I would be rolling with those guys. When school started in September 1966, I was transferred from the Lewis Jr. High to the James P. Timothy Jr. High up at John Elliott Square. That is where Rev. Henry Young's daughter Theresa was going to school. I damn near got her to do some wild shit in the wooded area by the school. I'm glad it didn't happen, or her Dad would have killed us both. She and I parted soon after that stunt in the woods.

I've always had a thing for tall red women. The woman who has my heart today isn't five-foot-ten but her qualities far exceed those of any woman I know today.

"Yes, it's you?" One day while walking to one of my classes, I saw the tallest long legged prettiest red complexioned girl in the whole damn school. We will call her DI. She lived behind the Norfolk House. I had to meet this sister. And I did meet her, through a friend named Seth Roberts. His older brother and my brother Kenny knew each other. Kenny also knew one or two of DI's cousins from going to school with them.

Di was kind of standoffish at first, but I had learned much about women from Star while in New York. Star and I would lie up in bed until three a.m. or later and she's hip me, as she'd like to call it, about women. Di was no match for me but I would play the same so long as I got her in the end. Di's mom was old school, meaning she had to meet your family if you were going to be seeing her daughter. I really understood and respected that, and so did my parents. Finally, the day came for Di's Mom to meet my parents. Not only did the introduction go down well, upon my mother seeing Di's Mom, she instantly realized she knew her from years earlier.

Other than Star, I had not been sexually active with anyone else. But looking at how physically attractive Di was, plus her smarts and popularity in and out of school, made her more sexually appealing. One of her best friends was also a very tall light complexioned voluptuous girl just like Di we'll call Monique. She lived on Washington in Jamaica Plain near the old Green Street Orange line train stop. Di and Monique and several others, Albert Pierce, Peter Rayfield, Kenny Kimble, Brent Jackson and his sexy sister Darcell, this close knit group of young teens used to hang out together after school at a local social center called The Norfolk House. All of us would get together and got to local house parties and gatherings throughout our hood.

Di and I started spending a lot of time with each other. Having already gone way beyond just kissing with Star, I wasn't so much pressed for a lot of kissing as Di was at times. Knowing Di had never experienced sex at that point, I truly wanted to be the first to blow her mind sexually, just like Star had done for me. Star taught me that it wasn't ever cool to pressure a woman to do anything she wasn't totally comfortable with. She'd say talk a woman through her inhibitions, don't make her feel guilty if she isn't totally ready. Let her know what you are asking of her, you are also willing to give back. Sometimes you have to allow her to feel the pleasure herself before you receive it yourself.

Those months in New York were a learning experience for me in many ways. Trust me when I say this. It's not always about receiving joy and pleasure. Many times when you truly give from the heart unselfishly you receive so much more back in other ways. Rather than do a full court press on this beautiful girl, I stopped the sex talk along the hands up her skirts and down her panties altogether. I fell back and gave her the emotional and physical space to think things through.

Di's Mom worked in Cambridge, MA for a major company. Working overtime was a regular occurrence. On one such occasion, Di had requested I walk her home from school. No problem. I took her books and placed them inside my book bag and we began our walk to her house, talking BS all the way. Upon arrival at her building I started to reach in my bag to give her back her books. Instantly, Di said, "Stop! Come up to the house with me Charles," is what came out of her mouth. I'm thinking to myself, "your Mom will be home by 4:00pm." But Di knew what I knew not – Mom was working late that day.

She reached out for my hand and smiled. This sexy super classy and very feminine gal. I truly love a sexy woman with no hang-ups about expressing her femininity. Di had all those qualities in her makeup bag (her personality). Once upstairs, she immediately took my book bag and coat, quickly disappeared with both in hand, and reappeared minutes later in a pair of bright red shorts, which I thought was a bit strange at that moment.

"Charles," she said, "do you want to watch TV or listen to some music?" That's the question she put to me that afternoon. I quickly picked up on her self-confidence as well as her movements and questions. So, I fell back and allowed her to lead. My response was, "whatever you decide is fine with me." Knowing her, I knew she'd choose music over watching TV.

Music it was. Watching her fix a glass of her Mom's liquor, I automatically knew where things were about to go. Music, double locks on doors, and comfortable clothing, spell S-E-X.

Di's actions were that of something she had heard about or seen done in the past. Whatever the case, she was emulating it to perfection. When she came in with our drinks, she had on her Mom's robe pulled tightly around her waist. Many women are the complete architectural design of their mothers, especially when the actual architect had good intentions and foresight. Di's mom was progressive beyond that time period. You could see the effects on Di.

As the music of the Temptations singing, "the way you do the things you do" could be heard playing low in the corner of the living room by the window on an old hi-fi, Di slid beside me and slowly kissed me while slipping her tongue inside my mouth. Upon withdrawing she said, "Charles, I'm ready. Please be gentle with me. You know you are my first." All I could do was smile in agreement. She truly was a virgin in every sense of the word.

Di lay back on the couch before me, slowly loosening the belt of her Mom's red velvet robe. As it fell open on both sides she asked, "do I look okay for you, Charles?" She was biting her bottom lip as she spoke those words so slowly and with total innocence. She needed to hear and know she was beautiful as well as desirable. I answered those questions beyond belief by placing a light kiss on both of her nipples. She just lay back and shivered, as she would describe it later. I so much wanted this to be her day and her day only.

I knew I only wanted her to feel the physical pleasure of the release that would soon flow from between her young thighs onto my tongue. So I began to slide my tongue down to the very beginning of her pubic hairline. Her hair was thick and curly. The aroma that emanated from her was pure woman, intoxicating as it was inviting. I slowly parted the thick hair covering my object of desire and need with my tongue. She cried, "that tickles" and then smiled down at me.

Never once did she say to stop. I slid both hands beneath her thick hips and forced her closer to my face, spreading her legs even wider, her body totally relaxing under my control. I nibbled lightly all around the outer area of her bird like nest, each nibble brought on a series of body spasms that cause her to bite down on her bottom lip each time. As I glanced up at her face, her eyes were tightly closed and both her hands were pulling on her hair at the sides of her head. While her eyes were still closed, I slipped one hand into the glass of liquor beside me and found several small pieces of ice. Easing them into my mouth, unbeknownst to Di, I searched out my intended target, her clitoris. When the coolness of the ice reached its target, she screamed, Stop! Stop! So I did.

As I started to move away, she softly said, "Please don't stop making me run!" I was confused by what she had said. She said, "Charles, I'm embarrassed to say it any other way!" I pleaded for her to discard her inhibitions by saying what she felt. She closed her eyes and said, "I don't want you to stop making me cummmm!" I said, "are you sure you want me to continue?" Her response was, "Yes, please!"

So I continued it again, this time I held her hard little clitoris between my lips and gently nibbled on it, and flicked at it with my icy cold tongue. Needless to say, she ran like water cascading down a continuous waterfall. Her entire body was in a spasm. She pushed me away and ran and locked herself in the bathroom for about fifteen minutes. When she reappeared she wanted to know where I learned that trick. A magician never tells his trick or who taught him. In her case, I lied and said, "I read it in Playboy magazine." We went no further that day. I was cool. My mission was fully accomplished.

The fourth time is when she said, "when are you going to, you know, do it to me the other way?" Then and only then, did I know for sure that she was totally over her inhibitions. This time, things were different. We started out with the sixty-nine position. We both used ice on each other. She used baby oil on my joint and on herself. Di said whenever she'd do herself she would use the oil on her two fingers as she slipped them inside herself. The first time entering her a pop-like sound happened. She said that lets you know you are the first. Then she showed me the blood. She cleaned herself along with me. Then we got down to business. She knew ahead of time just how to put her legs on my shoulders, around my waist, her head deep in the pillow. She even allowed me to go in her cellar without a flashlight. Now it was my turn to ask her how she knew about all those sex positions. She just said by being a good listener and a good peeker. It was not necessary to go beyond that point.

After we rested she made me lie on the bed as she sprayed whipped cream on me and licked it off as she slid me deep in her mouth. She said me cumming in her mouth reminded her of how her Mom used to give her warm milk with honey to drink at night. She said my cum was warm and thick just like the milk. The whipped cream taste on her tongue made the cum taste like honey. Di enjoyed it so much she got me hard quickly so she could feel like she felt when she had that hot milk and honey as a child. In fact, that became a ritual for us each and every time we did it.

What put a damper on things for a while was me getting caught naked hiding behind her brother's bedroom door. This is an actual account of what truly happened. Di and I had a silly beef about my old girlfriend Theresa. So Di said, *it's quits.* Heartbroken? Yes. But never let them see you sweat, was what Star taught me in New York. So even though I would see my girl at school or walking home with friends or alone, I just chilled and waited. You know when a relationship is really over and you know when it's not. I knew guys were slipping her notes and saying half ass slick shit to her, yet she stood strong against it all.

One day in the lunchroom, Di decided to break the ice. She came to my table after everyone had gone. She said, "So, asshole, when are you going to speak to your girl, or do you have a new one? If so, who's the bitch?" I answered "no" to her questions. Di said she was sorry about what she said and how she acted. She and Theresa had talked and Theresa assured her we no longer had anything going on. But if she and I were finished, she was going to start talking to me again. Di said she made it very clear that she and I were not finished.

Again, she said, "Are you going to talk to me, or are we going to fight right here, right now in this MF lunchroom?" She was serious. She slammed her tray on the table hard and people started looking at us. Di was as tall as I was and she would fight. She was far from being a punk. I said, "Okay, baby, we are back on. I'll meet you after school."

We met and I walked her home. We sat and talked on the steps until her brother came from school. She said her Mom would be working late tomorrow, and that her period was over a few days ago, and there was some things she needed help with, so don't go to school tomorrow. She was going to play sick like her period was still on. I asked her, "What do you need help with?" She just smiled and dropped her books and bent over, exposing her perfectly tight ass in pink panties. My response was, "You're right. You do need a lot of help." As we went through the door to her building she said she had a bag of ice in the fridge.

CB

Chapter 25 ~ Getting Caught

D i and I were having phone sex long before either of us ever heard of the term "phone sex," 900 HOT SEX! Back during those days, everybody had those long princess phone lines on their princess phones. Families back then had two phones, one in their parents' room, in her case her Mom's room, as we did. The other phone was usually in the front room, living room. That's where ours was.

There were two unique problems at center court here. Problem number one: teens back then would tie the damn phone line up for hours talking to their girlfriends about boys or talking directly to their boyfriend. Problem number two: All these phone conversations would be held in the damn bathroom because it provided maximum privacy. I can still hear my Dad saying, "Shake it quick, and get out boy!" Mom was like, "Pick up the damn cover and put it back down and get off the phone unless you want me to pick it up and embarrass you and Ms. Di."

The night before our meeting, we were doing our phone sex acts in our respective bathrooms. We would turn on the shower and flush the toilets when things got hot and heavy and we needed to clear our lungs, you know, scream.

On this particular evening, while Di and I were on the phone doing our thing, Di had her sponge banana all slicked down with hot baby oil on it that she had resting in a steel bowl with a lid on it. She would be butterball naked from head to toe sitting on the toilet with the seat down on top of a thick bath towel. Her legs were long enough to touch the wall facing her. She would put her feet flat against the wall while have the phone under her chin resting on her shoulder. In doing so, both hands would be free to frolic in her sandbox. Sometimes she would say she's not playing deep up in her "Play Pen."

As time passed, we got far more creative outside the confines of the bathroom. We made up games called floorwalker, store detective, Policemen, Drunk Driver, Doctor, Nurse, Dentist, Shoe Salesman. She loved playing Peeping Tom and Peeping Jane. She would crack the bathroom door while I'd pretend to piss. Our ultimate game was hostage and the blind fold trust game with a bowl of ice. Over the years, I have become a perfectionist and a connoisseur.

On this particular night, while she and I were on the phone doing what we sometimes did, her Mom picks up the phone being, "Inspector Gadget," she not only heard our moans and groans, she stayed on long enough to know we were meeting up the next day and planned to spend the whole day playing in her sandbox. Mom knew about her fixing us breakfast, and the drinks we planned to have. Di's Mom heard it all and we never heard her pick up or slip the receiver back in place. In order for her Mom to have known about breakfast and the drinks, she had to be listening through a lot of *fuck me Charles, lick me right there,* and, *I'm cumming,* and it wasn't me all doing the talking out loud and screaming. It was Di!

The next day, Di's Mom would leave early. Her boyfriend would pick her up, and drop her off daily. He had to drive from Talbert Avenue to their house, then on to Cambridge. They both worked for the same company.

The next morning, Di calls to say her Mom is gone and Raymond, her brother will be leaving in about ten minutes. Never once did her Mom let on that she knew we both were ducking school so we could have sex. She laid a mean trap for our asses. I gave my brother the slip at Dudley's and slipped inside Elite's Coffee and Breakfast joint at the corner of Ziggler and Warren Streets. I stayed in there with everyone else who was hooking school that day. It was a Friday. They were all going to the old National Movie on Tremont Street in the South End. It was cheap and the Truant Officers never came there searching for us truants. That day I had bigger things on my mind than any damn movie.

Rather than go through the station or wait on the Alston Union bus, I eased out of Elite's and walked up past Dr. Ruby's office to Dudley and Warren Street passing the Reverely movie theatre straight past the old Boys Club and on to her house. I eased past her Aunt's house real fast, quickly going around back and up the three flights to the back door of her Mom's kitchen. Through the door I could smell them pancakes, eggs and sausages. Back then, I ate plenty of that "Hit-in-the-head," "shot-in-the-head," "wrestled to-the-ground," "Grade A-swine." Those aromas were oozing down the steps through the cracks in her Mom's back door. I whistled three times as I neared her door. On the final ring the door was flung wide open.

Standing there with a huge grin on her cute face was my sexy Di in panties and bra. Without any hesitation she kissed me passionately as she squeezed my dick. Once all the doors to the house were double and triple locked, Di took my coat and cap. We did so much role-playing it wasn't funny. Here's an example. I'd say, "Damn, baby. On my way home from my night job I noticed how dirty my work clothes had gotten at work. I'd better take them off quickly and eat breakfast in my shorts." Di in turn would say she was hot due to the cooking she was doing, therefore she needed to remove her bra and panties. Looking at my tee-shirt she'd say it was too dirty to eat breakfast in, "Take it off!" That would be my cue to say, "Damn, baby, you've got grease on your panties in the back. Sit down in this chair and open your legs wide so I can remove those soiled panties." For some reason, they would always be pushed tightly inside her pussy, and I'd have to dislodge them with the help of my teeth, tongue and lips. Di would say she's been noticing how I've been coming home later each morning from work. "Why's that, Charlie?" "You are mistaken, baby." "Charlie, I need to check your dick and drawers out, before we eat breakfast. Now turn around and face me, Charlie."

After complying with her request Di would get on her knees and order me to stand before her while she slowly pulled down my shorts. Once they were down by my ankles, Di would rush out the room and get her brother's magnifying glass from his chemistry set that she had taken several months ago and never given back. After inspecting her Mr. Goodbar as she called it, she'd go over my drawers looking for strange spots and stranger's hair. Then she would end by saying, you have been a good Mr. Goodbar. And for that you can have ice cream after you take a hot bath. This was one of our games we did before we actually did anything physical. That day was no exception.

After breakfast we shared a Kool cigarette together, then she ran our bath water. She loved to play in water with herself, especially with me watching her get off with her banana sponge all slick with oil, a real turn-on for both of us. She would let almost all the water out of the tub, place her feet on each of my shoulders as we lay at opposite ends of the tub. Next, Di would bend her head and lick her nipple tips over and over. Then she would play with herself by sliding her fingers in and out of her. We would take turns licking her fingers.

For the grand finale she would get very serious and say, "this is how you make me feel, this is how I look when you are deep in me from behind when I've unlocked my cellar door for you to enter without knocking." Then she would slide that oiled soaked hard banana in her until I almost couldn't see it. She would move her hands away, pull her legs up close to her chest, and just squeeze her whole body with her arms wrapped tightly around her legs. The whole time she would be staring at me saying, "See how you fuck me. See what your Mr. Goodbar does to your girl, only you will ever bring all this out of me."

Upon releasing her body from her own grip, she eased the soaked sponge out and licked it like a lollypop. We rinsed off, had two stiff drinks of 151 Rum and went and jumped in her Mom's bed. First time doing that. Di went and got her diary and we went through each of our games, that Rum had us flying. She licked every inch of my body at least three times, while playing "Head Nurse Di of the Trauma Unit. At one point, Di said she wasn't 151 Rum drunk. Di said she was drunk alright. "Cum drunk" is what she was. The damn banana was cum drunk also.

We were both out cold in Mom's big bed. We slept for an hour like that. I woke up to a loud 'Bang-bang-bang' still a bit drowsy and even a bit unsure where I was. As for that noise, what was it, where was it coming from? Talk about being disoriented. Then, bam, it hit me. It was the damn front door. "Di, Di, wake up!" She's got the damn sponge still in her mouth like a damn pacifier. Now she hears the door, bang, bang, "Charles, it's my mother!" WHAT? We both jump up. She says, "RUN! RUN!" But where? "My brother's room." So I snatch up my clothes. All but my damn socks and one shoe. Di's Mom is yelling her name. "DI ! DI ! Open this damn door NOWWWWW!"

Di had all ten locks locked on the door. That was cool, but she also had the chain locks and the police lock on also. "Why?" Now that I'm hiding behind her brother's bedroom door with my clothes in my hand she goes to the door. She opens it.

The first thing her Mom says, "Di, why do you have on my robe?" "Ma, I was asleep..."

"That's not what I was asking you." Again, silence from Di. Next, I hear her Mom saying, "Who's been in my bed, girl?"

"Oh, Ma, I was laying..." And before she could say more, her Mother goes, "What's this? What's all this shit, Di? Oil bottle, sponge, soiled sheets?" Now, I could hear her Mother sniffing like that damn dog McGruff. Next, "Okay, heifer, where is he at?"

"Who, Ma? Raymond isn't home from school yet."

"Don't play with me, girl. I know your brother isn't home."

She's walking in every damn room looking, searching, and it's me she's looking for. The last room was her brother Raymond's room. Standing at the entrance to Raymond's room, she yells, "Charles Belim!" Then with me directly behind the door, she pushes it like she can't get through the entrance. Next thing I know, she's snatching the doorknob and there I am, standing naked. I dropped my clothes and was totally exposed.

For several long seconds, her Mom is silently staring at me. "Like, wow!" Then she says, "Come on out just like you are, and have a seat, both of you. And take off my robe, Ms. Lady!"

Now, here we are, both naked, sitting on a couch in front of Di's mother. Her Mom looks quickly at us, from one to the other and says, with a question, "Did you two do anything?"

Before I could respond, Di says, "No, Ma, we were just playing around in your bed. Ma, I thought it would be nice to play around in your bed and pretend we were married."

"And what do you have to say, Mr. No Clothes on? And do something with that thing of yours, it needs to go down or something!"

"May I use the bathroom?"

"Yes! And take your clothes with you!"

So, I go get my clothes and put them on. Coming from the bedroom, Di's Mom says, "Perhaps, if you use the bathroom quickly, your thing will settle itself down!" And she was correct.

Now that everyone was fully dressed, Di's mother addresses me first. "Charles, I feel you and my daughter have been seeing too much of one another lately. And I also feel your parents need to know about what went on here today. I'll be by to see them both. So, you two may say goodbye. And you can leave!"

As I stood to leave, Di stood right up in front of her mother and says, "I love Charles, and yes we did do it! Mom, you even know we did it, also. So, why all the pretending?"

Her mother's response was, "Both of you sit down -- and don't ever talk to me in that tone of voice ever again. Again, sit the hell down!"

We sat back down and then she said she knew all about us meeting today. We were like, how? "Those long bathroom phone conversations is how. A mother, a single mom, knows what's going on in her house. She better know! I know I truly can't stop you two from screwing, if that's what you want to do. I just want you to respect me and my home, if you, and when you, do it. And don't ever screw in my damn bed ever again! I'm the only woman that does that in that bed, are we clear?"

We both said we understood and we were sorry, and we truly were sorry for having disrespected her Mom that way. She went on to say, "It's time for you, Mr. Belim, to be prepared at all times." Then she got up and walked away and returned with a pack of super size condoms in a black package, which she handed me. "Especially, as large as you are down there." We all laughed. I asked, "Can we still talk on the phone at night?" Di's mom responded, "Charles, go home, boy and you both better be in school tomorrow!" Di walked me to the door and gave me a big long hard kiss with her tongue sliding down my throat. Halfway down the steps, she called me back to give me my gym bag and to squeeze my joint and wink!

Her Mom never once said anything to my parents. Two days later, I was coming out of my building and there she was, Di, standing there waiting in her orange fun fur coat, white boots, white gloves and white cap, as she handed me her books to place in my book bag. She said after I left, her mother made her wash all the bed linens, wash down the mattress and send her robe to the dry cleaner's. After everything was done, her mom said, "Now I can sleep!" Otherwise, she would have felt like she was in bed with both of us! Also, an appointment was made with her mom's gynecologist to be sure Di wasn't pregnant and to get her on the "Pill." A month or so later, I was invited along with her Mom's boyfriend to a family dinner. It was held out in Hopkington, MA.

During our chill period, we didn't do it as much as we had and only once did I use a condom. As for those pills, she'd spit them out or make herself vomit to get them out. Di said she "ain't no baby killer, plus God says when it's time for me to have a baby, not my mother, not even you, Charles!" Di was a very strong willed young woman, even back then. "In for a penny, in for a pound," was her motto, and mine, too.

Weak people I thoroughly despise. They are factored out of any equation of being predictable. My stance is predicated upon people not being who or what they are truly about. Weak people are cancerous to strong willed people, that's why I'm a good team player. Many years ago, Wilt Chamberlain scored one-hundred points and his team won. True, he accomplished a great feat, but in the real world, a true player allows everyone a chance to shine.

By Christmas and New Years going on 1966, Di and I were back in full swing again. During that cooling off period I was hanging hard in two spots even though I had an after-school job at Kornfield Drug Store at the corner of Williams and Washington Streets. It's still there, but it's a dump now. Back in the old days it was a Class "A" drug store. Those two new spots were the Mines Pool Room downtown and Jewels Pool Room on Blue Hill Avenue.

 C&

Chapter 26 ~ The Turn Out

First, let's go back to Kornfield's Pharmacy. My job title was 'Soda Jerk." That's a person who makes all those fountain delights. Fraps, milk shakes, floats, lime Rickie, banana boats, sundaes, etc. Back then, many neighborhood drug stores not only filled prescriptions; they sold alcohol, the drinking kind, whiskey, liquor on the down low. Kornfield's was no exception. One block down from them was another drugstore that did the same. The most famous was at the corner of Braddock Park and Columbus Avenue. I don't know about today, but when I was a kid there was a statute. Massachusetts Law called it the "Blue Laws."

Certain things could not be sold on a Sunday. Naturally, alcohol was at the top of the list. Aside from that, pharmacists were not issued alcohol licenses, not even for medicinal or therapeutic reasons. Not then, and surely not now! Those slight indiscretions just didn't apply to those places, and perhaps, still don't. Both places are still filling prescriptions on Sunday. Mothers are still perplexed as to how their men still wind up so damn "awesofied" shortly after picking up the Sunday paper.

My Dad was no exception. He would be drunker than 'Choota Brown' on a Sunday morning after buying the Sunday papers at a local neighborhood drugstore.

I truly did not like working as a soda jerk. I would have been on some chill shit had they allowed me to sell that liquor. But that wasn't part of the plan. So I chose those two poolrooms as a means to an end. I didn't realize the decisions made back then in 1966 and beyond would lead me on the road to the Federal Detention Section of the Charles County Jail in Maryland in 2008. Life is all about making healthy choices. Would I do anything differently based on my thinking now? Most assuredly yes. But in 1966, I could not see beyond those two poolrooms, the North End, North Hampton and a woman named "Star Child."

The "Mines Pool Room" was in the bottom portion of a building that is now the DMV of Boston, Mass. It was a large poolroom and it stayed packed with white and black hustlers. Charlie "Poncho" Brown, his brother Twinky, Black Jake, Marcus from the cathedral, Larry Searcy, Weasel Jacobs and Chico played pool in the Mines back then. I once saw Chico play in New York. For a grand a game they played 9 ball.

A lot of money changed hands in that poolroom, even by today's standards. Shylock money, dope money, poolroom money, hoe money, and last but not least, "Cannon Money." For those who may not be familiar with the vernacular, please allow me a moment to explain. "Cannon money" is proceeds derived from picking someone's pocket, plain and simple.

The early 1970s film, "Harry in Your Pocket," starring James Cobra, should give you some real insight. The storyline was about a pickpocket who worked basically the Midwest area of the country. Houston, Dallas, Kansas, cities that catered to the Rodeos, Circuses, Cow Shows, etc. Essentially, his thing was this. He was very well known by the police, yet they could never seem to catch him red-handed, so to speak. He would always manage to pass it off on one of his partners before the police could get to him. In reality, the game isn't quite played that way at all. Not for real. Not by white Cannons, or Latinos, and not by Blacks either, as you soon shall learn.

Jewels Pool Room was known for three things. Gambling, cannons, dope, selling heroin. The old man who ran the poolroom was Green Eye Jimmy's father whom everyone called "Pop." Pop kept a 22 long pistol on his hip. He had no damn problem putting one in your ass. Now if he liked you and you got out of line with him, he would shoot you in your ass or leg, as he did Ronald Stokes back in 1969. If you were a nobody who tried some shit on the crap table in the back room, there's no telling where you would get hit. And finally, it was noted for being a place where up and coming young pickpockets gathered.

The Mines Pool Room was also such a place. To this very day, Boston, Massachusetts is well known for pimping and hoes and some of the very best pickpockets in the country cut their teeth in Jewels and the Mines. In 1966, or actually when I was a shine boy down North Hampton, I met a guy named Rosey. He was about three years younger than myself. Never once saw him in anything but slacks and lizards or alligators. I mean, the brother was real sharp. I would ask who he was and what he did. I learned his name and that he was an in-town brother. That meant he was not from up the Hill like most of us who were shining back then were. He came out of the South End. By him coming through so much I would speak to him and he would say, "Hey, what's up," and keep it moving.

By 1966, I had heard so much talk about the pickpocket game I knew it was my calling. I was just waiting for my turn. Having been an ex-shine boy I already had some knowledge of how things basically went. At least I thought I did. Allow me to back up and give you a brief list of Cannon terms that basically describe the game in a nutshell. Many of the following terms are no longer in use because many of the older players are gone, deceased. The game is still alive and kicking. It just has new players with new terms. Where a person comes from also has a lot to do with the terminology used. Boston guys used many of the following terms, along with the old New York crew.

Dipping, the shot, the Wiz, Wire, Sticking, Shading, or Shade, Mall Busting, In the Bed, Prong ends up or down, In the Street, On the leg, On the Can-right or left, Upstairs right or left, Reach and Cop, the Spill, Double Stick; some of my favorites now, the come through, the raise play, putting a man on the Cin, long, Brick. All those terms describe a particular action that causes a person to get beat out of his money, or it tells us where it is as well as what is needed to be done to fleece a chump for his money.

The Brothers from Chitown, DC, VA, Cleveland, they simply say, "I play the game," or I'm a Cannon and I've come to play." The end result is always the same. We all go to major sporting events for one purpose, and one purpose only. "To break a Chump." The size of a man means very little. "Fleecing the chump out of his or her money." A Cannon will play King Kong in the Gorilla Cage if he's got a pack of C notes in his hip pocket. And if Jane ain't careful, she will get played also.

For many of us back then and even now, that was our way of getting back at the system, and a people who had put us in situations and conditions beyond belief. Many of us were not the type to stand on picket lines holding up signs and slogans, saying, "We shall overcome one day..." or we will wait on ours beyond the skies. Nor were we willing to pick up a gun and kill whitey, either. What we were able and willing to do was pick his pocket, his wife, her mother, his mother and their fathers. The unfortunate part is, before we got it all clear, the reality was that we had victimized our own people in the process. For that I do apologize.

Upon learning that oppression was, and still is, far worse than slavery, any day, for every penny, nickel, dime, quarter, etc. that our parents were denied for four hundred years or better, it was payback time. To show you how serious my crew was, the pimps would pray to the Pimp God for pimp blessings. Real down hoes would pray to the Ho God that a Ho had a good night on the hoe stroll. The Cannons, those who seriously played the "Wiz," they prayed to the "Wiz God." We prayed we'd beat a rich fat white man for a bale of C notes big enough to choke a horse.

My first wife wanted our daughter to be born in a certain hospital and then be placed in the Pink Room after delivery. (No, not Harlem Hospital, either.) The cost was $2500 for her request. On October 22nd, 1978, Charlene Belim was in that room with her Mom. Somebody got broke is all I got to say.

My man Seth who introduced me to Di has an older brother named Loren. It just so happens that Loren knew Rosey. In fact, they were hustling together daily after school. Seth introduced me to his brother Loren outside Jewels Pool Room. Then this familiar looking guy calls Loren off to the side for a minute, so I ask Seth who's the guy talking to your brother, he looks familiar. "That's Rosey. He and Loren are hustling. Remember I told you about him?"

"Okay, okay, right, you did." As he, Rosey and Loren, walk back to us, Loren introduces us formally. Then I said, "I remember you from down North Hampton. I'm the shoeshine boy. That was me." And that's how I met Rosey. While standing there talking, up pops Warren from Holworthy Street. It's a small world because Warren not only knew me and Kenny, he knew Loren and Rosey, too. He told them both he knew me for years and that Kenny and I had good names in the street. Warren moved with a group of guys who used to hide inside the ceilings of bathrooms in stores like the old Gilchrist, Jordan Marsh, etc. This was before dogs and motions detectors along with elaborate alarm systems. They would hit those stores on their late night openings, Monday and Wednesday nights. They never got busted.

Jewel's Pool Room was a den of thieves and everybody knew it. They had a "Creep Mob" out of Jewels whose specialty was creeping in Drugstores, hospitals, and medical buildings. They would take all the pharmaceutical cocaine. Those brothers and their women went all over the country. To my knowledge, only three of the original crew are still alive. Tom M., Dale K., and Deddie, who used to be with Loren back in the day. Two got killed together in a honey hole they had been beating at will by an expert Marksman Pharmacist.

The rest of that crew died from drug usage. There was a mean stick up crew that also came out of that poolroom. Their specialty was banks. That would also be my calling, but as you'll see, I added flavor and a twist and turn to my "G". You must truly understand, although I've never knocked the rough play, if that's your "G," I'm a player not a rough taker. My gun has always been the pen. I learned thirty odd years ago that the pen is far mightier than the sword. In place of force I use trickery and deception. That's why Jewel's Pool Room was a den of thieves and why I wanted in, in a bad way. One day Warren introduced me to a tall dark complexioned brother named Rico from Fayston Street. His mom was Panamanian. He and all his brothers would come to accept Islam in the years to come, as my brother and myself did.

Nineteen-sixty-six was the year I got hip, turned out to the game and we still use that term today with getting hip to the shot game. From that introduction to Rico, I met Earroll, Clyde (Pee Pee) Bacon, Ronnie kid Montero, whom I actually knew from a kid, who had just got back from Florida with "LaLa." I would soon meet big Shelly, he would come to have a set of twin boys with Bobby Brown's now deceased sister Bethy.

Dudley Station was another popular hangout, especially the Dairy Whip ice cream parlor. It was directly across from the Clock Tavern, opposite the tavern where Rent-A-Center is now. Eight's Coffee Shop was at the corner of Ziglar Street. The people who owned the Dairy Whip were white and they did their dirt, too. I did juvenile time with the female's brother in Shirley Industrial School for Boys in 1967. I served nine months there along with Rico.

After school was out, all the players and fly girls would meet at either of those two locations. Girls like Gayle Harris (Ronnie Harris' sister), Sam Manigault and her woman Lorna, Janet Blair, Debbie Collins and her sister Michelle. Then you had that crew of fly sisters from OP and Columbia Point. The last strong crew of female hustlers to come out of Roxbury and the surrounding areas, Theresa Mack, Angie S, Drucilla (Juey) H, Linda (Delilah) H, Beverly M, La Tanya J, and Kitty W, will be much spoken of in 'Plastic Money.' And, Miguel, I didn't forget your girl Barbara).

As for the guys, you might see in that town crew, Jerry D, his man Lester (Duck) H, not to be confused with Lester Mayo from Lenox St, Quinton L, Bad Foot Skipper Jordan, Ray Rose, David V from OP and the Hill, Bryant G, Charlie Johnson, Ricardo W, Mike C, Danny (Cully) Davis, Ernie Manigault, they will also be spoken about much in forthcoming books, Plastic Money, and White Face Black Game.

Many times you might see these guys all converge on certain bus stops within Dudley, stops like the Kane Square, Harvard Square, via Central Square, Alston Union, Brighton, even those all black bus stops. The biggest sting to ever come of Dudley Station was taken by my man Sleepy, he beat a man for six-thousand dollars going through the turnstile. That was considered a big sting back in the early 1960s.

The name I am about to mention and their relationship to the "Shot" as we still call it in Boston, Mass. is truly predicated upon their knowledge of the game called the "CANNON." That knowledge was passed down from these men who are now gone but truly not forgotten. Some of the guys I came up with learned directly from them, others through them. I knew most personally.

Amos Montero, Johnny Pimp, the little old white man, who used to collect tickets at the old Riverly Theatre, where area B Police Station now sits, Duke who used to take numbers in a store by the old Franklyn Park Theatre, the "Hat," a very sharp dresser who used to be down Shanty's. There were others going back to the old Skully Square days but I had yet to hear of their names or exploits. I never met Amos, but I did business with Johnny Pimp in 1969 through Sleepy. Duke, The Hat, and the old White Man, I'd sit with them for hours and just listen to them kick game and their personal love and respect for the Cannon.

Whether in the Mines Pool Room or in Jewel's Pool Room, most of the talk was about the Mechanics of the game. How to stand on a person's blind side, be they male or female and they not even know you are there, not even breathing on their necks. Paying close attention to whether they plan to turn around, simply by watching their necks and the rest of their body movements. Allowing a person to settle into a comfortable position before moving in on them.

Many times we would see who we wanted to play from a distance, we would never make eye contact with who we had sized up to play. If eye contact did take place and we had no one else with us, we'd just give them a pass or we might try to rock them to sleep by simply moving away, only to slip back up on them. Choosing who to play had a lot to do with how well that person was dressed. When it came to women, we'd check out her type of handbag (designer) and shoes, being an ex-shine boy I learned a lot about people based on the quality of their shoes. Men that are in business keep their shoes nice and shined, women wear good quality designer shoes. Also a woman's coat, if it's a good quality fur. And last but not least, if they are wearing good or expensive jewelry. Same for men. Many times what a person's reading -- *The Wall Street Journal, Washington Post.*

People are the same in Boston as they are in New York. Once you factor all those things into the equation, you'll be able to make good choices about who to play. Let me just say, I didn't know all these things when I first met Rosey and Loren outside Jewel's Pool Room in 1966. All my knowledge was learned over time. Nothing was instantaneous.

Let me stop once again to reaffirm my position. Yes, I am stepping away from what I've been about for the past forty-five years; but in doing so there are areas I just can't go into. You see, just because I've figured a way out of the box doesn't mean others have, or ever will, for that matter. I pray they learn how to think outside the box that holds them trapped to the confines of the box. I'm still a lover of game, I've just found a better game to play, and I'm doing it right this second. Writing my first of many novels.

Many of my former comrades truly know no other way of feeding themselves at this juncture of their lives. Stop pushing that glass ceiling and level the playing field once and for all, but truly "for all." All should not exclude ex-cons but rather factor them into the equation of hope and support. The truth is, Congress, the US Senate and all those special interest groups are truly playing con on the masses when they say they want to end crime. Do you realize the financial state this country would be in if crime took a "hiatus," for say, six months, a year? Can you imagine the implications of that hiatus on the economy? It would create "Pandemonium." So, don't be mad at my friend who is in your pocket, or using your credit cards, etc. Be angry with those who truly benefit from the crime and it ain't just the so-called criminals.

As I was saying, hanging around those spots, hearing guys and girls kick game, where to hustle, who to watch out for, shit, my mental plate stayed piled high! I learned about reckless-eyeballing from black people. I'm truly not prejudiced, I love white folks (I bought my last Cadillac de Ville with their money), but here's my question: As bad as black folks say white folks have kicked them in the ass, why when you saw me or one of my confederates sliding our young hungry hands in their bags or pants pocket you'd wake up the dead? Alert them? Why? Why is truly another sixty-four-thousand-dollar question.

When night falls and that same one you saved me from beating decides to slip on his "white cone shaped hood hat with the peek-a-boo eye holes" to descend on you and your family. Should I say, "Hey, brother, Jug Head Jones, here comes that white man and his crew you saved from being broke by me. What would you like me to do?" The answer to that has always left me perplexed to this day. Some will say of me, "Oh, he's an over the hill old fool who's living in the past."

Check out the video on Rodney King and his man who was beat mercilessly on the other side of the car that night. Check out the brutal videotaped murder of the brother who kicked the Teflon don, John Gotti's ass in Marion. He then was murdered by white skinheads. What about the case in Texas where two 'Good Ole Boys' (out of boredom) hogtied a Brother to their truck and dragged him 'til he was decapitated? And the state's attorney said race wasn't an issue. Or, perhaps you should read up on the Sean Bell case out of Queens, New York, 2008. Am I truly an old fool? Or are you a young damn fool? And no! I'm not advocating violence. I'm just saying, "Cut the bullshit." Don't make me out to be racist. I'm just keeping it Jiggie, baby!

Standing outside the Dairy Whip one Friday, I was broke, and said to myself, "Man, I'm not waiting on anyone to ask me, do I want to go out, I am going by my damn self!" No sooner had I started to walk into Dudley Station, I heard someone call my name. "Hey Charlie, hold up!" I turned around to see Rosey.

"What's up, Rosey?" His response is, "Man, I am broke!"

"So am I, my brother." Before I knew it, I was asking him if he wanted to hit a lick. Instantly, he was sizing me up. Then, finally, he says what I'd been waiting to hear all my life. Vicissitude is equated with change, a life style change at that. His responding "Yes" reverberated throughout my being, and can still be felt today as I reflect back to that day in Dudley Station. I was so elated I would have slipped my hand under the Pope's coattail inside Vatican City and played him for his damn sting (wallet). My adrenaline was at an all time high until he said, "Have you been out before?" The question seemed to linger in the air like smoke from a recent blaze. My first thought was to lie, but why, I questioned myself. Everyone had a first time, even Rosey. So, I 'fessed up as we used to say, and responded emphatically, "No!" His stare was long and hard. Then he said, "I had a first day once, also."

We walked and talked about the game on our way to North Hampton Station. I learned that his real love wasn't so much the game. Rosey wanted to be the next "Clay." He was a boxer and a fairly good one, as I would hear it said down the line. But, that day our collective thoughts were on a far different two legged target. We were on the hunt for "Chump Stew," male or female. It was almost "Tip Time/Rush Hour" in the Cannon vernacular. Once we arrived at North Hampton we posted up inside Joe Nemo's Coffee Shop. From this position we had a clear view of the flow of people traffic as they moved on the street.

One of our major concerns was the cops, two white, one black. The black of course was Black Stewart out of Station Four. The other two I had only heard about but had never personally seen, not up to then. Those two were MBTA PoPo's. They knew the game well. All they did was patrol the transit system. In the 1960s their office was a small room under the set of stairs next to the public lockers by the block of pay phones downstairs in Dudley Station. Today the MBTA police in Boston is a huge organization in South Boston.

After about fifteen minutes of waiting inside Joe Nemo's, a crowd started to gather at the Harvard Square bus stop going in the direction of Cambridge. As we watched the crowd thicken, I saw this woman, nicely dressed with shopping bag and a single strap purse step up to wait for the approaching bus. Rosey said, slow down, I see her also. He could sense my eagerness to spring. We eased out of Joe Nemo's. I said, let me play her. "I know I can beat her clean." I had my Newspaper ready, and double folded as we approached the crowd, not together, but not too far apart.

As the bus eased to a stop, the people on board began to move to the front and rear exit of the bus. On the ground the crowd was shifting to allow a pathway for those coming off the front of the bus. Now that the people were all off, those on the ground started to board. It was a mixed crowd, old and young, a lady with a baby carriage. My "mark" was behind the woman with the baby carriage, who she attempted to help.

Immediately, Rosey steps in tight behind me on my left side so no one behind can see over him or see what I'm about to do. I slipped the newspaper from my left hand to my right to cover her bag from anyone's view, doing so without ever looking. I slide my left hand in between the newspaper and quickly open her single strap purse. As I hold the open end of the purse against the newspaper, she begins to move. I begin to move right with her.

Never once does she realize I'm down on her ass. In the blink of any eye, I've located and latched onto her wallet. As she takes her next step, she's beat. Her purse is closed back tight as a drum. Her wallet was in between the paper. I stepped to her right because she was played on the left. I slipped around the front of the bus, Rosey close behind, crossing Washington Street heading in the direction of Shanty's Lounge in order to exit out on to the back alley. I knew I had reached a no turning back point in my life. "I had taken my first sting." My first fresh kill. It was a "bright red long wallet."

That first play earned us exactly thirty-three dollars and some odd change. The amount of cash was incidental to the monumental achievement and euphoria I was feeling. That experience was far better than sex would be combined with Di and Star together. The feeling I experienced as I crossed Washington Street to enter Shanty's Lounge, that feeling of power and control, was what kept me locked in the game until I said enough is enough in 2008.

As Rosey removed a brown no. 2 bag from his back pocket, he looked at me and said, "It's not so much about the money, but more about beating them clean." The no. 2 bag was used to put their property in and mail it back to them. He went on to explain that when you beat a person clean, that person has no real idea how they lost their wallet. You, on the other hand, are the only one who knows the truth. By mailing their belongings back intact prevents them from notifying the police that they were beat on the game at so and so location.

No college-educated male wants to go home and tell his wife "Sally" he got his pocket picked by two damn niggas at the damn bus stop on the way home. He's supposed to be Mr. Smart Guy, not a Nigga like me. So beat them clean each time and they will never be able to put shit together. That way he or she will tell themselves that they lost it somehow.

Now if you are ever caught in the act, give it back immediately. Running away with a hot sting is robbery in some states. In DC, Cannons are some of the best in the country. They are playing under a lot of pressure so they play a chump hard. Playing the Cannon takes plenty skill and raw nerve.

It's all politics in DC, it's the nation's capitol. You have big hat white folks and foreigners from all over the worlds coming to that city. DC isn't Mexico or Mexico City, the police ain't down with the lick, your ass is going to jail in DC if you get caught playing someone.

As we walked out that alley after breaking down that sting, and I got the odd dollar, "I had taken the sting," I knew I was walking out of one life and into another, and I was ready. As we eased our way over to a "Honey hole" of his on Huntington Ave, actually it was two spots. Rosey said, "Charlie, never finger fuck with the money, no matter how much is there. Always try to clean the sting with both of you present. Once you get a name for burning a sting (stealing), good and honest players won't do business with you. Also, Charlie, most Cannons are very superstitious. They feel if you burn them you not only steal your money and his, you bring bad luck to the group (mob as a whole). Now, Chumps will lie and say they had X amount in their wallets, so if you're busted, it's imperative that you have a solid partner in your corner."

As we approached Columbus Ball Park, Rosey said we are going to play the "Load on the Inbound" line trolley stop outside North Eastern University. He explained that it's always a big crowd of students and teachers all mixed in the same crowd. The students will give us good cover. No police, just young college kids. Everyone is polite.

We are going to play single load because of the size of the tip. It's usually a large crowd this time of day. Now, Charlie, if you can't beat your mark and close it back, don't play here. Find one in the crowd you can beat clean! Then slip back out the crowd and fall back on to the sidewalk facing the people loading the trolley. It's important that you are always in a good position to see everyone. People loading either have a token in their hands or the correct amount of change (twenty-five cents), so they have no need "women" to go into their purse for anything.

Charlie, be mindful that you don't play a student by mistake. "You'll only get practice, not any worthwhile money."

With less than half a street block to go, Rosey spoke. "Look, Charlie, at the size of that tip." "You're right!" I damn near shouted. "This is a honey hole, Rosey," I said. Instantly, I felt that same euphoric feeling I felt when I beat my first sting back at North Hampton station. I didn't quite understand it all then I just knew it felt good.

By the time we reached the crowd, I immediately zeroed in on a nice looking teacher type white woman about forty-five years old, holding a large brown strap purse. From the way it was made I knew I'd have to slip my left hand in between those two straps in order to play her. I was hyped. Shit, I wanted to beat her and again show Rosey I could play. Sensing my eagerness, Rosey slipped into the shade spot and quietly whispered, "slow down and play her, don't rush the play!"

Once she started to move with the flow of the crowd to load the trolley, I went into action, slipping my left hand between those straps and popped the latch on her purse and reached in and located her wallet without waking her up. She never felt the sting sliding out her purse, nor did she feel it being closed back tight. With her sting tightly held between a copy of the Boston Sun Newspaper, I casually back pedaled my way out the crowd to a safe position on the sidewalk. I cautiously placed the long brown sting in my pocket while I watched Rosey in action. As he methodically beat two people, the brother maneuvered with the precision of a skilled surgeon at the Boston City Hospital. I also wanted to master that same gracefulness and accuracy. Rosey was a real class act in action. Once his mission was completed, he moved to safe ground, my side of the street, where we both carefully watched the trolley make its way down the tracks leading into Symphony Trolley Station, the whole scene was something out of a movie script.

"Rosey," I said, "you're a bad MF."

"Charlie," he said, "you'll be better and you'll take the game further because of your passion for the game."

As we started walking and breaking down the money from those three plays, all three-hundred-twenty-five-dollars, I kept wondering why he said I had more passion for the game than him. As I write this now, I finally understand what Rosey meant so long ago. His goals and purpose in his world had changed...he changed. He wanted out.

Our next and final stop was Symphony Station itself, not on the inbound but on the outbound side. On our way there, Rosey again spoke about honesty, integrity and loyalty. The same pillars I learned from those guys in the North End. Those pillars would profoundly be reinforced once I stepped on Harlem soil in 1972. I have a home girl who recently published her first novel, "Street Covenant." I gave a guy 20K at her wedding in Boston inside the Prudential Center Mall in 1997. He didn't even know he had it coming to him. But, I knew and that's the important thing, more important than stealing it from him. We would wind up cutting 90k on that lick. The original play was a Cannon play with some twists and turns added to the mixture. Read "White Face Black Mind."

As we neared Symphony Station, Rosey schooled me on what to do and how to do it. I was to move behind him, watch and stay alert, because people can see what you are doing. We slipped into the station one by one at separate entrances and we never connected or said a word. Rosey pointed to his eye for me to look around and remain alert. Finally into the station comes a crowded car. People begin to disembark and head for the steps leading up to Mass and Huntington Avenues.

After several people pass, Rosey sets his sights on a tall white woman. Allowing her to get settled in her route to the steps leading to the streets halfway above to the top, that's when Rosey slipped in tight on her left. Stooping down very low, Rosey eased up on her, and I am one step behind him so no one can see who may be coming up the steps later. In one quick move, her bag is open unbeknownst to her, and he holds the open end with the newspaper so she's not able to feel the uneven weight. In the blink of an eye, Rosey removes the wallet. As she is about to step onto the concrete surface, he shuts her purse back and steps to her blind right side and up and around her he goes. I allowed a woman and a man to get between us for shade as we all worked our way up and out the station.

That execution of how again the game is played is a sneak creep play. The final is crucial because it's the getaway. Now, let me explain that fallacy scene that you may have seen in the movie, "Harry's in Your Pocket," and that profound remark, "Harry never holds." First and foremost, this game is not called pass the sting. This is called The Wiz, find a chump, beat them and get the hell away from them as quickly as possible.

Now, if you and I are out on the hunt for Chump Stew, someone to play, and one of us plays a person and beats that person, if either of us are silly enough to pass off that wallet to "Dingbat Joe" who gets out of sight down the block, you don't have anything to give back, if the person misses his or her wallet. How do you think either of the two is going to react if you are not immediately able to give them back their property? Someone is going to yell for the PoPo and someone is going to jail. Now, does it make logical sense to pass off the sting? No! That truly was an asinine scenario, but then it was only a movie. This book is about real life situations, not fiction. Now back to the story.

That nice white woman paid us two-hundred-fifty-dollars. We thought it would be a good gesture on our part to mail back her paycheck. She might be a bit short on cash. On the corner of Mass and Huntington Ave on the side going to Dudley Station stood a drugstore with a huge picture window facing on to Mass Ave. and the bus stop. Rosey and I posted up at that window, watching as the crowd grew larger by the minute. Between 4:00pm and 6:00pm daily it was a good spot to be if you're out working as we were that day.

After about fifteen minutes of waiting, a Chinese woman comes up from Symphony Station to await the Dudley bus. They are known to be super sensitive to touch but I sensed she was preoccupied with something by her facial expression. Being an "Ex Shoe Shine Boy" I knew how to read people's facial expressions. Those expressions told me I could beat her with ease. Some teenage kids who were ahead of her as the Dudley bus pulled into the stop, started horse playing and causing a bit of commotion in the crowd. This distraction was perfect because now everyone's in a huge rush to get on the bus.

As I dig in behind her, a big fat woman tries to use her weight to get between myself and Susie Wong. But, Rosey, out of nowhere, steps around me and steps real hard on "Ms. Lard's" instep, causing her to scream. I stepped around her fat jelly belly ass right in position and popped Susie Wong as Rosey fell in tight on the shade.

People who can't think quickly don't make good Cannons. It's a game for thinkers and improvisers. She paid us guys one-hundred-fifty and a gold ring that we sold at Baby Tiger's Gym for two-hundred. We totaled out at nine-hundred-sixty-three dollars, (four-hundred-eighty-one each), not a bad first day for a kid in 1966. The events of that day catapulted me into becoming a real Cannon. True, I didn't know enough about the game to go through the eye of a needle, but I was a true sponge when game was on the menu.

Now that the day was over, we agreed to meet the next day at 11:00 am at Spinellies Sub Shop on Dudley Street, directly across from a men's haberdashery called Callahan's. I had seen these pair of forest green silk and mohair slacks in the window along with this matching crisscross sweater, in suede that buttoned on the side. The sweater was seventy-five dollars and the slacks were selling for twenty-two. Now that I had some real money in my pocket I had to have them both and the matching socks.

The next day, Rosey and I met at our scheduled time of 11:00am. We got the same outfits, but in different colors. He chose blue and I stayed with that green. From there, we caught a cab to Sandy's Clothing Store on Columbus Ave. After the riots of 1968, Sandy's would close, along with Cy Stacy's. But around 2003, Sandy's old location would become the Shoe Fetish, a women's store that didn't do well. Sandy knew Rosey personally. Sandy's was directly across from the Harriet Tubman House. Upon entering the store, Sandy was up on his feet immediately greeting Rosey first and me second.

It was all for show, not as classy as Leighton's in New York. People didn't go there to browse, you came to buy or you didn't go in. It was just that simple. We came to buy shoes and a pair of Paris matching tee shirts and shorts in nylon. You could get them in an array of colors. I purchased a pair of nine-and-a-half-D green suede and alligator fronts, along with a size medium green Paris nylon shorts set.

Once outside, we planned to meet at Jackson's Fish and Chips on Columbus Avenue. Lorne would also be meeting us there. He went his way and I went to get a haircut and my second manicure. My first was when I went out with Star and her friends. No longer did I feel or look like the tin man character in the Wizard of Oz. The patch up eye and the half body cast was no longer visible. But most importantly of all, my emotional state was in better condition. In the coming years those Cartier wood and gold frames for sixteen-hundred-dollars would come to the once tin man along with many other amenities from ill-gotten gains.

Everybody played "Craps" in my projects, especially over at the handball court/racketball wall next to the basketball court. So, explaining how I came by the new clothes was not going to be a big problem for right now. Plus, I even gave a C-note to the house and fifty-dollars to my brother, so all bases were covered. After a nice hot bath and a rinse off in the shower, I put on some Champagne Cologne, for the first time. It still comes in a Champagne shaped bottle and you can still find it in many stores. Today, though, my favorite signature cologne is Amarige, which comes in a thick satin lined burgundy box with gold Arabic letters that says, "This is the most expensive and valuable cologne in the world." The top of the bottle is heavy gold plated. The price is five hundred a bottle and up. My childhood friend Mike Collins gave it to me on my birthday in 2004 along with some C-notes inside a birthday card. Those are the things that real players do.

After splashing on that smooth and seductive "Mack Oil" as we still call it, I stepped from the bathroom to my room to the smooth silky sounds of the Temptations' "Get Ready" album. On the cover you see the whole group in different stages of getting dressed. They all had on yellow shirts, brown ties, with brown silk and mohair suits. David Ruffin was the only one fully dressed. We may have been in different locations getting dressed, but once the needle of our hi-fi hit that vinyl and the Temps came alive through those speakers, my brother and I saw ourselves lining up with the Temptations to do what was known as the "Temptation Walk" as the music played.

Even Mom and Dad joined in doing their own rendition of the Temptation Walk. When I was all dressed, everybody wanted to see me in the living room to check me out. Boy, was I sharp and smelling good! My family's approval meant so much to me that evening. Reflecting back on that night stirs up many feelings and images of smiling faces now silenced by time. To be able to physically hear their laughter would fill my heart with much joy. Death is so final.

When I left 8 Adams Street that evening I did not once think about patches, casts, eczema, nothing negative, as I took the long way to Dudley Street to catch the bus down Mass Avenue.

I walked down Dudley Street past the Drugstore at the corner of Mt. Pleasant Avenue. A few doors down was a popular club called "The Place." The older Orchard Park crowd hung out in there. People like David Lewis, Vance Taylor, Charlie Johnson and his two sisters, Butchie Brown, the Hammond brothers, Mal Gomez from Mt. Pleasant, Tommy Reid, Perry Rose and his sister Barbara, Valerie and Deborah B, Mitchell Davis, and many others from the South End and up on the hill, Grove Hall.

The day I strolled past there was a hot day and the block was tight with people looking good. But, that day I was a few steps above looking and smelling good, and I got my props as I eased past one of Vance's sexy sisters. She's a Boston PoPo, or used to be. She made the remark, "It's raining Champagne all over the young brother..." I had a thing for that sister for many years, even when I'd see her in her PoPo suit.

As youngsters we have all these silly notions and ideas along with peer pressure. Especially when it comes to age. I knew Ms. Renita Tyler was a couple years older and that alone frightened the crap out of me. Being rejected by someone your own age ain't bad, but an older sister would have spelled disaster. Isn't it silly how we look back on our past. But once in our late twenties and up, age seems to take a back seat to feelings of the heart. Brother D. Lewis, you're lucky my self-confidence wasn't up to its full potential.

As I slowed to speak to those I knew, I could see I had their eye of approval. Back in the early to late 1960s Mass and Columbus was a black prostitute's haven, white girls didn't work that stroll. Being cute was cool, but being cute and a bad bitch is what got a hoe paid. A hoe had to be strong to work that stroll. Pimps back then knew that only too well.

Stepping off the Dudley bus and crossing Mass Avenue to the side where New York Pizza is now, I could see I was getting plenty eye action from the hoes. That always gives and up and coming fly player a boost in the ego department, and I was no exception. I had no idea what Rosey and Lorne had in mind for us that night. I only knew I was down for it.

Jackson's Fish and Chip was crowded that night as I approached the front door. The first person I saw as I walked through the door was my man Ernie's sister Sam. She was all up in this Redbone's face as she stroked the girl's hair seductively. Sam was notorious for knocking a player off for his woman. Sam was gay and a Cannon and people respected her. In 1980, she was brutally murdered in Elmont Park for something she didn't do. That night she was sharp with her streaked blonde finger waves with that fly burnt orange suede on. She stepped away from Ms. Redbone to give me a strong hug when she saw me come in.

To my right stood Rosey and Lorne talking to each other. Upon seeing me, they both started telling me how sharp I looked in my new outfit. I returned their compliment. No one had the big head, just three guys out all sharp. Lorne had on some soft cream, even cream lizards with dark chocolate running through the shoes to match his chocolate cap. Rosey spoke, asking us if either Lorne or I had ever been inside The Big M.

I thought about the time I shined a pimp's shoes in there and he gave me a two-dollar silver certificate for good luck. But I thought against mentioning it at the last minute. So my response was no. Lorne also had never been in there either. Rosey said we were going over there to meet the owner in a few minutes. Mud Kelley was his name, big Irishman, good man to know along with Mr. Corey. Corey's office is, "that's right, Charlie, next to Jackson Fish and Chip, where you saw the sign in the window that said twenty-four hour Bonding Nationwide. I came up in an era that taught us the imperativeness of having a personal relationship with a bail bondsman. The personal relationship in most cases would ensure that you could get out on bail based on your word in my town. Back then a man's word had depth and substance.

Upon entering the Big M, Mr. Kelley was at the end of the bar. Rosey spoke first. "Hey, Mr. Kelley." A smile crossed Mr. Kelley's large red face. Even from a sitting position it was obvious this Irishman was over six-feet tall and well over two-hundred pounds. He immediately responded to Rosey. But his eyes stayed locked on the two young sharply dressed guys with Rosey. As Rosey stepped closer, he extended his right greeting hand to this giant of a man known as Mud Kelley. After they shook hands, Rosey introduced us to Mr. Kelley, who again eyed us cautiously. Rosey read the caution in Mr. Kelley's face and then he said these guys are Cannons. Instantaneously, a smile came on his big wide red face.

As we settled in beside Mr. Kelley we learned that this section of the bar was known as his office. No one sat there except by invitation. He told us he also was a Cannon and he used that exact vernacular with a passion. When a Cannon and a lover of the game speaks about it, you can hear the passion in their voice. Looking about the bar you knew you were in a pimp and hoe bar, no question about it. Tricks and Hoes on one side of the bar and pimps and players on the other side. If you were white and entered that bar and didn't sit on the trick side of the bar, you were suspect. One of the barmaids would let you know you got no free peaks in there, so buy a drink and move to the other side of the bar. They'd let you know this wasn't a Peeping Tom bar. It was a Hoe Bar, cut and dry.

We learned that Mud Kelley came up out of the old Scully Square days in the early 1950s. The Government Center is there now, but from the 30s to the early 50s that was where all the longshoremen, Sailors, Charlestown Hustlers, Bank Robbers and all white Cannons hung out. Mud Kelley, Danny Keys, the McDonald Bros, Molly O'Toole and Sadie O'Keefe and Jake the Snake Paterson. I had heard about many of them from the old man Tommy Riley from the Riverely Theater. Later years he would work for my man Elkie's dad who used to own Hudson's Pawn Shop on Stuart and Tremont Streets.

Mr. Kelley told us stories about when men still carried "Nickel Notes and G-Notes on their hip." Yeah, he loved the game, you could sure hear it in his voice. As he blew out the smoke from a Cuban cigar, he was smoking, said he got a box right off a boat in Florida, he told us about two men, one Black, one White. I would meet one in 1972 in New York. We would do business together that same year and again in 1979. His name was Herman Hunter, aka Tee Baby, aka Bullets, from Harvey, Illinois. The other guy was Paul Hurley from Charlestown, MA. His brother was a priest. Big Hurley used to own a popular bar in a place called Chelsea, MA along with a couple of check cashing spots in my hood back in the late 1990s. Hurley and I met in 1996 while in Federal Prison in Allenwood, PA. Both of those men used to come through Scully Square. One a Cannon, the other a gambling man.

Rosey said it was good to know other Cannons, active and non-active, and he was right. You never know when you might need a friend. A couple of times Rosey had to lay low inside the club because of a hot chump he had beat. Mr. Kelley said to Lorne and myself that if we ever had to duck in and lay low, as he put it, we could do so. He had a downstairs section to the bar for special friends. Before we got up to leave, he made us all promise to stop by whenever we were in his part of town, as he put it. We had two drinks and left.

On the outside, we saw Lloyd the owner of The Trick House near the Big M. He was in deep conversation with two pimps, Wilbur Kennedy and Skippy House, about Hoe business, no doubt. I've known plenty of guys who were very good at their craft, but lacked polish and real respect for the game over all. Having game, respecting the game and being polished is what sets you apart from the squares and jap-slick chumps, those who are just in the way, slowing down the natural flow. They contort continuity, or attempt to, they think they got it going on, but they are truly in the way. We already had polish, we just needed to be shined a bit. Those introductions were just a part of the shining process, that's all. Many times, it's not about what you know but rather who you know and who knows you.

By twelve midnight it was decided we would go by Foot's after hour spot. Up to that point I had never been inside a real Pimp and Hoe spot. Foot's was legendary for having the best after hours spot in the hood during that time period. Having Mob ties and the story floating around that he had laid to rest a hood tough guy for trying to rob him, all that drama made him a man of respect in and outside the hood. His spot was one block down from Williams Street in the direction of North Hampton Street; in short, a block from Kornfield's Pharmacy. The Spot was up a steep set of steps that led to what was once a large apartment. Many of the walls had been completely removed to create more space. No one was searched but once inside you understood why you weren't.

The Boston Police were there in uniform. It was like a damn movie! Police kicking it with a hoe -- no bullshit! People talking, drinking and listening to music; some people were sniffing cocaine right out in the open. In one room there was a bar where black and white socialized without incident. I recall seeing Sonny Berry, Skippy House, Ronnie Fox, black Sam out of Philly who would become Muslim years later. "Hakeem Abdul" and I would meet in Philly in 1977 and remain friends until his death in 1994.

The gambling was in a very large room. Foots sat at the end of a long table with a green felt covering. Directly in front of him sat a huge fish and tackle box with several shelves. The amount of money I saw on that table was just unreal. So many fifties and C-notes were in stacks as high as a loaf of Wonder Bread the long way. The damn fishing tackle box was the same way. Next to the box was the biggest gun I had ever seen in my entire life. Behind Foots were three stone faced white men standing in complete silence.

Rosey was somewhere talking in another room. As I watched, I learned the game they were playing was called "Georgia Skin." That night would be my first of many nights to come that I would watch that game being played. And yes, I too would learn how to Skin, as it is called. Several people can play at one time. There are two sidemen, one controls the cards as they come out the wooden shoot that holds all the cards in place. In Skin there is no shuffling of the cards by hand. The cards are all walked face down in piles of five and tens, then they are all gathered and placed back in the box. They are cut first by the sideman, then handed back to the side man with the box. Then he slowly withdraws a card from the box and turns it face up for all to see. If someone likes that card, say it's an Ace, any Ace, then they take it and start placing bets that his card will outlast the rest in the deck. Then another card is withdrawn in the same manner. You can let several cards come out, or pass, before you choose a card to play. You try not to play a dead card, one that has already been played. You can bet who you want, however amount you choose.

By now, both sidemen would have chosen a card to play. Each time a card comes out the box, you are expected to lay a bet with someone. Whenever one's card has been played, meaning if you are holding an Ace and the next card has played but the Ace and the King, then the side man who is turning out the cards from the box will pull out the remaining cards to show whose card came up first. Now, let's say all the remaining three Aces are running tight (close together, that's called the "Cub", the Cub is always barred) meaning it's not held against the person who is holding the Ace. Some people can walk the "Cub," meaning set the deck for the cards to be very close, near the end of the deck. That shit could cost you your life in any Skin Hole.

Foots was considered a "Soleman" – a professional swindler. If you can't recognize the cheat when it's going down, you surely can't protect yourself from it. I'm not saying Foots was cheating, I am just saying it's always best to be the house because the house never loses. Skin is a very fast game, you must be able to keep track of what has fallen, and who you are betting with each time a card comes out the Box. Also, I would learn how to play "Coon Ca'n, Cee Low."

That first night in Foots' Spot was truly an experience. The only other two spots that could come close to Foots' Spot was a spot in Harlem called the Big Tack/356 – not to be confused with "Gaynelle's Spot" – "Across the Track" -- which also became the Cookoo's Nest" back in 1976-77. The other spot would be Andres in Miami on 7th St, NW, a real slick spot. Can't forget the Garage that used to be on 75th Street and Exchange in Chicago. Still even to this day Foots' Spot is the only spot I've been in that Black and White gangsters played Georgia Skin. Not to mention the fact that uniformed police hung out and fraternized with hoes. It was truly a sight to see.

As we were leaving about 1:30am, on our way down the stairs leading to the street, a police with all type of insignias on his cap and jacket passed us on the steps. He inquires, "How's the action tonight?" We respond, "Very good," as we step past him into the cool breeze of the late night air. At the corner of Washington and Williams we all part company promising to get together the next afternoon.

My girl was beefing because we were not spending a lot of time together. She thought I had been spending time with someone else. She was 100% right. Her first name was "Cannon" and her last name was "Game" and she was all consuming. Knowing she couldn't relate, I just played things off by using her Mom's words that, "we need to cool things." We don't want her to tell us I can't come over at all, do we?

What my "new girlfriend" was offering was a lot stronger than her offer of sex. Sex is measured in minutes, time, how long you can last. Game is measured with a far different yardstick. Game would give me and take me places and expose me to things sex couldn't. Players ain't tricks, and we don't need money to have sex. We need game, strong game, to get and hold on to what sex can't give us.

Waking up the next day and reflecting back over the events of the previous night created an adrenaline rush that went all through my body. Everybody at the breakfast table wanted to hear about my night on the town. I gave Mom and Dad what I knew they wanted to hear. That night when I got in, I woke Kenny up and told him all about the thing and people I saw and were introduced to. Kenny just wanted me to be careful and to enjoy myself. But he missed the point, it wasn't about me going out to have fun, it was about me coming up. Nothing else mattered.

On Sunday about one o'clock that afternoon, we all met at the Dairy Whip. We decided to take a ride on the Blue Line to Revere Beach and hang out at the Himalaya. It was a popular ride at the beach where teens and young adults gathered to hear the latest sounds coming out of

Motown.   It was strange to see the white girls out of Revere and East Boston dancing on the concrete by the Himalaya as the Motown sounds came over those speakers.   They may not have been able to take you home to meet their parents, but on that small piece of concrete by that ride called the Himalaya, the color of a teen's skin, be it black or white, meant nothing negative when "Little Stevie Wonder" started singing "Finger Tips part one and two."   Many friendships began at that Revere Beach ride.

There was one white boy I remember well, Charlie Hamell.   It was nothing to see him in Roxbury or downtown by the King of Pizza trying to get down on a black hoe.   Event he Sullivan brothers from the South End, Bobby Devlyn, Frank Casearny from up on Parker Hill and his pimping ass brother.   Saw him at 100 Centre Street, his black girlfriend had a beef for playing the Con game.   Back then we didn't think about hipping any of them white girls to the Cannon, only thing that guys wanted to do was put them on the Hoe stroll Downtown.   Putting them down with the "Griff Games" would come much later in my life and the rewards would be great.   There's nothing like sending an all American White Woman in the jug in the Hood and she's never questioned about why she's taking out so many of them "New Big Faces."   But all that's talk for another book.

On Sunday, I learned that playing women, picking their pocket, required a bit less skill and nerve than playing a man.   With women, you know she is carrying a wallet or loose cash inside her purse.   Once it's open, you feel for it, you remove it and close it back.   Not so with men.   The vic may be six-foot-five and two-hundred-fifty pounds.   You may only be five-six and one hundred fifty pounds.   He on the other hand may be wearing a raincoat, topcoat buttoned up to his neck with or without a vent, you know, that split in the back.   Now, let's factor in the location of his wallet on this person.   Is his wallet in his back pocket?   Which one?   Front?   Coat pocket?   How does a Cannon overcome all those possibilities in a matter of seconds?   And yet still beat his man clean and send him on his way?   It's another sixty-four-thousand-dollar question to be answered.

CB

Chapter 27 ~ Playing Men

Before I get into this chapter, let me be perfectly clear for those who may not take the necessary time to think before they put a bad bone on a brother. I am not waking up the dead, as they say in the game (exposing the game). That part was done the very first time someone's hand got caught in someone else's pocket.

I trust my readers are beyond naivete, and acknowledge that we do share our experiences, good or bad. The Cannon Game is by far not a New Millennium Invention. The game itself was around 2000 years ago. My old comrades and I did not invent the game. We have only taken it a bit further along than they did 2000 years previous.

The way the game was played in 1966 isn't how it was played in 1972 when me and Ernest Manigault stepped off that Greyhound bus. And how we played the game in 1972 took a 360 turn in 1976. And when the 1980s came along the whole mechanics of the game changed. Now that we are living in a new millennium it is fair to say that the Cannon Game has seen a new form. So if you think what was applicable yesterday still is today, you are seeing things incorrectly. The basics will always stay the same, "stick your hand in a vic's pocket and take his shit and hope you don't get busted!"

My experiences and exposure belong to me and me alone. Now, if you're doing what I did back in 1966, 1972, 1980, I can see why you might think that the brother is giving up the game. Perhaps my brother you should work on elevating your game up a bit. As you can see, I'm working on elevating my "G." Now, with that all said, let me get started again. In order to stick your "raw duke" (hand) in the pocket of a complete six-foot-five-inch, two-hundred-fifty pound stranger, that takes an abundance of raw nerve by itself.

So, let's say you are beyond the nerve part. So, now what's your plan of action, you know you haven't a damn clue where his wallet or loose cash is located. Remember, it's winter and cold out and his coat is buttoned all the way up to his damn neck and no damn vent's in his overcoat. That is what I was taught. We call this move, "Fanning a Chump," searching him. There are a couple of ways this is done, depending on the setting you're in. Now, let's say you are playing single load, alone. What you want to do is position yourself in front of him, if you're in a crowd like "waiting to board a bus, train, going through a crowded entrance to a doorway."

Now that you have positioned yourself in front of him, with your back to him, drop one hand and unbutton the two bottom buttons on his coat. Easy, but quickly, by slightly leaning against him or just keep him stationary by not really moving. Once that is done, ease behind him without ever allowing the two of you to have eye contact. Actually, once you've opened his coat at the bottom, you can "while still in front, fan his front pockets with both hands for a wallet or a brick of cash."

Let's say you located his cash and wallet in separate pockets when you fanned him. Now you must decide which one to take once you are behind him. But, wait! Let's back up a bit. You know exactly where the wallet is but that cash is another matter. Allow me to explain. You have to determine a couple of things based on touch only. Was it old money or new money? How would you know that without physically seeing it? Very simple. Old bills spread, new money is tight, unlike old money. Secondly, was the pack large or small along with being old or new? More than likely, if the pack is large , so are the bills in the pack. White folks don't go around faking about carrying bricks in their pockets, not at all. If you fan a brick in a white man's pocket, you can bet he's carrying big notes as in C-notes. That's how Wall Street white folks get down.

Say you've come to the conclusion your man is carrying a brick in his front left pocket, so you position yourself behind him so you can slip your left hand up under his coat that you previously unbuttoned while you were briefly in front of him. If his pockets are deep I suggest you "Riff the money." Take your middle finger on your left hand and lightly pull up the inside material of his pocket at the top, the pocket lining. By doing so, the money will rise to the top of the chump's pocket by using the riff technique. Now if it's a short pocket, the best play to execute is the "whole hog." Stick your duke, your hand, without any hesitation in his packet and take that brick "peep it to make sure you don't need to replay him for his sting."

Many Cannons who play "A single load Game" (play alone) miss a lot of money. There are some Cannons who are cut above the norm when it comes to playing the "single load." Two such Cannons names must be mentioned here, "Boston Joe and Matches," two "Bad MF-ers." No bull. Their individual as well as collective feats and techniques are legendary in the annals of the cannon game.

Now if your man isn't on the front right or left and you've unbuttoned his coat, go up under his coat from behind and fan him on both sides of his ass. As soon as you locate his sting, crack his latch, unbutton his pocket, and settle yourself. His wallet's position in his pocket will determine how you'll have to prepare to take it. Are the open ends up or down, or is the whole wallet in the bed (sideways)? There is another possible scenario.

Years ago, 1976 to be exact, I was down in Miami for the first time, and on every damn city bus as you got ready to exit at the back door, once you looked up you could not help but see the big sign saying, "Beware of Pickpockets." It also showed a picture of a wallet and it had a comb in between the two open ends. We had a big laugh. By then I was up on them "Cracker Jack tricks." All we'd do is move the damn thing, the comb, to one side, stand it up or take it out, slide it back in, minus the wallet. So much for the comb trick.

Oh! I also saw it at the Mardi Gras one year along with a sign saying, *Don't put your wallet in your back pocket; put it in your front with the comb.* We watched a white man tell his *(little Johnny this is how you protect your wallet)* Son how not to get beat by the long finger Boys. After all that bullshit I beat him as he and son were unloading at the front. Someone stopped to ask the driver, *how do you get to the Big Gray Dog Bus Station?*

I slipped out the back door. He stepped down and started walking, took a self fan, couldn't explain to self or son what the hell happened to Daddy's sting! Now, if those open end s are facing up at you, you have to pinch them together as you start to bring up the sting to break the sting off from the pocket. If the ends are facing down in the back pocket, you just get a firm grip and ease it up and again break it off. If it's "in the bed," sideways, straighten it up and take it.

If you are playing two deep, you and your partner, one of you is the wire, the other is the stick. Whenever the Stick is being used his job is always to keep the man straight. Never allow him to get past or around him. All of the sticks moves should be very natural. When he makes body contact, it should always be to the upper body of the person being played. If the man is being played on the front left, apply body pressure to the upper body on the right. Never lean on the money, or the Wire's hand is jammed in the man's front pocket and he will feel it. When you hear a light kiss, or cough, you know he's been beat and it's time to let him go. Also, you must move very fast because if he misses his sting, the stick is always the one he comes to because he was the one closest to him. Never do they suspect someone from behind being the culprit. The wire has to keep the vic in eyesight until his man slips out of eyesight of the vic. If the vic does blow his sting, miss it, the wire has to be close enough to kick it back.

Sometimes you may have to walk the sting back yourself and hand it to the person you just took it from, with a story how you came by it in the first place, if your partner is in a bind. But before it gets to that, try and give it to a stranger to return. It looks better if another person, (white, male or female), returns it, than a black person.

The upstairs play is really playing at its best. It requires putting your back flush against the back of the vic's chest, keeping him straight. The stick will turn to face him on a side angle as if he's trying to pass the vic. Using his own hat, briefcase, etc., he raises it up to the face of the vic, preventing him from seeing the other hand sliding inside his inside suit or top coat pocket. One hell of a play when you see it in action!

Sometimes, chumps will tell you exactly where their valuables are by the things they do; such as constantly touching a particular pocket. It could also mean he's holding big or he's been beat before and he's very uncomfortable being where he's at. You can play him or give him a pass. Before I would give him a total pass. I would have to give him a fan just to see if he is holding big. Now, if he's holding a bank, let's say two or more packs in one pocket, you know it must be a fast and tricky play. You can't just take his money, he won't go for that so easy. But he will allow you to trick him out of his money. In this type situation it would be an excellent idea to have a woman as the stick rather than a man. She would play what we invented in New York as the "Fallout" play. It may sound corny in name and even look corny in action, but believe me, when you realize the ten-thousand dollars you had a minute ago is now gone, it's not so corny any longer.

What the stick does is pretend to slip and fall. Being a man, he automatically reaches to help her get up. She will ask him to help her up because of her injured leg that got twisted when she fell. He is going to use (that's the key word) both of his arms to help her up. She is going to lean right up against his pelvic area in a rubbing like fashion with her ass. That will keep him totally off guard, with both arms extended away from his body so he can't check his pocket. Once she hears the signal from the wire that he has beat the vic, she says, *thank you, I can make it from here*, and she moves away very quickly by ducking inside somewhere. Perhaps even taking off her coat, or putting on a hat that she had in her handbag.

Those were some of the things that were taught to me that Sunday at Revere Beach long ago. I would never physically see that play in action until 1976 in New York. A brother named Steve Brody from Washington DC is credited with helping me perfect that play. I am perhaps the best at playing that play, even now. One must have an abundance of creativity and a love for the game to play as hard as I once played. Many of the things I learned on that Sunday would take days, weeks, months, even years to perfect, and executive to perfection. I would learn how to read a person and instantly know what would be required to beat him by his body language alone. Being able to play a man was and still is the ultimate feat in the world of a Cannon.

In 1966 I had yet to reach that level of playing. In 1972 I came up out of the Minor League to play in the Major League of Game. In 1976 I was on a World Series Team. From then on I only played on an All Star Team of Players. Beyond that came being inducted into the "Hall of Fame of Game." Now it's 2008, and I am writing my memoirs of the

Game I once played so well. Hustling with Rosey and Lorne, etc. was feeling my way through, trying to find my place. As you continue to turn these pages of my life you'll see where this game took me as well as those who suffered because of my selfish decisions.

Back to the game! I also learned another key component to the game that Sunday. It's called the "Shade." The shade's job is crucial for if the Shade isn't on his job, everyone stands a good chance of going to jail. As the stick gets in position to the "Vic" and the Wire eases in behind the Vic, the Shade must first look around at all those who are near them to be sure no one is watching what is about to take place. Once he is comfortable then he slides in behind the wire on the side he is playing the Vic on so no one can see. On our way home that day we boarded a crowded train, a big fat guy loaded with us. Big Boy had to stand the whole ride holding onto an overhead strap like the rest who were standing. Rosey looked right in my face, while rubbing his left index finger in his own eye, which was indication to me that he wanted to play Big Boy at State Street Station.

In front of Big Boy sat a woman holding a young baby about two years old, directly in between her legs was a folded up baby carriage. From the sweat running down Big Boy's face, it was obvious he was tired of holding onto that overhead strap, he wanted that seat occupied by the woman with the child on her lap.

The train slowed down as it entered the station, and the woman began to gather up her belongings in order to get off the train. Sensing her readiness to get up Big Boy reaches out to help the woman with her baby carriage. At that point, Lorne began to make his move as though he wanted to take the seat also. But, in reality what Lorne was doing was sticking the man.

Lorne says, "Ok, you take the seat, Sir," and Lorne squeezed between the "Vic" and the woman. I am behind Rosey tight on the shade. By the time Loren cleared the man (passed him with some body contact), Rosey had beat him. As we stepped off at State Street Station, the man was settled into his seat, never realizing he'd just been beat. Now that is perfectly executed game. That was my first experience with playing a man.

Rosey had told Loren and myself about a month later that he wanted to pursue his boxing career. Through his friendship with Mr. Kelley, he would get the backing he needed to pursue his dream. For whatever reason his career never took him to where he wanted to go. After Rosey squared up Loren started pimping. I stayed with the Game.

Back in OP there was a group of guys two or three years younger than myself. One of those guys we will call "Shorty" had a speech impediment, he stuttered sometimes when he spoke. We met when my family first moved to the projects through a mutual friend. The Crew he ran with was all "Till Players" and those brothers knew their craft very well. Their motto was "You never leave a Black Face." Essentially, what that meant was this: cash drawers are usually all black, so if you take all the bills out each slot you are leaving a black face, alerting the cashier.

Those guys used to go to this place on Massachusetts Avenue that sold and repaired cash registers and electric cash drawers with keys. Those brothers taught themselves how to open the cash drawers without them ringing any bells or making the slightest sound. Those guys even stole the keys to many standard machines used in Sears retail and auto department. Having those keys allowed them to go all over the country playing Sears' stores. A brother named Milton Farmer was the best of the best (only one other brother came close – Barlow out of Chi'town) who ever did it. He had one hell of a crew, Raymond G, Donald Green and his Bro Shorty, Neal B, and Franky Rogers. Most of that crew is deceased. Those of us who know them still speak of them with much reverence. Milton was known to go up on the roofs inside OP and throw money off the roof to the younger kids – and I mean money! Two other names must be mentioned; Kevin Copeland and Carrie Fox also played the game.

One day while on my way to look around some of the stores around the Dudley Station area, I ran into Shorty coming out of Woodrow Wilson Court in the projects by the big ball field. We had a brief conversation about project gossip. Then he said, "What's up with you today, Charlie?"

"Man, I am on my way to get a sting. Why?" Up until that point he had given me the impression he was "double breasted" (played the till game and the Cannon). I had no reason to doubt otherwise. So when I asked the question, what's up with you, his response was I need some work. Without thought or question, I said, "You want to go up to Dudley with me?" He responded, yes.

There was this store called Robell's that was near Dudley Station that stayed crowded along with Woolworth's and Dutton's. Robell's was my first stop. As we were about to enter Robell's, Shorty sees a guy he knows by the name of Mike who is a clerk in the cosmetic store next door. The name of the store was Carol's Cosmetics owned by a brother named Frog. I knew his brother Ronnie and sister Joe Alice. She had an adult daughter by a guy I used to hang out with named "Lester Mayo." They, along with my sisters, came from the same bricks, Lenox Street Projects.

When we stopped, Shorty introduced me to this younger version of myself, I mean the brother had on a pair of Pepsi Cola thick eyeglasses and we even had a similar build. Down the line many people would ask, "Are you two brothers?" No. Unbeknown to me then, I had already met his Mom, Dad and two of his sisters long before we met that day. In years to come, he would also develop love for the same game I was about to execute that Saturday...the Cannon.

Our love for the game would take us from Boston to Toronto, Canada, and even to the Super Bowls in 1984 and 1985 played in Palo Alto and Tampa, Florida. At one point we even lived in the same apartment building at 49 West 85th Street between Central Park and Columbus Avenue in New York City. On the day we first met, my mind wasn't on forging friendships. It was on a "Vic." I never gave it a second thought that that day might actually be Shorty's maiden voyage, his first day going out on the stroll. He had led me to believe he could play the game.

Upon entering Robell's department store, I told Shorty, "You go down one aisle and I'll take another." Actually, I thought he jive hesitated when I made the statement about splitting up, but I didn't give it a lot of thought. My mind was focused on finding someone to beat.

Moving down the aisle to the back of the store my eyes immediately locked in on this three-hundred pound fried hairdo toy cop trying to rap to an equally big black sister with nine-hundred ragamuffin kids trailing behind her. Seeing that picture I knew we didn't have to worry about his fat tub of lard.

Looking around I spied this lady in what looked like a nurse's uniform. She was all alone looking over different sets of sheets that had the "Red Tag" markdown sticker on the package. She was totally oblivious to my presence, which allowed me to stoop down as if I was tying my shoe. Doing so gave me the cover I needed. I was able to open her purse, and take her sting along with a tan envelope that had the see-through window. Looking through I could clearly see it was money. Quickly closing it back I slipped away like a thief in the night. As I made my way to the door that led to the street I looked over to my right and saw Shorty, basically still in the same spot I left him at.

I immediately exited the store and crossed the street so I could watch the entrance. I wanted to be sure Shorty could see me and I could still see him. After about ten minutes out comes Shorty, looking up and down the block before looking straight across the street, finally noticing me. I nod for him to come on over. I just knew this Negro had beat at least two or three people based on the length of time he spent in the damn store. When he finally reached me, I asked, "How'd you do?" His response was a dropping of his head as he said, "I didn't get one."

"Listen, my man," I said, "that's cool. You keep what you got and I'll do the same." Finally, he came clean about that day being his first day on the stroll and how he always wanted the game. A part of me kept telling me this joker is lying. He got a sting or two on him, but when he offered to let me search him, I declined. I told him, *players don't search one another, we search Vics.* Quickly, we took a shortcut through a side street leading back to our projects. Once we hit Harrison Ave, we cut through a building leading to Batan Court.

Inside the building, I said, "Hold up, Shorty," as I pulled out the wallet I had taken. "Check it," I said. He found eighty dollars along with some loose change. I broke down the money with him, then I came up with a tan envelope. Man, when he saw that money, he went to stuttering and stammering and spitting like an MF. The money in that envelope came up to five-hundred dollars. That was the money I had taken by myself up to that point. I broke that money down the middle because that's how I learned to do things going back to those days in the North End shining shoes. It's not about what he lied about, playing fair and being a player is what it was all about that day when I broke bread with Shorty.

It's 2008 now, as I sit in this cell writing this book while I await sentencing in US District Court in Greenbelt, MD. I'm compelled to say many, not all, of my peers no longer are about fair play and respect for this thing of ours called game.

For me, I'm cashing in my chips. I'm done! Cash Charlie out! My next two books will lead up to that end. But, on that day in the hallway, as I broke down that sting, I had no idea that my honesty and integrity would perhaps be mine alone. Shorty was so happy to get that money he started talking real clear after a while. From that day on, we would break down many stings in the coming years.

Sad to say, we took everybody's money. If you got caught in the line of fire, you got fired on, played. I remember a book back in the 1960s called "Soul On Ice" by Eldridge Cleaver. He was one of the many staunch supporters of the Black Panther Movement on the West Coast in the 1960s. In his book, he describes a mindset that is so very true even to this very day. He was sent to prison for rape. The real interesting thing was a statement he made in his book.

He said that in order to hone his craft, perfect his pussy taking skills, he assaulted black women first as if their bodies didn't count, raping one of our own held no significant value or importance, simply because his intended or ultimate victims were to be white women. Back during the

1960s, our ultimate goal was to play whites only. Yet we also honed our craft on poor black folks down Dudley Station and the surrounding areas. How can you justify tricking and robbing the same people you claim to love and who are just as disenfranchised as you? In short, we count less, so rape us, our women, and rob us, Black People, first! Practice on us first, make all the blunders on us before moving on to the real kill, "The White Man!" In reality, all we did was set the stage for what we see our youth doing to each other in any City, USA, with guns and knives, etc. In 1972, a play in Philly would cause me to stop playing anyone Black.

Boston Cannons and New York Cannons utilize a play called "The two blocks back play." What it consists of is this: If a play went down that resulted in a blowout, "Vic woke up that he was being played," and broke bad even after you kicked his sting back, we automatically knew to go back two blocks in the opposite directions of the play and wait. If no one in your crew showed up, we'd go to a pre-designated spot, "50th Street and Broadway Chuck Full O' Nuts Coffee Shop" and wait there. Having those safety nets in place ahead of time saved many of us from a beef. Bostonians and New Yorkers were the ones who used that tactic.

After that day in Robell's, Shorty and I started hanging out in a popular poolroom called The Mines, along with Jewels and Wolf's including the famous Apollo Poolroom on Columbus Avenue in the South End. By doing so, we got the opportunity to meet other young players such as ourselves.

Many of the young hustlers from the South End played a different game than those who played the Cannon. They played a game called the "Trick car game." It went like this. When the white tricks from suburbia came to the hood, Massachusetts Avenue, the Big M Bar to devour the treats that lay deep within the thighs of black prostitutes, before he would get out of his car they would take out their wallet, remove how much they intended to spend on a girl. The rest of his cash would be left in his wallet. He'd call himself hiding the rest by stashing it under the floor mat or under the seat, etc. Those brothers from the South End would be hiding inside hallways, doorways all along Mass Ave, watching them tricks' every move.

Once the trick did his stash act and went inside the Big M Bar to purchase his weekend delights for the night, the guys would use coat hangers to pull up the door latches and slip inside the car to get the money. What used to confuse the tricks was his wallet would always be in the exact same place minus the cash. I even went down on the avenue a few times myself to get some late money. It was real funny watching a guy blow, get beat. He would come out of the trick's house, all puffed up after getting off, get in his car, light up a cigarette and reach for his wallet. Some would just slide their wallets right back in their pockets and drive off. Then you had those guys who for whatever reason would just open theirs up.

Seeing those contorted facial expressions take shape was a real treat. Guys would look in their wallets five, six times before they would get out the car, get down on his hands and knees and start searching the floor of the car. Others went so far as to try taking out the front seat of the car on busy Massachusetts Avenue at one or two a.m. I have seen tricks look in the back seats of their cars for their loot, same for the trunk, look under the car. The two best were watching them search themselves and finally beat up the dashboard.

Many big stings came out of those trick cars back in the 1960s. Jerry D and his two brothers, Noah B, Victor White, Malcolm, Skip Jordan, and many others were the recipients of those stings. The drawback to that whole scheme was too many people would claim to be down on the lick for me, actually it was a local hustle, and if you weren't raised down there, those guys truly didn't want you knocking their hustle. Plus, many times you would have to be out there at two or three in the damn morning. That was not my thing. I was still attending school and living at home. Also to me, that shit was really "Nighttime Burglary of an Auto."

"I ain't no cat burglar; I'm a Cannon," I would say to people.

03

Chapter 28 ~ Meet the Boston Crew

One day after school a group of us guys and girls were inside the Dairy Whip when Ronnie "Kidd" Montero comes in with two other guys. Now, let me tell you about Ronnie Kidd that day. Ronnie was six-foot-three, light complexioned and real stuck on himself. I had known his family going back to the Julia Ward Howell School days. He was always hustling and staying sharp.

That day in the Dairy Whip, Ronnie had on all lavender – crocodile tie ups, matching socks and slacks the same shade, lavender short sleeve shirt, dark lavender sport jacket that I had seen in the window of Lebo Brothers, and he had a process!

The brother stepped through the door full of confidence and cockiness. Self assured, that's the best way to describe the Kidd. Rico was always the quiet self-centered one, Mr. Laid Back. He, being dark in complexion, always loved cream, or brown as his color. His outfit was all cream and dark brown with dark brown suede and ostrich slip-on shoes. Clyde was the smallest of the trio and the oldest. Pee Wee Clyde had on a wine colored outfit with matching lizards. He was always smiling and talking fast with that deep Alabama accent that became part of his persona. Rico and I had met prior to that day up at Jewel's Pool Room but Pee Wee I had not previously known.

Kidd was talking shit and flashing his bank, big Rico, who was Kidd's height, just played that laid back persona of his. Pee Wee was up close and personal in some sister's face. After all the fanfare was done by Kidd, I was again introduced to Rico and Pee Wee also for the first time. Kidd says, "Charlie, I've been hearing good things on you." So now, you're reaching.

My response was, "Not like you, Kidd, but give me a little time and I'll be better than you." I knew that statement didn't sit well with Ronnie Kidd that day. Rico and Pee Wee both laughed; Kidd remained quiet. We all agreed to do some business. Rico said to come by Jewel's and so did Pee Wee and it was genuine. Shorty and I knocked around a couple more weekends, but I really wanted some heavyweight action to sharpen up my game and so did Shorty. So, we agreed to separate and get back together down the line.

Weasel Jacobs was making a name for himself in 1966. I only knew of him from the Mines Poolroom. He had a real good one-pocket game and a nine-ball game as well. On this particular Saturday, Weasel was playing a heavyweight name, "Big Jake" down the Mine's Poolroom. To me and many others, Jake was one of the best Black players around the town at that time. He'd play white boys for big money, and he would even play up in their hood. The brother had a rep for not being a nice guy either. I just happened to be in town that day to pick up two pair of slacks I had made to order at Bedford's Tailors. I ran into a guy named Al Harris as I was exiting the train station at Essex Street. "Hey, Charlie," Al said as I came up out of the station.

"What's happening?" I responded back to him.

"Man, I'm on my way up to State Street Station to play the rush tip," was Al's reply. "What about you, Charlie?"

"I got some slacks to pick up. Who's downstairs in the Mines?"

"Weasel and Big Jake are going at it hard, Charlie. Listen, Charlie, I got to get going. See you later."

"I think I'll slip downstairs, Al. Talk to you later."

Stepping into the Mines that Saturday afternoon was like stepping into a morgue. All eyes were riveted on one game only; I mean no other table was in use but table #6, the table Weasel and Jake had on lock. I had to actually nudge my way through the thick crowd to get a peek at the action on the green. They were playing "One Pocket." Jake could play, no doubt about it, but his real strength wasn't his stick, his strength lay within his ability to intimidate his opponents. His mental intimidation game gave strength to his pool game, and he knew how to put pressure on a weaker, less aggressive type of player.

Weasel wasn't yielding, though. He, too, could play. In the middle of the game, Jake cracks, "Let's up the bet five-hundred to fifteen-hundred!"

"Man, you can't call a bet like that in the middle of a damn game, Jake!"

Jake responds, "Put up or blow the bet!" (The whole game.)

"Jake, you can win all I got all day, but you can't take a dime from me. My money comes too damn hard!" Weasel finally comes back with.

"Okay, mother fucker, it's a bet!" cracking slick again Jake says.

"Money on the wood makes all best good, mother fucker!"

Talk about tension, man, it was thick. Fuck picking up my slacks, I had to see how this shit was going to play out. Suddenly, Weasel pulls out his bank and throws it on the green, but he's three-hundred short of the fifteen. Jake immediately reaches for the original five-hundred from the overhead light of the table. Just as Jake is about to touch the money, a voice from the crowd says, "Bet covered, play pool!"

I threw down three live Presidents (not dead ones on the table) on the green. Dead men don't talk; only live ones! Both men looked at me hard for several long seconds. Jake had pure venom seeping out of his nostrils and eyes.

Fifteen minutes later Weasel and I walked out the Mine's together, both winners in our own way. Weasel won the game and I won his friendship for life.

As we were rounding the corner in the direction of my tailor, Weasel says: "Man, why did you cover my bet, we really don't know each other?"

"That's where you're wrong."

"What do you mean?" he quickly said. I went on to explain something I learned on my first trip to New York from a hoe named Star.

"And, what's that, Charlie?" he asked me.

"She said, 'always try to look out for your own kind.' I'm a Cannon and so are you, Weasel! I don't have to know you on a personal level to do you a solid. (White folks look out for White folks all day, don't they?) Jake back there is a bully and he's not even a player. He's a taker, an intimidator; we play for our money. He, on the other hand, doesn't. He may have a wee bit of polish on himself, but he doesn't shine like we do."

We stayed friends from that day up until his death. Shit, I even had a fling with one of his sisters in 1969, "Patty." I learned much from him.

Rico and I finally did some business a couple weeks after Weasel and I had that talk. Big Rico had a flow that was unreal. To see him twist and turn on a city busy was like watching an Olympic figure skater like Nancy Kerrigan, or a swan gliding on a lake. To see him play a man was a hell of an experience, his speed was deadly quick, a step ahead of plain fast. The Kidd, "Ronnie Kidd," didn't like playing women. To the Kidd, playing women was beneath him. That's how the Kidd was.

EC was another tall brother who could reach real good, he gave up the game to become a Pimp, spent some time in Detroit, then came back to the Beantown to pimp for real. He, along with Rico, Pee Wee, Ronnie Kidd, Weasel, Ernie, the list goes on and on, have all gone back to Allah. This book is about them also, and the impressions they made on my life. Even now, I can see each one vividly in my mind's eye and hear their unique laughter still.

Ernie's sister, Sonia, (Sam as she liked to be called), was the first female I ever hustled with. Because of her small size she would slip between a crowd very easily. Plus she was very sexy and young looking; people took her to be a child many times, but she was far from being a child. Her hands were so tiny and she was very light-handed when she played a woman. We beat a lot of people on that old water town line coming out of Harvard Square back in the 1960s. Her brother and I became life long friends until his death in 1989. My very first trip to the West Coast was with him. We put a real hurting on San Francisco and Chicago. Philly was our honey hole out of town though. Our biggest single sting was taken in Philly in 1980.

One day, unbeknownst to me while I was in Dudley Square hustling, actually I was playing a woman at the old Equilstation bus stop on the load up, as they get on a bus, I was seen playing a woman, by 'Dis Aunt' who lived right next door to her. Boy, that shit created a lot of ill feelings in both houses for many years to come. I was branded a common thief. Thief, why, yes! As for the common part, I'm not so sure about that. Years later, 2000 to be exact, the Boston Herald along with the State Superior Court of Boston, Massachusetts and Special Prosecutor's office at Ashburton Place did in fact charge me with being a "Common Known and Notorious Thief," a phrase that was used back in 1966 became a real life charge against me in the year 2000.

Her aunt put pressure on Di's Mom to stop me from coming around, but it only lasted a short while on her Mom's part. But her aunt and cousins, now that was a horse of a different color. She and I would rekindle that old flame again in 1976 for a short while and those old feelings of dislike would once again manifest itself at a family reunion held by her family.

In December of 1966, Loren and I went to New York during school vacation for the Christmas holidays. I found my old friend and introduced her to Loren. We even went to the Cheetah that night where the Winter Garden Theatre is now at 50th Street and Broadway. That was a really fly club in 1966. One night on 8th Avenue and 42nd Street, Loren and I are on our way up the stairs to this poolroom. As we get right to the top, Charlie Johnson, Gary Stevenson, and Pedro Nunez are coming out at the same time. Seeing them in New York would really bring us up a few notches on the Boston Cannon scene. I felt ten feet tall after that encounter.

The next day we are down at Macy's at 34th Street and Herald Square taking stings like we have a license to steal White folks shit. Unknown to either of us then, 34th Street was the training ground for the all-new

PPC personal. PPC stands for "Pick Pocket Confidence" games. Not being New Yorkers or New York Cannons, not even knowing any, was a total disadvantage for us both. Back then as well we know. Now, New York and San Francisco has the best "Bunco Squad" by far to this day. And in December of 1966 before Christmas the squad in Midtown was very active. They busted us around 1:30 in the afternoon on 34th between Fifth and Sixth Avenues.

You can always tell a true New Yorker from a visitor. New Yorkers say 6th Ave, while visitors say, "Oh, you mean Avenue of the Americas." We were not going to reveal we weren't true New Yorkers so we never said we were from Boston or our real ages.

We used the 47th Street hotel as our address and said that we were eighteen years old. By claiming to be eighteen we went directly to the Brooklyn House of Detention on Atlantic Avenue. That was a wild spot in 1966. The police slapped the Cowboy shit out of me for not having my shirt tucked in my pants. We were housed on the Fifth floor.

One evening our floor went to gym and to our surprise we see Charlie Johnson and Frank Aruzo. Charlie was going with his fine sister Minerva. In 1966 she should have been a Playboy Bunny.

We did about two weeks and got cut loose with time served. Star had all our clothes from our room and put them up in her spot. We went to the hotel, got a shower in her spot, changed and went down in the hole (subway), and beat us a few people and got our shit and came back home. Everybody was upset because I had missed my birthday and Christmas, still they were glad to see me.

My brother got married in 1966 and in January of '67 my very pretty and smart niece, Deborah L. Belim, was born. By March of 1967, I knew everybody in the town who was playing the game. By this time, there was a new club in downtown Boston called The Sugar Shack, and that's where the action was. All the latest talent from Motown came through the Sugar Shack Night Club in the 1960s. I wouldn't get to go there until 1968. β

Chapter 29 ~ En Route to Shirley Industrial School for Boys

I n 1967, I was really starting to feel like I actually understood this game, The CANNON. I had been back to the Big Apple, got busted, saw Star in the process. Not to mention having also survived the "Old House of D in Brooklyn on Atlantic Avenue." What's so crazy about that whole experience, Loren and I should have been at some juvenile facility in the Bronx. You got it. "We lied about our ages." Still I hadn't done the ultimate "beat the man on my own and by myself."

One day after school I decided to post up at a bus stop inside of Dudley Station in my hood and wait on the Humboldt Avenue bus to pull in. I knew based on the time of day it was that it would be a large crowd by the time the bus pulled in. "Nigga buses" are historically slow in any hood USA. Like clockwork, the bus was late and the crowd had grown in size. While waiting on the bus I had decided to play someone on the "load up" rather than waste time riding then play someone as they attempted to unload.

As the bus pulled into the bus stop for the large crowd to board, I quickly nudged my way in the crowd to play this well dressed black woman in her mid-forties, I beat her quickly and attempted to do a back peddle out the tip. However, the force of those jockeying to get on the bus forced me to load. One particular guy who was built like a Sherman tank began pushing me extra hard it seemed from behind. Knowing I had a fresh kill in my pocket, the woman's sting, I tried to be cool and not attract attention to myself.

The Sherman tank was pushing me up onto the bus so damn hard I finally turned around to face him and say something. When I saw that nasty look in his eyes, I knew this Negro was trouble just waiting to happen. Now that I was forced up on the bus and its doors closed as it eased out the station, I immediately went to the back of the bus to avoid the vic I had beat and the Sherman tank. My intention was "get the hell off this bus at the first available bus stop outside the station. Nearing the first stop outside the station I reached over a lady's head, pulled the cord indicating my desire to get off at the approaching stop.

Maneuvering my way through the crowd, I again came face to face with the Sherman tank. Knowing I had a fresh kill in my pocket really made me anxious even more to get away from this damn fool in a hurry. Fate had its own agenda. What happened was this. The bus driver had to come to a sudden stop in traffic. To prevent myself from falling on top of the people already seated, I reached for the first available overhead strap holder, but the bus jerked, and I bumped into the guy from the station who forced me on the bus. After politely apologizing, the next thing I know this damn fool is knocking me upside the head saying I am trying to take his wallet. That crazy MF jumped all over my ass. I lost my damn glasses.

Now, here is the part that I still can't figure out after forty some odd years. He beat me out the emergency exit. Now, mind you, the emergency exit is a door that is part of a seat that you can sit in. I was thrown out that door into the traffic at the corner of Moreland and Warren. The woman I beat never missed her sting, at least not to my knowledge. Being thrown out the exit wasn't bad enough by itself. I landed on the hood of a damn car going down Warren Street.

Somehow, I managed to roll off the hood and came up on my feet and ran down Moreland Street. I didn't even realize I still the sting until I got to the park near Copeland Street. The three-hundred dollars in that sting was well earned that day. Black folks will fight hard for their money, even harder still if they think you almost got away with it as the guy did. After that experience I never went anywhere near that bus stop for any reason.

It's so very true playing poor Black folks can be extremely hazardous to a Cannon's health. Dr. Ruby here I come for a new pair of headlights. For the next week while my glasses were being made Di was my seeing-eye dog. She had me looking in some hell of a hole that whole week.

The day I picked up my "new headlights," my seeing-eye girl Di met me down Dudley. I gave her $250 to get herself a pair of shoes and a dress. We had planned to go to the Sugar Shack the following Friday to see Gladys Knight and the Pips. The whole town was talking about the coming show. None of us at school had been there and we had planned to make it a big night. Rico, Gail, Ronnie and Pat from Glenway Street were also going. Everyone was expected to dress very sharp. Two days before the show, I decided to put some work in. It was mid-April and a nice day weather wise. I had a 1:00pm dental appointment at the old health center on Savin Street. I left school at 12:00 noon.

On my way to get a bus at Dudley Station, I did a detour and got the bus to go up Dudley Street in the direction of Columbia Road. Back then that was a good area to work, plenty stores and crowds in the streets. Near the corner of Dudley and Columbia Road was a large Woolworth's store that sold everything you could think of. They even had the long lunch counter like the one across from Blair's on Washington Street. They had the one-dollar picture booth and the Rocking Pony for 25-cents a ride in the front of each store. Those picture booths always stayed full of kids making funny faces each time the camera flashed.

Rico and I had taken a couple of stings in there a couple of weeks earlier. They had a store Security Guard who stayed mostly by the exits trying to catch the kids stealing candy. On this day as I entered the store I didn't see him anywhere. So I took that as a good sign. Immediately I went to the Home Furnishing Department, the pickings were always good in that location and today was no exception.

The section was jam packed with women White and Black alike. They were having a sale on bed linen and all the women were busy reaching for bedding. I, too, was busy reaching, but not for any bed linen. My object of desire was that big Black bag hooked onto the side of this woman's baby carriage. It would have to be a fast play.

The very next time she reached in that pile for a pack of colored sheets, I slipped my hand down into her black bag and felt for her sting without taking my eyes off her. Once I had a firm grip on her sting I came up and out with it all in one motion. My gym bag was unzipped so I slipped it in and eased away. For some reason the door to the street seemed further than usual. Then my hands started to sweat and my mouth went dry.

Finally, I was at the door and pushing it open to fresh air and freedom. Not once did I ever take a gander back over my shoulder, or look left or right for that matter. By not doing so, I broke a cardinal Cannon rule. Had I looked back just once, even just before I took that sting, I would have seen that black-reckless-eye-baller had a beam on me from the next aisle over. Black folks—Black folks, my people.

Sometimes we are in everything but a damn hearse! Like I said, I never once looked back coming out the store. If so, I would have seen the security cold-trailing my dumb ass. I made another crucial mistake. I went into an unknown Irish Pub to clean out the sting, not knowing whether there was a back exit available. Never do you do that shit! Also, I should have done one of several things, got off the main street quickly, crossed over rather than walking a damn straight line that led me directly to station #9, the PoPo's house. When I came out the pub, the security guard was flagging down the Police. The reckless-eye-baller saw the whole play and alerted the store security.

The police put me in the car, went back in the pub, found the damn sting in the bathroom stuck behind the toilet. Also, in my haste to clean out the sting, I overlooked two new crisp fifty's tucked in between some photos. Talk about having a bad day, shit it was way beyond a bad day. Soon, as the police got my silly young ass inside the shakedown room at Station Nine, I was immediately strip-searched. Not only was the Vic's money, ninety-five dollars, found on me, so was my own personal tucked away C-notes found inside my secret pocket inside my pants. All money confiscated automatically became their loot.

When it came time for the good guy-bad guy routine, I had been pre-hipped dating back to the North End-North Hampton Street days, and last but not least, my baby "Star Child in New York." After two detectives finished running down the "Boo Game," I politely asked, "May I have my one phone call? Oh, and by the way, officer, I'd like a lawyer." I overheard one of them mumble under his breath, "Smart-Ass MF-ing Nigga" as they left the room.

I spent the night in a cold ass cell, with no blanket and no heat. Next morning, I was arraigned in Dorchester's Juvenile Court. My whole clan showed up for support. "Little good it did." The judge continued my case for two weeks and committed my ass to the Department of Youth Services in Roselindale, Massachusetts.

The Youth Services Board, as we called it back in the day, was run by some sadistic MF-ers, let me tell ya'll. We had to address all the male staff as "Sirs" only, not Mr. so and so. One particular staff member was Pete Larose. He was mixed, as they'd say during those days. Chinese and Hispanic, yep, he was one of many who hated any and everything black with two eyes. His thing was taking a youngster for little or no reason and throwing their ass through the day room window. You'd land in the hallway all knotted up and broke the hell up. For some reason, I managed to escape his wrath. Freddy Martin, a childhood friend and I had long agreed if Larose ever did that shit to us, we'd kill his Kung Fu ass and escape to New York.

Then, there was this Irishman from the then "White side of Mission Hill Projects. Back in the early to mid 1960s, whites still lived in Mission Hill. Mr. Timothy's family was one of the last white families still there during that period. One day, he caught me talking in line in the lunchroom. Immediately, I was sent back upstairs to my room.

Several minutes later he showed up, while he stood there telling me all about the do's and don't's, out of nowhere this crazy MF-er "goes berserk and punches me in the mouth." Mind you, this cracker was well over six-feet tall and must have weighed at least 250 pounds. Man, I had blood streaming down my shirt out of both nostrils. Now, check this out. The crazy bastard offers me a damn cigarette after he fucked me up. I refused it, and told him I'd get his ass back one day for what he did to me. Before he finally got elected to public office, Blacks, Older Blacks in Mission Hill would get wind of how he was treating the youngsters at the Youth Service Board in Roslindale. Those brothers fucked his ass up one day and ran his whole family out of the projects.

On my return court date on the pickpocket case, the juvenile judge at Dorchester Court found me to be a delinquent and I was sentenced to serve nine months at a place called "Shirley Industrial School for Boys" in Shirley, Massachusetts. My thinking was really warped and distorted.

I actually wanted to see what Shirley was all about. Somehow, I equated Shirley (jail) with being a young player. Yep -- a player of the Cannon game, and a player. Going to jail for me had nothing to do with me making a bad judgment call. To me, it was an unwritten passage to manhood and a life of crime.

Here's the real irony. I've heard guys say, myself included, man I did a good six months at so and so joint, or my ten years went by with east up North. What are we really saying? That's an individual question that requires individual answers. I can only speak for myself, no one else. It has taken me three state and two federal sentences, "old law and new law," for me to acknowledge certain truths. True, I made tons of money, had a new home given to me as a wedding present by my first wife's father, had the flyest apartments in the city (407 East 88th between First and New York Avenues; 49 West 85th between Central Park and Columbus Ave), did the brunch thing at Tavern On The Green inside Central Park. Not to mention fly cars. Oh, but let's not forget those "buts." We all know about the ones that nag and gnaw at us like a bad toothache. For instance, when two of my beautiful daughters were sexually violated, one was by a family member, the other a member of my Mother's church.

You already know the why's and how-comes. Yep. I was "stuck like Chuck" in a New York State of mind, too busy being a player and a Cannon to protect my daughters. Being in that mindset caused me, due to being busted on a beef I honestly played absolutely no part in during 2000, not to be present at my fiancée's funeral and my mother's several months later. I have no qualms about my decision to stay silent regarding that beef; I'm not a rat. My issue is this: I should have done the right thing -- put my children far up the ladder of importance -- perhaps I would have saved them from being molested.

When hindsight is applied, many of our, my own included, selfish desires come to light. Regardless of the outcome of my present federal case, I will stand tall and take my lick. In doing so, I also must again say, "I'm turning in my player's card" that I've held onto so tightly at such a high price. Today, December 18, 2008, I announce to the world that I am through placing myself in harm's way of the penitentiary. But, in April of 1967, "hindsight was under deep cover," as you shall continue to see.

Upon my arrival at Shirley Industrial School for Boys, it was like old homecoming week. I knew over half of the joint. My cousin, Joe Bell's co-defendant, was there. He, along with one of the "Tate Bros.", was in Concord Prison, Ronnie Kidd's Bro Roy was there, Johnny Stevenson, Sterling Bradley, Danny Terrance, Bobby Devlyn and last but not least my man Rico (Ricardo Wilson). He came to Shirley right behind me. Those months at Shirley shot by very fast. My whole family came on a regular basis, they always do when you're young, but by the time it's your fifth state or federal bid, they don't come as often, and in many cases they don't come at all.

I've only done one state sentence in Massachusetts, 2000 to 2003, and that was for a beef I played no part in. I served that sentence at Shirley Medium, a stone's throw from Shirley Industrial School for Boys. While at Shirley medium I used to gaze up the hill at the old Administration building and reflect on those months I spent up there in cottage #5. Every day all of us Cannons would get together and talk shop about the game. Rico and I saw ourselves playing our game on Broadway in the greatest city in the world – New York – while others daydreamed about seeing themselves in Cali (San Francisco). Others saw themselves downtown Boston only.

We, Rico and myself, not only saw ourselves at major sports events, Kentucky Derby, World Series, we also saw ourselves in the thick of the crowd as the ball dropped on New Years Eve in Times' Square.

In our hearts, minds and souls, we knew we'd one day get our opportunity to play the game we were destined to play, The Cannonnnnn!

For fun, we'd hone our craft by playing each other. When we got down on the staff it was for real and so were the consequences if you got caught. We, Rico and I, never got caught.

Heroin. My introduction, verbally, that is, came about while at Shirley. Heroin is the only drug I know that is known by so many names until it ain't even funny: Dope, Black Tar, China White, Bone, Raw, Pee, Doogee, Blow, Scagg. In Boston in 1967, it was called "Scagg" in the Grove Hill section streets like Intervale-Brunswick-Devon and Blue Hill Avenue itself. Those were the dope stores of the 1960s up on the hill.

I sincerely believe those locations should have been called by some other names: Criminal, Isolation Prison, Madness, Separation, Divorce, unloving self, Emotional and Spiritual Death, and last but not least, Physical Death. Those are the rightful names that should have been stamped on each bag that was sold throughout our communities in America.

I hear a brother way in the background saying, "No one put a gun to your head and forced you to buy it!" Not knowing who your father is or where he is, is a form of that gun. Not being allowed to drink from a White's Only water fountain is that gun. Not being allowed to sit in a particular seat on a public bus is that gun. Not knowing how to read or write is that gun. Being told you are not only second class, but a third class citizen is that gun. Seeing your Mom or other female family members scrubbing floors so you could eat is that gun. Let's not forget the "Willie Lynch Syndrome" for added effect. And in the end what you get is a beat down person who doesn't even know how prone he or she is to use a mind and body-altering chemical. In many cases, it will hold that person hostage until they die. Back in 1967, I didn't know any of those effects.

One day, while walking in the big yard, Rico says, "Man, they got this shit called Scagg; it gets you high all day for just ten-dollars and most times two people can get high on one bag." Naturally, I said I never heard mention of anything like that. He said they had just started selling it right after I got busted. He said you can snort or mainline it. Then instantly, I knew what he was talking about. It was the stuff that killed George Kelly and his friend the day they bought that "Kool Aid" from Kenny and myself on Sherman Street. The way the brother was campaigning the usage of that shit was like it all belonged to him.

I left Shirley at age Sixteen on December 16th, 1967, not thinking about "Scagg" or anything remotely connected to using it either. My father met me at the bus station when my bus got in that Saturday morning in December. Three days later I turned Seventeen. I registered for a special after school program at Dorchester High School. From there, I transferred to Boston English High School. After completing the tenth grade, I didn't return that September. I was one of the disenfranchised. My life became totally consumed with playing the game. Shirley was over and done with and now it was time to move on up in the game – start playing Men.

છ

Chapter 30 ~ Downing My First Man

By the summer of 1968, Rico was home. Shorty was in Shirley, and I still had not completely made my Bones yet (beat a man), but it was soon to come, that was certain. Having gotten busted in April of the previous year, Di and I never did do the "Sugar Shack thing." So, the week of July 4, 1968, we stepped down the stairs into the "Shack" for the first time to the sounds of the Isley Brothers singing "This Old Heart of Mine." The joint was jammed with people, white and black alike. We had very good seats for the show.

That night, I knew I was truly in my element in every sense of the word. Now, I was going out daily and doing okay. I could even afford to give Mom a couple hundred weekly. Kenny always got his fifty-dollars C-note when he needed it for whatever. With all that was going on each time, I got behind a man, I would hip him by rushing the play. Over anxious is what I was and that's why I kept hipping men. One day, I was just so determined to beat a man, I just sat for at least an hour or more in Arlington trolley station, just observing people and how they moved about while waiting for a certain inbound trolley.

That day I really became a reader of people. The less preoccupied a person, the more likely they are to look about their surroundings. Many people who are not totally comfortable being in those stations could be victims of past crimes or someone they know was in fact a victim.

But then here comes Mr. And Ms. At Ease," the one who's system savvy, knows what to be aware of. They are very beatable. You just have to trick them out of their money. And last we have "Mr. and Mrs. Preoccupied" with whatever and just don't see everything or everybody around them. That is who I was looking for that day as I sat in that station.

Then the rush started to flow down those steps to the platform below. And then I saw him with two bags, one in each hand, and a newspaper, trying to read it as he stayed close to the railing coming down those long steep steps to the bottom. He was so oblivious to his surroundings, he never looked left or right, as he got right up into the thickness of the waiting trolley crowd. This guy was so in a hurry to get on the trolley before it even stopped to let passengers off, he was already pushing and shoving.

As he started to maul the crowd, he never once noticed the figure easing behind him. In his haste to get to the door of the trolley, a woman pushed him and he dropped his newspaper. As he was standing back up from retrieving it, a hand fanned him on his front left and there it was -- very soft thin wallet, sitting at the very top of his short pocket. Once it was gripped hard, I could feel the tension in my left hand, sweat was starting to form under both of my armpits. Then he did what I had heard people say, "he beat himself!"

By me having a death grip on his sting, he stepped forward and away from his sting, leaving it in my left hand in midair. All Cannons remember their first kill, be it male or female. Without any hesitation, I eased that sting in my pocket so damn fast and backed out of the tip as he stepped onto the inbound trolley that day. When I saw him comfortably seated and the doors completely closed, sweat really started to run like a faucet from my armpits and down the back of my legs as I quickly rounded the corner to come up the escalator. Talk about a long distance to the top level! Man, it seemed like it took an hour to get up to the top, then through the turnstile and up one more flight of steps to the sidewalk and freedom.

I crossed Boyleston Street, went to the corner of Arlington and Newbury and walked up Newbury until I saw a cab. I had forty-dollars of my own money, so I knew I'd be able to pay the cab on my own. I directed the driver to take me to Cy Stacy's, a men's clothing haberdashery, one block from the famous Big M Bar on Mass. Ave. Quickly, I paid my two-dollar fare, got out of the cab and went inside Cy Stacy's as the cab drove off down Mass Ave. Once the cab was out of sight, I walked the short distance to the Big M.

Mr. Kelley was posted up at his regular spot at the bar. Seeing me, he quickly motioned for me to go downstairs fast. He no doubt thought I was being tailed. Several long minutes past before I heard his heavy footsteps coming down the old wooden stairs. Here's this big powerful Irishman with rosy red cheeks smiling and holding a serving tray with a bottle of Johnny Walker Black Label Scotch and two glasses.

As he sat down, I ran down the whole play, blow by blow. The excitement in his old eyes was just un-fucking-real, especially when I got to the part about the vic walking from under my grip on his sting. I wanted someone to share that moment with, someone who truly understood what I was experiencing for the first time. Another Cannon! That sting held six new crispy C-notes, plus two fifty-dollar bills. I offered him the two fifties, which he took with a, "Charlie, I'll keep it for you, in case you ever need it."

We sat there for at least an hour talking about game the same way I had done years earlier while shining shoes in the North End. I kept that wallet right up until I went to prison in 1973.

Back then, many of us had heard the name "Sleep." Like many young Cannons my age, I, too, had only known the name, not the man. All that was to soon change. One evening, I was sitting in a popular restaurant, Muslim Ak-Bar's, on Blue Hill Avenue. It was owned by Brother Gordon, a mean spirited, no-nonsense, Nation of Islam brother. He was famous for making two things: Barbecued beef sandwiches and Arabian Punch drinks. Brother Gordon's menu was far better than the Hickory Pit or Herb's Restaurant on Blue Hill Avenue. Herb, along with the owner of the Hickory Pit, were rumored members of the Nation of Islam as well.

I had just slipped two case quarters into the "pic-a-low" (Juke Box) to hear the mellow sounds of the Temptations sing "My Girl." Looking up in the direction of the door, I saw Rico, EC (Errol Crawford), Ronnie Kidd and this real tall stranger I had never seen before. The stranger had to be at least six-foot, five-inches. As they came over to greet me, I was in awe of the brother's height. I had no idea who he was. After all the hand slapping and fanfare was over between those I knew. Finally, Ronnie says, "Charlie, this is Sleep."

We immediately extended our right hands to each other. His persona appeared genuine as his huge hand seemed to swallow up my small hand within his. From the little I learned about him that evening, Sleep had recently been released from Walpole State Prison on a robbery charge. In actuality, it was a con game beef made out to be a robbery. Being recently released, the brother was thirsty for some pro work. No question about it, he got just what he wanted based on the company he was with that evening. The following year, I would have the opportunity to break bread with him myself. A long friendship would eventually develop between us based on those two encounters.

Later that same year, 1968, Mike, the younger version of myself who Shorty introduced me to the day we went to play Robell's, would meet and develop a close friendship with a brother named Cully. Their newfound friendship also would bring them both into the Cannon game. By the end of summer that year, 1968, heroin was starting to move its way into our community of Roxbury at an alarming rate. Many older brothers were returning from Vietnam on their first tour, and many came home hooked hard on that "Asian China White."

In a matter of a few months, heroin was being sold in every poolroom in Roxbury, South End, Dorchester, Mattapan, and beyond. Jewel's Poolroom was heroin alley and up there it sold for ten dollars a sack. Down at Wolf's Poolroom in the South End, you could buy New York "duces or tras" for five dollars each. The Rainbow and The Wine Cellar's price were ten dollars. That's where all the White Boys came to cop. Many of us younger guys had heard that if you snorted a sack of good dope, you wouldn't cum and you could sex a girl all night, or at least for several hours. There is some truth to that belief. However, they left some things out, like, eventually, if you continue to use, you won't even have a desire to do it even for five minutes. It would kill your nature, and you may have trouble finding it, or it just might have trouble standing at attention.

I took my first sniff of heroin in 1969, got so damn high after I got past that burning sensation from the "Iron/quinine," I must have crashed about ten times that day while I was high. Quinine is what gives you the rush. Today's dope isn't cut with "Iron," they use a lot of "Morphine base" and Oxie's to stretch it, or when it's not that good. So, you not only have a heroin habit, you got a Morphine habit, a synthetic drug habit and it is much harder to kick. That shit has destroyed many lives. Some close to me, some not so close, and some from my own family.

You don't have to always lose your life to be a casualty. You can still be walking and talking, yet be dead emotionally, spiritually and financially. Take it from me -- I know exactly what it feels like to be in that state of decay. True, I wasn't privy to those realities the day I took that first sniff. And nope, it wouldn't have made a difference had those realities been in my conscious mind, I still would have done it anyway. Today I do know the answer. In spite of all the slick hipping I was receiving back then, none of it measured up to the acceptance I sought from others. That is why I took that first sniff.

Today, I know it's not about people accepting me, but rather it's about me accepting Charlie for who he is for himself. I can't change having been born with Cerebral Palsy, crossed eyes, eczema, or red hair. Today, I can honestly say I'm okay with who I am. In the summer of 1968 I still had a long way to go before I reached December 19, 2008, my birthday.

One day while riding the old Tremont Street line in search of a sting, I caught sight of another Cannon on the bus I had never seen before, so I decided to get off when he did and introduce myself. We both unloaded at Massachusetts Ave and Tremont Street. While waiting for the traffic light to change, I introduced myself and told him I was also a Cannon. I learned his name was Leroy Myers. His accent was laced with a deep Southern twang. The brother was from Richmond, Virginia. He was a small built guy, very dark, and about twenty-five years old, not more. I learned from Leroy that he and two others had been coming to Boston for five years. Those two guys I would meet later in my life. Out of all the names he mentioned that day I only knew one and that was Sleepy.

As for the guys out of Virginia and Baltimore, I wouldn't meet them until the big race at Pemlico Racetrack in 1972. I did, however, know Big Cut and Little Cut, Ball Track and his partner Tony out of Virginia. They weren't Cannons, they were "Creep Thieves." Leroy and my partner Ernie would both wind up in Concord Prison in 1969, both would be sentenced to five years and both would do only one year. Upon their release, we would all do business together in the coming years. Especially in New York, Baltimore, along with the Super Bowl of 1983, which was played in Tampa, Florida in January of 1984.

On the evening of Martin Luther King's death, April 4th, 1968, I was over Di's house listening to music when her Mom came in the back room to tell us of the news that had just flashed on her big black and white television screen. Many of us knew MLK had been asked to come to Memphis, Tennessee to support the Black striking Sanitation Workers in that racially divided city. After seeing the footage of the reaction to his death in many US cities that evening, her Mom became fearful for me being out late. She suggested I go home before things got out of control.

Taking her advice, I left for home. Upon reaching Dudley Station, I encountered a group of all white police in full riot gear. They had the biggest and longest "Nigga Beaters" I'd ever seen in their hands. On each of their heads were these menacing looking helmets, their pants were tightly tucked into those polished nigga kicker boots and they wore black leather jackets. The whole aura was something out of World War II in Germany.

For a split second, I thought they were German SS Soldiers. Each one's face was ashen in color and their eyes had this piercingly strange look of part fear and part hatred. They were in two long rows and each person had to pass in between those lined up police in order to exit the station to get into OP. Whoever is truly responsible for that Brother's death just didn't kill a dream. The word "assassination" is more applicable. I'll explain.

King's death far exceeded the mere physical assassination of a man. The perpetrator attempted to assassinate a dream, not of one man but of a people. A God given right. A right to be treated equally. But, the "assassin," and the "assassin's bullet, missed their intended mark. True, it killed a man, but here at this moment in 2008, and thirty days from this writing, this great country will have its first African American Commander-in-Chief. Walking through that long line of menacing looking police that April 4th in 1968 in Boston, no one could have convinced me I would live to see otherwise. But January 20th, 2009, will come to pass. And not only for people of color.

Prior to the death of Dr. King, a James Brown concert had been scheduled at the old Boston Gardens at North Station. A few months prior to my arrest, a friend gave me a copy of that famed concert on DVD. Seeing that concert brought back many memories to me. I was actually in that audience, and thought I saw myself in the film. I was one of the many screaming teens that night. The Mayor, as did the police, wanted that concert to go on so the Brother could not only do his thing, but the powers that be also wanted him to address his own people personally. He accomplished both that night.

Many of us felt back then that every time we successfully slipped our hands into a white person's pocket and took their money it was looked upon as a blow for the cause. That's cool, but what about them poor black folks? How did they figure in the scheme of things? Oh! I know – "just collateral damage, casualties of war." Did they count? These are questions I've been asking Charles H. Belim (Abu Bakr) since that era and even as the era was taking place. It's really sadly comical how we justify bullshit. Yep. We was taking black folks' money also, sad to say.

ଔ

Chapter 31 ~ Getting Ready for Easter

In 1968, I had not accepted Islam (taken my Shahadtan yet), so the coming of Easter meant a lot to me, and many others as well. I was hustling, and by now the whole family knew it. Even our family in Alabama, Georgia and Detroit. Still, Pop gave me a couple of C-notes to help me get an outfit.

I took the money and ran directly to the "hole" (Filene's Basement). I'm sure I could have put something together with that two-hundred-dollars plus what money I had. But what I did was buy this "Brown Shadow Stripe Silk and Mohair Top Coat" for two-hundred-seventy-five-dollars. The whole house was upset at me. Literally, I was told, "Don't come back in this damn house without a suit of clothes and your hair cut or done."

You see, in 1968 I had a "Real Barber Shop Process" straight out of "Mop City Barber Shop" where "Nubian Notions" sits right now. "Mop City" was the hot spot in the town. Happy, John, and Goodstuff were the Barbers. The police stayed in that spot looking for us Cannons whenever someone got beat in or around Dudley Station. The Friday before Easter, just two days away, I was standing outside Shanty's Lounge talking with some of the older guys when this white woman, perhaps twenty-five years old, walked by. All the older Players started saying shit as she was passing.

She wasn't a bad looking white broad at all. Looking at her you instantly knew she was a "hippie." Long stringy blonde hair with a white flower sticking out the side, cut-off jeans and dark brown handmade moccasins on her feet. She was obviously high off some form of LSD by the way her eyes kept jumping around. I watched her go into Folsom's Market at the corner of Washington and Northampton. By then, all the older guys had gone back inside Shanty's Lounge or just walked off. Not me.

I decided to wait on her to go back in the direction she came from. After about twenty minutes I saw her coming out of the market and heading in my direction. Keep in mind that I ain't never been down with the robbery game, but that particular day I was pressed. Shit, I had to get myself a suit, plus get my hair done!

Somehow, I knew she had exactly what I needed, so I posted up at Uncle Ned's Pawn Shop, you know, window shopping. I watched her pass me from her reflection in the pawnshop window. As she attempted to cross Mass Ave in the direction of the Olympic Flower Shop, the traffic light changed. She couldn't cross; that was my cue to spring into action. And I did. Quickly, before the light changed, I walked right up beside her and said hello. Her first words to me were, "Why do you have that stuff in your hair?" I lied by saying, "It's my natural hair." "No, it isn't," was her reply, as she handed me her bag of groceries.

Together we crossed Mass. Ave, me holding her bag in one hand, while she held on to my other hand. Sometimes, we've got to play out the hand that's dealt us, and that's exactly what I did.

After crossing Mass Ave, we continued to talk, mostly about the war in Vietnam, though she did the majority of the talking. I was trying to figure out how to beat this Hippie broad out of her loot. I didn't want to strong arm shit for real, plus I ain't seen the color of her money, yet. Shit, she might have been broker than my black ass. That's the type of shit that was whirling around in my head that Friday before Easter.

As we were about to cross West Springfield Street, she said, "I need to stop at the corner store on the next block to get some smokes. Folsom's Market charged too much." She added, "Their price was eighty-five-cents a pack. The corner store only charges seventy-five-cents for a pack of Winston's."

So into the store we went, still hand in hand. Once inside the store, she immediately chose her brand and a pack of "Zig Zag" rolling papers. She turned to me and said, "Do you need anything?" I responded, "Yeah, a pack of Kool's." When it came time to pay, I expected her to pull out some bills from one of her jean pockets. That wasn't the case at all. In a slurred and barely audible tone, she said, "Baabbyy, pass mee my wallet inside the shopping bag." *Bingo! A wallet!* I thought to myself. Fool, hurry up and get this dizzy white broad her damn sting so you can peep her ends.

Soon as my hand made contact with her sting inside the shopping bag my fingers felt that familiar feeling that spelled M.O.N.E.Y. That's right, it was bulging out her sting. Instantly, my mind was counting C-notes. Silly, right? I know. After a few seconds, I came up with her sting and handed it to her. It was a long green cloth sting. I guess in her haste to get back to her place she didn't pay much attention to how she placed the money inside her wallet.

As she fumbled with her sting to pay for our cigarettes and rolling papers, I finally got a bird's eye view of her cash. Seeing all them crumpled up twenties, tens and fives spilled out onto the store counter spelled three things: a brand new Easter suit and shoes and a fresh "do," as in process!

I knew I had to get those ends from the hippie broad, not on the rough side, though, but on the smooth side with a twist of trickery and a sprinkle of deception. She lived three blocks from the store in a loft apartment. We had to walk up a steep set of stairs to reach her loft. Once inside, she and I went into her kitchen area. Mind you, she never did remove her sting from the bag except to pay for the cigarettes and such in the store. So, when she said to place the bag on top of her cluttered makeshift kitchen table her sting was still inside the bag. Rather than remove her groceries, she said, "Let's have us a good smoke. Have you ever smoked marijuana from a water pipe, handsome?" That's what she called me. "No," I replied. Secretly I didn't want to, either, I just wanted that goddamn sting!

Taking me by the hand, she led me into another cluttered room with a dresser and a waterbed strewn with clothes. On the floor near the bed was the strangest looking thing I've ever seen. She said it was a Moroccan handmade water pipe, and it had two long tubes that interconnected into each other. The bottom portion of the pipe was a big bowl filled with red wine. Quickly she packed the pipe with some dark reddish weed and fired up the pipe.

I was sitting there looking at this crazy ass bitch's face as it began to contort each time she drew on the pipe. I'm like, "Man, I don't want any of that shit." But then I heard a voice saying, "Don't bring your black ass back in this house without a suit and your hair fixed or cut!" With that voice ringing in my ears, when she said, "Pull, baby, pull," I did just that on my tube. That shit was powerful and strong. I got instantly high. Then reality hit me like a ton of bricks. *Negro, you're up in a damn loft in the South End with some crazy ass white woman who's zonked out of her mind. You'd better get that sting and get your ass out of there.*

As I was still pulling on the damn pipe, the crazy bitch shimmied her ass out of her shorts and was spread eagle on the waterbed. Yep, you got it. She was beckoning for me to have sex with her. *If she thinks I'm getting naked with her ass, she's crazy,* I'm thinking to myself. Thinking fast, I ease down my slacks and hit her. I don't have to even consider cumming. Three to five strokes and the bitch is out cold. Now, I'm really in an MF-ing panic. *Is the bitch dead or in a coma?* All I kept thinking about was *"Rape charge and Charles St. jail!"* Man, I pulled out of her cracker ass, ran to the bathroom and cleaned myself up, ran to the kitchen, snatched her sting, and down the steps I went, three at a time.

Two steps from the bottom landing, the damn door to the street is opening. *Oh shit, it's the MF-ing police! Nigga, you're going to jail for rape and robbery on a zonked out naked white woman!* That's just a flicker of the thoughts that flashed in my mind as that door opened. Fate dealt me a fair hand, though. It wasn't the police, just another hippie – a guy.

I quickly mumbled something about her being upstairs asleep as I eased past him in the hallway. Once I was outside that building, I ran like Jesse Owens did in the 1936 Olympics. At the corner of Tremont and West Newton Street, I got myself a cab straight to Logan Airport. While riding to Logan, I counted out twenty-five-hundred-dollars in twenties, tens and fives. Now, I had my suit and process money.

Thinking back to that day now, boy, that was a wild MF-ing stunt all in the name of Easter. As soon as I got on that plane, I ordered a double shot of gin. Less than an hour later my plane was landing in LaGuardia Airport in New York. Stopping a "Red Cap," I asked, "How do I get into Manhattan?" "Take the next Q33 bus right here to the subway station."

At the station, I got a train into the city that never sleeps, "New York City!" To my surprise, while walking up Broadway, I ran into Frankie Clarke and Kevin Copland, two hustlers from my hood. They had just come from Leighton's shopping for shoes. Kevin had just purchased a pair of "Rainbow colored Alligators." He took out the box to show me. Boy, they were MF-ing pimpish! I happened to be on my way to that same store.

I come from the era where players put plenty emphasis on looking and staying sharp. With young players today, their swagger and style of dress ain't what it could or should be. Suits, ties, shoes, "dress shoes" that is, are a large part of a players "G." Easter of 1968 was no exception for Charlie. The brother was sharp. Blue suit, powder blue shirt, deep blue silk tie and dark blue lizards. I was so busy that afternoon, I didn't get the opportunity to do any running around. On my way home, I did feel a bit guilty about not looking up Star.

Once I got home that evening, the whole house was sitting in the living room, waiting on my ass. Soon as my family saw them bags from New York, all those frowns turned into instant smiles. Everyone had their hands out. Yep, I got taxed!

The next day, Saturday, I was one of many young players waiting to get their new Easter process from my favorite barber in "Mop City Barber Shop." My barber was a brother named "Happy." In the late 1980s, Happy would receive a fifteen-year sentence in Federal Prison for being an Armed Career Criminal. He was my cellie at Danbury Federal Prison in 1990.

During our short stay at Danbury, we would reminisce about "Mop City" days. One such story is this: We young Cannons had heard many of the older hustlers tell stories of how big hat white folks used to tote Nickel-Notes and G-notes in their stings, even a handful of blacks carried their share of them.

While waiting for my turn that Saturday to get my hair processed, in walked Skippy House, Melvin Gains and Sonny Berry. Skippy could have passed for Barry White's clones, curls and all. His persona was always loud and obnoxious back then. Many pimps have that aural, he was no exception. Now Sonny Berry, he was a no-nonsense nigga point MF-ing blank' Before you thought about confronting him you'd best have your life insurance paid in full. Melvin, I had known since I was a kid along with his whole family. He was "Mr. Laid Back," quiet and calculating. He used to own thoroughbred racehorses down in Miami back in the day.

On that particular Saturday before Easter, when they came by the shop Skippy was talking shit soon as he hit the door. Hearing his loud voice all eyes immediately focused on him and his crew at the door. The best way to describe the scene, is to ask my readers, those who are familiar with the tune "For the Love of Money" by the group the O'Jays to picture the song playing in the background while all these bills are floating in the air. And no, they weren't fifties or C-notes. Skippy, Sonny and Melvin were throwing Nickel Notes and G-notes up in the air.

The whole shop was in a state of pandemonium at what they were seeing. I was totally mesmerized at what I saw. Melvin actually let me hold one of them G-notes in my hand to examine their authenticity. It was the real deal. I've never forgotten how those bills looked in all these years. Years later in 1972, two very close friends of mine, after beating a case in BMC (Boston Municipal Court), these young gun "Cannons" beat a vic for three thousand in Nickel Notes along with four C-notes. In 1980, Ernie and myself would top what they took.

After seeing Skippy and his crew throw that money in the air, I knew I was playing the right game. Shit, I was ready to play his big fat ass that day. Sometimes you just instinctively know certain things about self and your capabilities as well as those of others. Seeing those bills, I knew my turn was coming down the line. My turn has certainly come and gone many times, only to slip through my hands like running water. It is so very very true. "He who ceases to plan, plans to fail." My plan was only to get "X, Y, Z," never to truly look or think beyond the above, when I did see flickers of positive change and the possibility of greater things.

I'd allow other negative influences to cloud my path of vision. Now that I've decided to free myself from thinking my life in the streets, I can see hope over the edge of the box I allowed myself to be imprisoned in for so many years.

In plain English, it's called, "thinking outside the box" of emotional, spiritual, financial and physical imprisonment. People usually project themselves to others, (and self included), based on how they see themselves in that mirror of the mind that only they can see. That's not to say that outside influences can't play a major part in the scheme of things.

As a teenager and even beyond my teen years, into adulthood, I had little understanding of life beyond taking a sting. Prioritizing and accountability were not part of a hustler's vernacular, especially those who played the Cannon game. Just because you suddenly learn one plus one equals two, not three, and you've been accustomed to thinking it equaled three for the past forty some odd years doesn't mean you change your thinking instantaneously. It's a process that has to come into focus. Sitting in "Mop City" Barber Shop in 1968 I had no such knowledge of the things just spoken of. So when my barber's chair became empty, I eased into it to get a new process because the next day was Easter Sunday.

By September, Shorty was home from Shirley, and looking fit and anxious to get back in the swing of things. His first weekend home we went to work. By then, many of us had gotten hip to a place downtown near the expressway called Haymarket. It's an open market. There are a few actual stores but most of the business is done in the open behind makeshift stands. You can buy every kind of fresh fruit, vegetable and fish. The place has been there since I was a small child, from what I've been told. The crowds are just unreal, people come from out of town just to see the famous market.

By noontime until about six o'clock pm, they are open for business. Everything is cash, no checks, no credit cards, no travelers cheques, just green money exchanges hands down there. So we went down there and got us a couple of good stings and left. Let me tell you, that spot is still there to this very day. I'm just going to leave it at that. We hustled off and on for the remainder of 1968. But for the most part, I hustled with Pee Wee, Ronnie and Rico.

In 1969, The Temptations were hot with their release of "Psychedelic Shack" and "Run-Away-Child." You'd hear those tunes daily on WILD on the AM dial. It was Temptation blitz on the airwaves. Ronnie and I had an unwritten contract in '69 on the work side. One day we were on a bus out of Egilston Station going to Mattapan Station. It was really crowded. We beat two people and were about to get off at the Wellington Hill Street stop. The last person we had just beat took a natural "fan" and missed his sting and broke bad. Now the woman I eat was beefing as well. The people on the bus were screaming and hollering, "Get them two fried head MF pickpockets!" "Don't let them off the bus!" "Close the doors! Call the police!"

Someone said, "I got my knife. I'm sick and tired of them niggas robbing me and other hardworking black folks on this damn bus route! "Ronnie panicked and pulled out his knife to force the man back and make the driver open the front door so we could get off. Naturally, the driver complied. Unbeknown to us, there's a pregnant black woman standing at the bus stop, waiting to board the bus.

Once the door opened, she stepped on the first step. As she was about to put her foot on the second step, I was in such a damn hurry to get off the bus I didn't realize she was pregnant. Ronnie was right behind me talking about "Hurry the hell up and move!" so he could get to the street. The next thing I knew, the woman was flat on her back on the damn ground. Ronnie and I stepped over her. She was hollering and screaming, "Someone help me, please! I'm pregnant!" I didn't realize it at the time, but my oldest sister and her husband had recently purchased a home on Wellington Hill Street.

In our haste to get away, we ran right past my sister's house and she saw me clear as day. I seemed to stay on the radar of family controversy even back then. Once she saw me, she called "Rose," my younger sister. From there it was a snowball effect gone wild. The whole damn family knew I was being hotly pursued by the police out of Station #3 on Morton Street.

Being young and with strong wind, I eluded capture that day. Ronnie and I would have another close call down the line together. This time it would involve a motorcycle cop and a chump we played who also woke up as we exited the Essex Street train station in downtown Boston. We ran right into the motorcycle cop, breaking from a hot chump. The PoPo was getting ready to get on his "tricycle and peddle off!" We had to fight that big Irishman to get away. I gave that brother some air after that for a while. Hustling with him was seriously hazardous duty for real.

A couple hours after that shit went down, I was sitting inside "Frankie O'Days" talking to my man's dad and mom when Sleepy and Bullets came in the Bar. Bullets was a living legend and meeting him was a treat. The two of them had been slipping around the outskirts of the city playing.

That day we had a long talk while sitting at the bar listening to Jimmy Smith's cut "Who's afraid of Virginia Wolf" in the background. That's the type of spot it was in those days. Sleepy had heard about our first blowout only. Then I replayed the second blowout. All this time, Bullets sat very silent. Then he said, "Kid, you're not playing the Wiz." That was the first time ever hearing that term used to describe the shot or the Cannon.

I learned we, Ronnie and I, were putting ourselves, and others, in harm's way.

"You are robbing people and that type of shit will get you an asshole full of time. Cannons don't carry guns or pull knives on people, we are playing on the stroll. That is a No-No! The police respect our game and how we execute it. They frown on people who snatch and grab stings by force. When a chump wakes up, give him or her their shit back, it's rightly not yours. Stop trying to beat the whole bus, train, or trolley. All you are going to do is hip someone; then others will start checking their stings to be sure they are secure. People remember people who almost took their sting, and others remember you as well. Fighting chumps will get you a lot cf time, also. Remember, you are playing a sneak game, focus in on one person, learn to pick a good man and play him hard but never rough. Stop reaching at everyone you see."

"Some of us are very good at the mechanics of the game but that's all. You must also know what to do after the sting comes off. Keeping your stick and yourself safe is far more important than taking the sting."

That talk from him that day in Frankie O'Day's taught me a lot. Not only have I applied it to the game, but other areas of my life as well.

What I thought I knew I really know at all. And what I didn't know I now realized I didn't know. More importantly, I stayed mentally absorbent. I was open for constructive criticism. In 1972, we would meet again in New York. A few days later Sleep would give me some pro-work for real. He played areas outside the city like Watertown, Medford, Sullivan Station, Cambridge, Lynn Lawrence, Worcester and Springfield. This is how we played: absolutely no blacks at all under no circumstances, and no women either. His wife Lillian who was white would drive their big station wagon behind as we worked. Her job was to trail the bus we loaded. Keep in mind we never would load at the same buy stop together. That way, no one could put us together.

We never spoke a word to each other. Eye movement and jesters were used only such as brushing your shirtsleeve or jacket sleeve took the place of saying NO. If he wanted my attention he would simply act as if he had something in his eye. To get me in position where he could play a man, he would slightly pull on the collar or lapel of his jacket coat shirt.

All that dressing up in those slick outfits was a no-no. I learned how to blend in, not stand out. He taught me how to really stick a man and read them good. How to not only play the chump in question, but the driver, the people on the bus, the ones getting on as well, to see if they flashed any type of identification. How to watch out the side windows of the bus, train as it comes into a stop. I've seen police come up on a bus through the back door and slip into a seat.

One of the most valuable pieces to the game he gave was, how to use a shot coat or have the tailor put in a shot pocket making it a shot coat. Rather than cut a hole in the lining of your coats, you can buy coats that will allow you to put your hands through a slit inside the lining. No one will ever see your hands as you fan a man, because for one, your coat is open, to give you free movement and cover to play.

All that playing with a newspaper is a tip (it draws the PoPo and reckless eyeballers). I can honestly say I had on OJT up close and personal by a professional Cannon named Sherman "Sleepy" Cottman. He also is no longer with us. Nor is his wife. The reason Lillian rode behind those buses was to pick us up after we downed a chump. We also played medical buildings, hospitals, office building entrances, hotels, at certain check out and check in times, and the C-note window at all the Race Tracks in New England, such as Rhode Island and New Hampshire. He knew his craft very well, without a doubt.

Going to New York was like going home to me, and I've loved going there. Over the years, I've come to know Manhattan and the Bronx far better than I know my hometown of Boston. So that is why I took a few days off in 1969 to spend in New York City. Plus, I wanted to see my old friend Star.

After checking in at the Hotel President on 48th Street between 8th Avenue and Broadway, I got myself a good meal at Mama Leonie's across from my hotel. Then I took a short stroll down 8th Avenue to see some of my old haunts along the way. Nearing a popular bar named the Sea Garden, a pimp spot between 42nd and 43rd Streets, I heard a familiar female voice call out "Charlie" twice. To my surprise, as I turned around, sitting in the driver's seat of a brand new 'Lack 1969' was Cinnamon. Damn if the cinnamon color of her car didn't match her skin and hair color to a tee.

Stepping to the car I could clearly hear James Brown singing "Licking Stick." Leaning out the driver's window Cinnamon gave me the biggest hug and kiss on the mouth I'd had in a long time. I had to remind her I was no longer that shy kid. We both laughed. Then she got serious and said, "If she ever went back to men, she'd have to be with me. I said, "You know you're way out of pocket for talking like that. By all means, I should charge your ass for those remarks." Again, she and I both laughed, but deep inside she knew I wasn't joking one damn bit.

Riding up 8th, Cinnamon finally told me Star was busted doing sixty days on the Rock – Riker's Island. She was due out in two weeks. She and Butch finally purchased their own Brownstone in Williamsburg, Brooklyn. Now they were saving to open their own seafood restaurant. By 1973, they'd do just that. She got a little pissed when I passed on going to Brooklyn with her to see their new home. I put her off by saying I'd hook up with them tomorrow. My thoughts were elsewhere, locked in on a good blow of cocaine a certain Cuban had at the same hotel I was staying in. After spending another thirty minutes riding, she dropped me off at my spot.

I blew my brains out sniffing all night. By 2:30pm the next afternoon I was in a cab to La Guardia Airport. I would not return until the Summer of 1971, the year of my brother's death.

Arriving home, I decided to go see the group Sly at Harvard Stadium in Cambridge the next evening. All of us, I'm sure, are familiar with that inner voice, the one that speaks to us about shit we shouldn't do. Yet we, on many occasions, find ourselves throwing caution to the wind and do whatever we have a mindset to do.

As much as I wanted to go see Sly and War, something kept gnawing at me, *Charlie, don't go, bad decision.* I went against the grain and played a game with myself. *I'll go but I won't do any hustling.* That's what I told myself. In order to get to Harvard Square the quickest way, take the Orange line to Washington St. station, change trains by going to the lower level and get the Red Line train to Harvard Square. Real simple shit, something that wouldn't take a rocket science major to figure out.

As the train was coming to its stop inside Washington Station, again that voice was speaking to me. This time it was saying, *Don't get off. Stay seated.* Paying the warning voice no mind, I began to stand up to get off the train. That's when I saw them. A mob of them, in fact, the MF-ing Police. Fuck them, I said as I make my way to one of the exit doors.

Once on the platform, I've got no choice but to go in their direction in order to get to the lower level where I can get the Redline train into Cambridge.

Just as I'm about to step on the second step leading to the lower level, the mob of MBTA Police are all over my dumb ass. Let's go, Charlie, you're under arrest for armed robbery and assault. Man, I ain't no damn armed robber, and you people know that. Quickly, they placed me in cuffs and hauled my ass off to District #3 on Morton Street.

The next day, I was arraigned in Dorchester Court as an adult. That old bitch Judge Sadie McGuffey set my bail at twenty-thousand-dollars cash on both counts and sent the case downtown to Superior Court. The beef involved the blowout Ronnie Kidd and I had at the corner of my sister's street. Charles St. Jail, here I come!

Because I wasn't twenty-one, I was housed in what was known as the Boystown section of the old jail overlooking the small yard. Charles St. Jail was a filthy deplorable place up to the day it closed its doors in the late 1990s.

The jail was made in somewhat of a semicircle five tiers high. One section was right above the old kitchen, the high security section consisted of a dozen gray steel slab cells on the second landing. The other section was near the entrance to the outside yard.

On the ground floor of each section were several long gray tables that served as dining and recreation tables. Back then, you were only allowed out your cell for one hour a day plus meals. During meals, birds would fly all over your head and shit on you at will. No TV, radio or phones. You had to cover your toilet with wood or cardboard and put your shoes on top to prevent the rats from coming up out of the toilet at night.

Many guys got bit for failure to do that simple task. To compensate for the despicable conditions, on Sundays, Captain Royal (who was black) would allow us to eat a home cooked meal from our families when they came to visit. We'd eat on the guardroom floor that also doubled as the visiting room. Some of the city's most racist police worked at the old Charles St. Jail. They were not above taking a person to one of those unused cells on the flats in the back, hogtie your ass and beat you damn near to death. My Nephew, "Big Truck," gave them a run for their money. He may have lost the war but he sure won the fight. Two months would go by before I got cut loose on that beef.

One day, I was sitting in the 'Bullpen' when the turnkey calls my name and says, "the case has been dismissed." To this day, I don't know if the Grand Jury dismissed it for lack of a positive ID, or what. Ronnie said he was questioned and cut loose before I got busted. I was in New York when his encounter took place. How they knew to stop me and give me that beef is still puzzling me. The person that saw me and absolutely knew who I was is my sister. No, I'm not pointing fingers, just stating some facts. In my life, I've had an ex-wife tell the police I had a warrant on me in 1979, all because she slipped and said she had an outside relationship.

I've had one of my kids put the PoPo on me out of anger. My niece's husband, a Massachusetts Trooper assigned to the State's Attorney General's Office, placed a call to my federal parole officer saying I was "selling dope" based on what one of my daughters told him regarding some money she saw me give someone. A guy from DC got a case in New York in 2007 unrelated to me, yet when he was interviewed by the detective Fraud Unit out of Midtown North, he told them he knew me and we did certain business together. His name is George Reid.

Someone from my hometown of Boston, Mass. who has "diarrhea-of-the-mouth" contacted Detective Steven Blair of the Financial Fraud Unit and told him Charles H. Belim is the guy known as the "Professor and Ring Leader of the Wig Mob." All I've ever earned is a GED at FCI Petersburg in 1987 and 70 college credits from Brewton-Parker College out of Mt. Vernon, Georgia between 1989 and 1990. So, how could I be classified as a damn professor when I've never taught school!

A guy I've known, (as well as his whole damn family), since he was five or six years old named Mike Spike and his woman, Dawn (aka Silver Fox), gave the Midtown North Detectives information on my whereabouts. He gave them information on a bank move I used many years ago that only he and I knew of. His woman Dawn gave four signed statements saying I gave her checks to deposit into four different accounts she played. I thank Allah I wasn't on film with that Rat.

My co-defendant, Carol Silva from Boston, Mass., is all over my present criminal complaint (federal in Greenbelt, MD), making statements about me providing her with over 50 different bank account numbers, names and counterfeit drivers licenses. She claims I took her from Boston to Maryland, VA and DC to execute this scheme. People should truly not have a problem understanding me when I say I'm done. Finished! So, quite naturally I'm a bit paranoid of people now because of experiences. I don't allow anyone to engage me in any crazy conversations about banking business. In my third book, an entire chapter will be on Rats and how they slither around us players, snatching tidbits of information to scurry back to their chief confidants, the police.

But in 1969, I didn't look at people that way. After spending time at my girl's house I eased down on Blue Hill Avenue and got myself some dope. By now, I was sniffing quite a bit of dope like a real sucker.

Perhaps, two months or so after being released on that case with Ronnie Kidd, I got busted in Washington Street Station for attempted Grand Larceny. Check this shit out. True, I'm there to get me one, no doubt about that. But before I can get down, I do a double check of my surroundings and I make the PoPo. So, I decide to just board the incoming train with the intentions of riding one stop, getting off and waiting on another crowd and a good person to play. My other option was to come out and reload on the inbound side. As I attempted to load, the police rushed in on me from both sides. *What am I under arrest for? Attempt. You reached out and opened a woman's purse.*

I made bail by calling Corey, the Bondsman, whom I met through Rosey before he stopped hustling. The case was held over to the Superior Court. The case didn't get called for about a month. When we did go back, the DA's offer was five years at Concord. He and everybody with him was crazy if they thought I'd accept that dumb shit. The DA's version of what took place and our copy of the police report wasn't consistent with each other. The PoPo was saying something far different.

The police report says I opened or attempted to open an unknown woman's purse on a crowded subway platform at the height of Friday's rush hour. One officer said I used my right hand; the other said my left hand. The DA said, "Right hand" to my attorney. So, we said, we are picking twelve. I explained to my attorney that I couldn't physically do what they suggested because I didn't have the strength or the coordination. Once they saw the shape of my right arm, he also knew we had them so long as the police got their heads together on me using my right hand.

My attorney subpoenaed my medical files from the Boston City Hospital. The DA continued running the "Bo game down" about the police getting up on the stand and swearing I used my right hand and the other said left. With some slick talking by the DA, the officer changed up and says my right also was used. My attorney's theory was this. Very few people are in fact left-handed. Most are born right-handed. And that is what the DA wants the jury to think.

Now remember, there isn't a victim to deny or confirm anything. In comes the "Monkey Wench" that was tossed in the wringer. My attorney requested that I stand, face the jury, and remove my shirt, revealing my right arm and the scar left from the two major surgeries. I was further instructed by my attorney to raise my right arm, straight up in the air. I could not do that without the support of my left hand. Due to the plate being in place of the bone is why I couldn't extend my right arm all the way out, or up on its own. All my medical files were also introduced. Those files were irrefutable.

The jury stayed out all of ten to twenty minutes. Upon the jury's return, the smiles on their faces were clearly the indicator that we had won our case. The Foreman of the jury said, "Not Guilty!" I've had three jury trials in my life; that shit is very stressful.

The whole time my case was in Court I never once realized how sick my Dad was. He never complained about his foot at all, at least not to my brother or myself. While at work, he had injured his big toe on his right foot. He never would go to the hospital. He soaked his foot and put them damn steel toe boots right back on and went to work daily. He was one of those men you'd see tearing up concrete in the street with a one-hundred-pound jackhammer in his hands. Cold or hot, my father did his thing out there.

After his day job, he'd go to the hospital and work his night job. His work ethics were impeccable. By this time, he no longer drank at all, not even a beer. Mom finally got him to go to the hospital for his toe. He was on antibiotics and told to stay off his foot and not to put that damn steel toe shoe on until his foot had completely healed. That shit lasted three days only, and then he was back at work in those boots. A week later his whole foot was swollen.

The antibiotics were no longer effective. Then we learned that Gangrene had begun to set in and the only way to save the foot was to "amputate his toe." When I went to see him, he put on a good front, but I knew he was in pain. So I said, "Pop, you want me to get you a drink?" He just looked at me and quietly said, "No."

ß

Chapter 32 ~ Stroke and Death

Strokes run rampant in Black and Hispanic communities throughout this country. Poor health care, no health care, poor diet and eating habits, drug and alcohol use and obesity. These are many of the main culprits that lead to this medical condition. Many times just having a regular scheduled Blood Pressure check up will give us an abundance of information about prevention. As to what was the actual cause of my Dad's stroke, to be perfectly honest, I don't know.

All I know is two days after visiting him, he suffered a massive stroke to the right side of his body. Being paralyzed and unable to talk was an insult added to injury.

To see your father so totally helpless and totally dependent on others and not being audible was very painful for all of us. Due to the stroke, the doctors said it wouldn't be a wise decision to amputate at that time. That put Dad in a catch-22 situation.

Having the amputation so soon after the stroke could kill him. Not having the amputation would cause the "Gangrene to spread" up his foot to his leg. One of the worst things I've ever personally experience was to sit and watch that Gangrene eat my Dad's leg away and not be in a position to do anything about it. His eyes expressed his fear and pain, not his voice. That was forever silenced by the stroke itself. Finally, after much pleading and prayer, the doctors went ahead and amputated. Not his toe, not his foot; it was his leg, from the knee down, that was gone.

True, his life was saved (by Allah's mercy and grace only) but the price was tremendously heavy for everyone. All he wanted to do was go to work and support his family. Now he couldn't do that any longer, nor could he even express his feelings. Not one of his high and might sisters, nor his daughters for that matter, cared to even bring Dad to their home for the holiday.

Not one of them "uppity Negroes" offered to give their brother a meal. My sisters were no different. Mom played game. Neither she nor us had planned to let him go with any of them from the start.

Sometimes, families ain't worth the blood that ties them together. My Uncle Albert, Kenny and myself went and got Pop, took him home to 8 Adams Street, apartment # 497 in Orchard Park Housing Project. The year was 1969, two days before Christmas, and Dad stayed home until after New Year's 1970. And that's the truth.

Not one, I mean, not one of them uppity ass Negroes ever offered him a get well card, or a pair of slippers; nothing for Christmas. Shit, they never even bothered to place a call to our home phone number.

All of my Mom's family was there for Christmas dinner. We had a hell of a good damn time. Dad smiled as tears streamed down his face, and Kenny and I wiped them away with our hands. I went absolutely nowhere, except to the corner store for cigarettes.

Di came over a few times. That was one of the best holidays I've ever experienced with family. Memory of the actual date we took him back to the hospital eludes me now that so many years have floated past me. Still though, I know it was shortly after New Year's Day in January 1970. It was a very cold day, that I do recall.

As I close my eyes now, in between the writing of these words, I can vividly see Kenny and I helping our father out of his clothes as he desperately tried to help with his single functioning hand. Kenny's voice still rings clear as day in my ears. "Daddy, Charles and I can do it, you just sit tight!"

Now, tears dripped from all our eyes. At last, he was sitting up in his chair in his blue flannel pajamas. As we were about to leave, my father reached for my hand. He indicated he wanted a cigarette. Not giving it a second thought, I took out an open pack of his Chesterfield regulars, shook one out, lit it and placed it in his mouth. We stood there watching him draw on that cigarette and blow out the smoke. Now he was okay. We gave Dad a hug and left.

Chapter 33 ~ Dad's Death

L ife is finite. Death is infinite. I sometimes ask myself, *Why is it that life has a beginning and an end, but death only has an ending?* A few days after leaving our father with that cigarette in his left hand, my mother received a call. I believe it was from my sister, Claire, saying our father was dead. These are the details surrounding his death as told to us by our mother.

Somehow, Dad died because of a lit cigarette falling on him in bed, or while he was sitting up in a chair in his room. Not knowing what actually happened, it is possible it happened due to the cigarette I gave him the last time I saw him.

Dad had his own room a short walk from the nurse's station. How does a person just burn up so badly in a damn hospital to the point that no one knows anything until he is almost burnt to a crisp? Then upon discovering his badly burned body, ships him off to the Burn Unit at the Boston City Hospital, without notifying or contacting the family at that point either? Mind you, not one person even bothered to contact our family at the point that they should have.

My father's niece, who to this day is still married to Lawson Riley, (the owner of Riley Funeral Home), was a nurse at Boston City Hospital in January of 1070. A nurse working the Burn Unit was assigned to Dad after his being there several days suspended between life and death. This woman realized no one had bothered to come see about him since being in the hospital.

Somehow, some way, she recognized the name "Gibbs," my father's last name. Immediately, she contacted my father's niece, who worked on another floor below. She came right away to see this patient for herself. Due to the condition of his burns he was not recognizable. Yet the name, age, and one limb amputated recently, was identification enough for her. Calls went out all over the city. My Dad had many relatives. The Belim family was the last to be called.

Thinking back to that day, the day I came in from hustling, happy about life, my girl, having made a few hundred, what could be better? Nothing could upset my day, so I thought.

As I opened the door to enter our apartment that day, I immediately saw Mom, Aunt Tee, Uncle Albert, and my brother Kenny. They all just stared. No one said a word for what seemed like eternity. Then, my Mom spoke these words: "Charles, your Father died today at Boston City Hospital."

You know when you are about to have a tooth extraction the dentist will administer a pain reliever to numb the pain. I wasn't afforded that luxury. My heart was extracted without being sedated, so consequently I felt all the pain as I stood before those I loved and respected, minus one. My father.

Everyone processes pain differently. Sometimes our processing can take years, and at times it has. Death is so very absolute. Death never dies. Only life dies. The living are caught between those two inevitable worlds.

Our apartment suddenly became small and stifling. I had no choice but to quickly remove myself. When I left, I knew where I was going and what I wanted.

I went to buy some dope in order to medicate the pain I felt. I learned many things, good and bad, from those guys in the North End down Shanty's and from Mr. Kelley. No one, though, taught me how to deal with death. Perhaps, they knew not how themselves. Back then I knew nothing about allowing myself to feel pain. I ran from pain, straight to heroin, only the medication was not long lasting.

Even after taking my Shahadatan, I still didn't understand that it is okay to feel pain. Working through and accepting pain brings about growth and acceptance. Using heroin only stagnated me and kept me hostage to my pain and anguish. Holding oneself hostage is a hell of a feat for a person. And I did just that with regard to my father's death, my brother's death, Theresa's death, and my Mom's death.

Honestly, from 1970 to the writing of this memoir, I often told myself that, "I killed my Dad with the cigarette I lit for him." Islam and writing "Shoe Shine Boy" freed me up from feeling somehow responsible for the deaths of aforementioned people. Now, I can finally move on with my life when I am finally released. Knowing that it is okay to feel pain, I'll never use again. I am allowing myself to see other options. In 1969, and the years to follow, would be hard for me when death came calling for one of my family members.

At my father's funeral, not one of his daughters, sisters, nieces or nephews, spoke a kind word of condolence to me. I was his flesh and blood. Now, that is some real deep nigga shit. My girl Di held me tight all through the service. If any investigations were done as to how he could have burned up so badly that his body was never on view, is not known to me. If his wife (Claire's mom, sued, I don't know that either) did get any money, she never offered or gave me shit.

I'm the "Bastard Child," according to his family; perhaps, not so much in words, but rather in their actions toward me. Their idiosyncratic ways and manners have little, if any, negative effects on me today. You can't pick them, you just got to give them love from a far off distance until they grow. Dad was laid to rest and we all parted at his gravesite.

In 1969, my brother took his Shahadatan, "May Allah be Merciful with his soul."

Back then I didn't know the difference between the "Nation of Islam" and those who were "Sunni Muslims." In fact, I had never heard the term Sunni Muslim during those days. But through a woman named Shirley Ford, my brother was introduced to Islam and for that act alone, I thank that sister from the very bottom of my heart.

I haven't seen her since my brother's funeral in 1971; however, I did serve time with one of her sons at "MCI Shirley" in Shirley, Massachusetts in 2002. We were in the same unit, Unit "F." We spoke daily about Islam and his Dad, who was once the Imam at the Masjid on Shaumont Avenue in Roxbury, should I ever go when I'm in Boston. He never once mentioned his Mom's name, and I never did ask him if it was Sabria.

By the spring of 1970 much had changed in the lives of Earline's two sons. By then, both had habits and both would be arrested back-to-back and sent to Bridgewater Detox in Bridgewater, Massachusetts. Roxbury District Court, along with many others (Courts) throughout Boston were looking at different ways to deal with addicted criminals. Rather than send them to prison, the courts gave us a shot at accepting a treatment program.

CB

Chapter 34 ~ Bridgewater State Hospital

It was obvious to everyone by 1970 that Kenny and I were using heroin. You can't tell a partially true story. If you attempt that feat, you have done a grave injustice to the truth. Nor can you paint a half complete portrait and call it complete. The truth must prevail. So with that said, I shall continue.

Leaning on Dudley Station and its daily commuters was bound to cause me big problems one way or another. By mid March, I was stopped and searched while leaving the station because a "Reckless-eye-baller" saw me play a woman and beat her. Busted! Wallet on me and two bags of heroin in my secret pocket inside my sport jacket.

The next morning I was arraigned in Roxbury District Court. And Judge McKenney, who years later got disbarred for his Cocaine usage and womanizing, was my judge. Those two bags of dope established that I was a user. Judge McKenney said to me, "You got two choices. Now, if you are smart, you will realize you only have one logical choice. This is your deal today only, so please listen very clearly. Five years Concord, or the Drug Program at Bridgewater." It was a no-brainer. I took Bridgewater.

First I went through their ten-day Detox Program during which time I saw a barrage of shrinks. They would ask all types of loony-tune questions, like do you like girls or boys. (I started to ask his monkey looking ass the same shit he was asking me, especially as heavy as he was breathing!) Did your mother abuse you? I said, "Yes, yes," and his eyes lit up. He said, "How?" My response was this.

"When I was young, she never could slice the damn "loney" meat even when she made our school lunch. She also would use the Wonder Bread bags for wrapping paper and she'd put our lunches inside big brown bags to take to school. Mister, all I ever wanted was a 'Lone Ranger lunch box,' but all I got was a brown shopping bag from Blair's Supermarket down Dudley!" I said, "I am traumatized, and that's why I use drugs…"

He wrote all that down in shrink jargon for the court. After taking the "Merdox" (Methadone) for ten days and saying you needed the program, upon returning to Court, the Judge would sentence you to Bridgewater for drug treatment. Your Court case was placed on file, in short, you received no Criminal Conviction. No matter how many cases, (Warrants) you had, you being in Bridgewater assured you of no prison time. Many of the Charlestown, East Boston, South Boston, Roslindale Stick up, B &E Crews, were all there, with us out of Roxbury, etc. Yes, my brother was there with me. He just did the detox. I stayed about four months.

That was a real loony-tune joint. They would tell people if you don't follow the rules you could be sent back to Court, your Court of commitment and re-sentenced to state prison. Not likely, not for a fight or missing group or stealing food out the damn kitchen. Plus, far too much money was flowing for drug rehabilitation; they wanted the program to produce clean, non-addicted addicts.

Bridgewater wasn't only for drug addicts. It also housed the Criminally Insane (the famous Boston Strangler was there at one time). The DD Unit, the Treatment Center for sex offenders, the Profile Juvenile Center, and us, the "Dope Fiends." Behind the Green Door was where the criminally insane were housed.

Whenever we went to school we had to go through the green door section to get to the education area. We would have to walk down those narrow hallways to get to class. Passing those one man shoe box rooms, with glass windows -- or was it plastic – seeing men, young and old, lying half naked and some totally naked, in the fetal position on tiny beds, in a bland room void of life. Some barked and howled at nothingness, staring blank faced as we passed them. Others in the distance meowed like cats in the night. Many had been placed there by families who just didn't know what or how to deal with them. Others had been deemed just plain crazy by legal definition of the Courts, and the State of Massachusetts.

Bridgewater was known to have a dirty crew of Walpole CO's whose greatest ambition was to cross an inmate (patient as they'd call us on the surface) whom they felt was unmanageable (a black or poor Irish). The inmate would be given "Thorazine." Those of you who have ever been in state or federal custody have seen the effects of it, some first hand. I personally know a guy, Leonard C. (Fat Nard), who was on it for being deemed too aggressive. His recreation was hitting white boys with a two-piece (knocking their ass flat out), then throwing them down the "laundry chute."

Now, you know whites love a laugh when it's at our expense, but it ceases to be humorous when the joke's on them. Man, them white folks had that brother so damn meek, you could have placed a bowl of warm milk before him and he would have gotten down on his hands and knees and lapped it up. He was turned into a "Putty Cat" (pussy cat). All his aggression and hostilities were gone.

My assigned job was in the kitchen. I liked that job for three reasons: Reason #1, I got to eat all I could eat. Reason #2, I got a chance to steal shit to sell to other people. Reason #3, I got a chance to steal all I couldn't eat there, and bring it out with me. Blacks $3.00 for fried chicken. White boys, $5.00 for the same fried chicken sandwich. Supply and demand. There was plenty demand so the supply price went up for some folks. Each five-dollar piece represented a piece of cotton my mother and family had to pick in Georgia. You must know "an even swap ain't no swindle."

Now, about those classified as defective delinquents (DD for short). They were adults who functioned like little kids on a string all tied together. All of them wore Farmer Brown uniforms with patch pockets and straw hats. One was named "Egg Head" because of his enormous size egg-shaped head. We would offer him chocolate candy bars if he would act like "Elsie the Cow" and run his head into the wall. He would comply and we would all bust out in laughter. Bridgewater was a crazy place and still is to this very day.

After being at Bridgewater for about four months, I was given a weekend pass to come home. Being home went much too fast and when it came time to return, I didn't want to go back. At the last minute I went on down to the old Trailways Bus Station to return to Bridgewater. But in all honesty, this is what truly happened. Plain and simple, I fell asleep. And didn't wake up until the bus got to New Bedford, Massachusetts. Immediately, I found a payphone and called Bridgewater to explain what had taken place. The person on the other end of the line was not sympathetic to my situation at all. In fact, the person was very nasty. He told me I was way past the time allowed out and I'd better get my ass back there fast. As he was still running down the murder game, I just politely hung up on his dumb ass.

I went outside the station and smoked myself a Kool cigarette and the "chase is on." I purchased myself a return ticket to Boston. Mom just said, "Now what?" I said, "I don't know just yet, but it ain't Bridgewater." Di was all in tears about me not going back to the Loony-Tune Farm. In fact, if you want someone to go, "You go in my damn place and I'll write to you!" She changed that tune quickly enough.

After about a week of slipping around the town, I went to work one day and ran into a Probation Officer from Roxbury Court. He knew I had been sent to Bridgewater because he had done the probation report. He was like, "How long have you been home?" I said I got released the day before on good behavior." His response was, "that's why I haven't received your release report yet." Naturally, I said, "You're right, Sir." He wanted to let me know if I needed anyone to talk to, he would be happy to listen. Now you know that was not going to work. My mother already had one white man coming in the house, surely I did not need a white "big brother." I took his card and said, "I'll keep that in mind," as we shook hands and parted.   ∞

Chapter 35 ~ Time to Get Ghost

M om's best friend was "Sue Johnson." In 1970, Sue and her husband were living 60 miles Northwest of Chicago. He was in the US Navy as a Chief Petty Officer, assigned to the Naval Training Center at "Great Lakes, IL." All Mom did was make one phone call to Sue and it was a done deal. I was on my way to Chicago by the weekend. Mom didn't want me back in New York where she couldn't put her hands on me if she needed to.

The winter of 1970 was brutally cold in Chicago. I arrived in Chitown on a cold Sunday morning in November. I had exactly one-thousand-dollars stuffed inside a pair of socks hidden deep in one of my two suitcases. Walking the few blocks to the train station to catch a train that would take me the sixty miles to Waukegan, IL. Was out of the damn question. It was too damn cold. After standing outside the Greyhound bus station on Randolph Street for at least thirty minutes, I finally was able to flag down a cab. To the train station we went.

The train ride to Waukegan took about one hour and yep. Aunt Sue was late. Forty-five minutes would pass before she showed up to get me. Bob was assigned to the USS Kitty Hawk, he was out at sea that winter. Their place was nice and quiet, too damn quiet for my rambunctious eighteen-year-old ass. I had to get out of there. Shit, I wanted to see Chicago, so I packed my shit and headed for the city, "Chicago!" Prior to leaving Boston, my Mom had give me her cousin's phone number and address in the city. Cousin James, James Steed, lived on the South Side. I went directly there once I got back in the city. I knew James had kids my age, so I figured, *Shit, they are family, why not check them out.* Man, cousin James didn't have kids, he had a damn tribe! And they were sleeping everywhere. Thanks, but no thanks. "We kin folks, boy," he kept saying as I got my shit to split. YMCA, here I come.

I went to the "Y" on Wabash Street in the loop. Got me a clean spot, bath, toilet, all in one. I showed my YMCA card and got a discount, $38.50 a week. Sue and cousin James had the number to the "Y." I deliberately didn't call home because Mom would be upset to find out I had left Sue's house. On my third or fourth day in Chicago, Sue left a message for me to call her immediately. So, I called. My Mom had been notified I had left Sue's along with my refusal to stay at her cousin James' place. To cool her out, I had to call home and promise I'd go back to Sue's house until I could find a job and a studio apartment. I stayed around Chicago a few more days to learn the city. I knew from the tips I saw that I'd be back to get myself a sting.

Upon returning to Sue's house, she immediately started telling me how I needed a real woman to slow my ass down. I was like, okay. Where is she? "Don't laugh, boy, Aunt Sue got just the right woman." Little did I know she wasn't joking one bit about finding me a woman. Unbeknownst to me, Sue had a friend named Shirley who lived a few miles away in a town called Zion.

Every street in the town had a biblical name. This friend lived on Ezara Street and it was in the middle of no man's land. Many of the blacks who lived there were from a place called Calhoun City, Mississippi. Yep, they all seemed to know each other. When I met Shirley, I was nineteen and she was twenty-seven with a son named Sean who was eleven-months old. Shirley's youngest sister, Ann, also lived with her. She and I were a year apart in age.

Women are very devious, (not all, just some). For example, as soon as Sue agreed to let me stay with her, the two of them hatched a plan for me to meet her. Fearful their plan might get derailed again (by me returning to Chicago again) it was immediately decided that upon my return to Sue's she would bring my young dumb ass by Shirley's for us to meet. That is exactly what took place. Sue said to come take a ride with her. Just like my Mom tricked my ass the day she slipped off with me in tow to meet Bill the TV man, Sue was now being just as slippery as my Mom was back in the day.

The ride to Shirley's place took about forty-five minutes, due to weather conditions that November day, a few days before Thanksgiving. Shirley must have been posted up at the window watching for us. Sue only had to knock just once and the door flung wide open. Standing there in the doorway that frigid November day was this tall copper tone sister with shoulder length black hair smiling directly into my eyes like she had hit the Megabucks ticket.

Watching her eyes I could see she was not just giving me a regular once over. This sister was devouring me with those beautiful large brown eyes of hers. As She was about to introduce me, I immediately began to extend her my right hand. She paid that jester no mind as she stepped forward and put both arms around me as if she'd known me all her life.

Being a Cannon, one reads body language quickly. She was saying non-verbally that she was available, not in a sexual way, but in a way that says, "I'm locking." For one thing, she saw my hand coming up to greet her and she ignored it to put her hands on me physically.

Once that was accomplished, she held me and slid her hand down my back. Like I say, being a Cannon, you learn to read body language. To cap things off, she smiled over at my Aunt Sue as she stepped aside and allowed me to enter her place ahead of she and Sue. Again, I read women well.

Our coats and hats were taken and we all settled in for small talk. How long will you be staying, have I had any luck with finding a job. Questions like that. Oh, do you have kids? Shit, she basically knew from quizzing my aunt. Then she asked if I had made plans for Thanksgiving, and before I could say "yea" or "nay" Sue said she had been invited to some old friends of her and Bob's. Now, they were both looking at me quizzically, so I finally said that I hadn't made any plans. With that said, Shirley said, "I'd like to extend you an invitation to my home for Thanksgiving dinner, provided you are sure you have no other plans."

Now, it was my turn to toy with her. So I said, "On second thought, let me get back with you on that invitation. Do you have a number where I can perhaps call you later this evening?" Shirley looked at Sue with a befuddled expression. I wanted her to know she was not the shot caller. I was. She was twenty-seven and square. I was nineteen and city-slick and a Cannon.

After we left, I told Sue her friend was a bit aggressive and that's why I didn't jump at the offer of dinner. I'll give her a call around 9:00 pm to say yes I'll come for dinner. With that said, we drove home laughing and talking shit. Aunt Sue was real easy to talk to. As time passed, I would find out that Aunt Sue and Shirley's younger brother were seeing each other on the down low. He lived next door to Shirley.

I arrived at Shirley's about 1:30pm Thanksgiving afternoon. Shirley had gone all out in the cooking department. I ate so much I went and sat on her couch to nap, but she insisted I go lay across her bed, and I did so. Having sex with her wasn't even on my mind, not that she wasn't desirable. I was just a bit spooked by the age difference, plus she had a child.

As I lay there, she came in and removed my shoes for me. I knew instantly where this was going. Especially when she cam in again in a bathrobe and said she wanted to relax awhile. So she lay beside me and we talked. Not once did I make any attempt to sex her. I just allowed myself to follow her lead. After a few more minutes, she said, "Your pants will get all wrinkled, you can take them off and I'll hang them up." Her eyes said the rest.

We had sex, but nothing wild like Star or Di, just regular sex. For her, that was enough, but in reality it wasn't, as you shall see. The next day, Aunt Sue came and got me after she spent an hour next door talking to Jack, Shirley's brother, about Mississippi. Right! As time passed, Shirley helped me get a job busting suds at a placed called the "Prime Time Supper Club." The job paid short money, however, I ate free and good plus I left with a brown bag each night full of food.

Zion was a dry town, first one I had ever been in at that point in my life. The Prime Time Supper Club's bar was situated outside the city limit. You couldn't enjoy any form of alcohol during your dinner meals. Shirley worked at an old nursing home on the main floor. The two upper floors had been converted into a hotel. That is where I first lived.

Shirley would sneak up to my room, sometimes twice daily on the days I was off. By now it was obvious why the sister was sneaking up the back stairs. It sure wasn't to change sheets or bedpans. I guess it's fair to say the sister spent her time between the sheets more so than changing them. Even country girls have a right to get their freak on.

Naturally, I gave her all the creative room she needed to express her alter ego. Things kind of got out of hand, job wise, because she was missing in action far too much. So, what we decided was I'd move in with her. Naturally, it was a wee bit cramped. Living with Shirley was my second experience living with a woman. Star was my first. Doing the square thing did have its appeal in many ways. I got to play Daddy!

From what Shirley shared about herself and her son's father was actually vague. They had met while she was living in California and working at a dry cleaner. According to Shirley, Sean's dad was a police officer from New Jersey. When you're nineteen what do you really know about decision-making, not a hell of a lot. Thinking back to those days I have to truly laugh at the majority of the decisions I made or went along with. One of the worst decisions I've ever been a party to has to do with my brother. Even now, thirty-eight years later, the echo of my voice telling him, "Kenny, you can't stay a few days," still rings in my ears even now as I commit this story to paper.

My brother also had some legal issues in Boston of his own going on around the same time I did in 1970. Some time in January of 1971 (around the second week), my brother showed up at Shirley's (not my place, but hers) somewhat unannounced, and on the "1:00am" as I was. To further complicate the situation he had a white boy with him. As to how they hooked up has escaped my memory over the years. By the time I found out, he was already in Chicago waiting for the train to Zion.

Having had no prior warning nor about his excess baggage (his white friend), I just said my brother's in Chicago, and he's going to come out to meet you and see me, etc. She was cool, at least on the surface. However, I could sense her apprehension in her silence and movements.

Shortly after 3:00pm, Kenny and his friend arrived, hungry, tired and apparently high. I knew she did not know, and no way was I going to tell her. She didn't know I used, although I only got high once the whole time out thee, and it wasn't around her.

After Kenny and his friend ate, Kenny wanted to shower and kick back. He just naturally assumed he could stay, and I understood his reasoning, we were brothers, why would he have to ask if he could stay? I never had to do that at his house. Before I could respond to his request about the shower, Shirley called me into the bedroom and said, she "did not feel comfortable with Kenny and his friend being there."

Then she said these words no one wants to hear when they are on the run and a thousand plus miles from home, allowing the words to flow from her lips, "Kenny and his friend have to leave." Okay, I can truly understand the white guy having to leave because he could have slept on the pullout couch. She chose not to hear any of what I was saying.

Naturally, I had to be the one to say, "Kenny, you can't stay." That shit cut deep into my heart as it did his. Had I been stronger, I would have said, "Well, we all have got to go, then," packed my shit and left with them. But, I took the cowardly way out and yielded to that bullshit. The shit we do when we are young, dumb and full of cum. It's truly amazing when I think back to those years. My whole family went wild about that incident.

Kenny left and went and stayed with our Mother's cousin James in Chicago. Kenny and I would meet in Chicago to hang out together many times. Not being allowed to stay at Shirley's would come up and we would have nasty arguments over it. While staying with James, he decided to get clean. James was cool about it and got him into a hospital that had a Detox ward in it and he got clean. Shortly after being released from the hospital he left Chicago for Detroit. His woman, Shirley Ford, had moved there with her daughter. Shirley also had a brother there named Bobby. ☙

Chapter 36 ~ Becoming A Father

In February of 1971, Shirley found out she was pregnant by me. Now the conversation turned to marriage at least on her part, not on mine. I was having difficulty enough dealing with her being pregnant. Marriage was just a bit too much. How Shirley managed it is beyond me, and how at twenty years of age did I allow my dumb self to go for what I'm about to share is even more silly.

Sue must have mentioned something to my Mother about Shirley having discussed the possibility of us getting married. My mother told Sue she'd kick her narrow Georgia ass all over Chicago if she signed her name (forged) anything relating to marriage. Sue knew to keep her distance from that marriage. Shirley kept telling me how our child should have married parents. Now all that shit sounded good but who's ready for marriage at age twenty to a woman he only met a few days before Thanksgiving? The stuff you do when you're twenty and sometimes even when you're twenty-seven, can truly amount to nothing but stupidity.

Shirley knew this older woman who owned a small Breakfast type restaurant at the corner of our street from her hometown. She talked that woman into going with us to Waukeegan, IL to pose as my guardian at the Post Office in order to get an application for Marriage. At that point in my life, marriage was the last thing on my mind. She should have had enough sense to know that herself. That cliché, "The blind leading the blind," was very apropos.

Once we had the blank license in hand, Shirley immediately started telling me about some Minister she knew from her hometown. She could reach out to him at a moment's notice, and he'd be more than happy to perform the ceremony. She knew far too many helpful people from her home for my money. So this is what I cam up with. I would sign all the paperwork using the name "Seth Roberts," Loren's brother's name.

In short, I married my damn self and she went along with that dumb shit. We truly had blinders on our eyes and peanuts for brains. Then I said, once we got to Boston, (yes, we came to Boston, dumb, dumb) and settled in, we would make it all legal. She went and told her older sister (Rae Townsend) who lived in Chicago that we had gotten married.

When these people came to visit us they had to know it was all a "sham" especially once they saw my young ass. I didn't even shave nor did I even have a moustache or hair on my face. That sister had an ulterior motive and it had nothing to do with what I had hanging between my legs either. I was pussy drunk and acting like a real sucker. No one had the ups on the other when it came to being foolish over the other.

In two months we were on our way to Boston along with our fictitious marriage license. The day we arrived back in Boston was one to go down in the history books about black folks from Orchard Park Housing Projects. My mother was known to have a sharp tongue throughout the projects, and a short fuse to go along with her tongue.

Our arrival that day was expected, the house was jam packed with people from our building. The alcohol was flowing and the music could be heard outside. Someone from one of the apartments facing Adams Street must have seen us as we were getting out of the cab because by the time we were rounding the corner to start up the final landing to our apartment, Mom was standing at the very top of the landing looking down on us. At five foot ten and a half and one-hundred-eighty-pounds, she must have looked like a not so friendly giant to Shirley.

Mom had a glass of whiskey in one hand a Kool cigarette in the other. Let's not forget that "don't fuck with me" expression on her face. It was obvious she was happy to see me, however, she kept looking beyond me in the direction of Shirley. When we finally got to the top landing, Shirley wasn't quite sure how to address my mother. Finally, she gave her a hug as she said, "Hi, Ma!" Mom being Mom said, "Honey, you're a bit too old to be calling me Ma! Plus, I'm still young, baby." Immediately, Mom laughed to ease the obvious tension looming in the air.

Once inside the apartment, everyone introduced themselves. All the neighbors seemed to have that "damn, she's old" look on their faces. Quickly, Mom pulled me in her room and said, "Baby, if you wanted an old woman, I would have got you one from the projects!" That was how my mother got down, no cut card. Earline didn't need one. Naturally, Di's name came up. She had been calling like crazy. "Why did you tell her you had gotten married?" Immediately I showed her the license. Mom just looked at me and started laughing. "Boy," she said, "don't you know I know your handwriting and I know that boy Seth also? What she do to you? God help your crazy ass."

We stayed with my mother for about two months before I found us a nice two-bedroom apartment on Quincy Street in a private house. Our rent was only eighty-five dollars a month. I actually put forth good effort at working a legit job even though I was slipping around taking a sting here and there. Shirley went through a rough pregnancy with our first child, Melanie, plus she didn't have a lot of love for Boston. She was a good southern sister at heart.

Boston was wild and much too fast for her liking. The pressure of parenting overwhelmed my young ass and I picked back up and started sniffing again. A couple times I almost got busted while hustling. Even though I had the beef for failure to return to Bridgewater, a chippie, using again, a daughter on the way, and last but not least, a woman and a year old step son to support. I hung in there and didn't abandon ship.

Di knew I was back in town. Yes, I had been deliberately ducking her. How was I going to explain this situation I had gotten my now twenty-one-year old self into? One day, I just couldn't duck the sister any longer. She came down to the projects and found my dumb ass. After telling her the story, she said, "Perhaps the baby isn't yours, Charles." That's a thought that had never crossed my mind. "You're acting like you love that old woman. What about me, Charles? What about us?"

Those were the exact words Di expressed to me that hot summer day as we stood inside the Dearborn Schoolyard. Di knew me only too well. She knew I couldn't just up and walk away. After crying, she cursed me out about how she had stood up to her family for years, not allowing them to say anything negative against me. She even spoke about accepting my using. Man, this sister was hurt beyond belief. Di and I parted that day with many mixed feelings between us. The spring of

1976, we would reunite. She would seek me out through my family. We would meet up in New York City.

One day, I had been hustling all day and everything I touched just turned to shit. I kept hipping people or someone would see me and wake the people up. Finally, I beat a man on the load in Kenmore Square Station for two-hundred-twenty-five-dollars. I caught a cab and went shopping at "Star Market" on Boylston Street. On my way home, I took a cab by Wolf's Poolroom, got myself four of them NY Duces for five-dollars each and went to our apartment on Quincy Street.

I got home with fifty-dollars, food, etc. Shirley said, "Is that the best you could do? Sean," her son, "could have done far better," she said. I said, "Bitch," if you weren't pregnant, I'd kick your ass for talking to me like that. A half hour later, I left to go to my Mom's house for a few days. By that Monday, I was back home and at my regular job as a maintenance man at a Tri-complex set of Apartments that connect to the "Prudential Center."

Those words she said to me cut very deep and I have never forgotten them. She never worked at all in Boston. I took care of everything. We didn't have a big bank, but we didn't want for anything basic at all. Had she not been pregnant with my daughter, Melanie, I would have left her ass for saying that shit. We were not married, not in any sense of the word.

 C8

Chapter 37 ~ Death of a Brother

Looking back over that time in my life with Shirley I see clearly we were a total mismatch without any commonalities between us. My brother's death and funeral truly made me see the light.

In early June of 1971, my brother came back home to see my mother and myself. He was drug free. He and Shirley were living in Detroit along with her only child then, a daughter named Waleah. He was living a Muslim life now along with Shirley. (Yes, he, too, had a Shirley -- Shirley Ford!) On his last visit home, I wanted to bridge that gap that existed now between us due to me telling him he couldn't stay at the apartment in Zion.

We met at our Mother's apartment. On the surface it appeared we had buried the hatchet. However, once we got outside the house it was clear he was still feeling something. He said he wasn't ready to forgive me for not standing up for him. I didn't want us to part on a negative note. So, I refused to walk away from my brother without us putting that behind us once and for all.

He was waiting for Uncle Albert to show up to take him by a friend's house named Rosco Thomas to pick up some personal things that Shirley had left behind when she and Waleah left for Detroit.

We stood outside arguing in front of our mother's apartment, neither knowing this would be our final conversation in life that evening. The finality of life comes upon us so swiftly at times, "even in the blink of an eye." Death takes only lives, not prisoners. Its' mission is only to take.

Uncle Albert finally arrived and we both climbed into his station wagon. As he drove off, we continued to argue, even as the car slowed to a dead stop at the corner of Mass and Columbus to pick up Rosco. As Rosco attempted to get in, Kenny said, "Why don't you go on home to your make-believe wife and son?" My first reaction was to hit him in his face, but instead I just looked at him with deep contempt, and got out the car.

I watched as the lights changed for the traffic to begin crossing Mass Avenue in the direction of Columbus Ball Park. As Uncle Albert's car and smoke from his exhaust disappeared in the sea of traffic, I slowly turned my back and walked away, not knowing I was seeing my brother alive for the last time.

On June 18th, 1971, I woke up early at my mother's place, full of sweat and disoriented. Then, out of the blue, my brother's face appeared, looking blank faced, not saying anything. Before going to work, I asked my mother if she had spoken to Kenny that week. Her response was, "No. Perhaps you should give him and Shirley a call."

On June 21st, 1971, I was hanging out up in Grovehall near "Castle Gate Road." When I looked up, I saw two girls I knew from Charlame Housing Development, where my sister-in-law and niece and nephew lived. They were calling my name out loud like they had gone crazy. Pam spoke first, "Charles, you need to go home." I was like, you need to go home, you and Voila know you shouldn't be up here on the Avenue this late at night. Then Viola said, "Tell him Pam, tell him!"

"Tell me what?" I said. Pam was just standing there looking blank faced. Finally, Viola said, "Charles! Kenny is DEAD!!"

I knew I heard every thundering syllable of each word that came out of her mouth. Yet, my response was so delayed, the reality of those words refused to release any response from me.

Finally, I said, "You need to find something else to joke about." Then I heard someone, one of them, say, it happened in Detroit this afternoon. Instantly, I became frozen in time and space, oblivious to sound and touch. Then I remembered hearing my own agonizing screams of "No, No!" What flashed before me were our last two conversations, one outside my Mom's place on Adams Street, Mass. and Columbus Avenues, and last but not least, Zion, Illinois, when I said, "You can't stay!"

Pam and Viola walked me down Warren Street that night to my street, Quincy Street. They each gave me a strong hug and we parted.

Shirley was up watching TV when I came in. As I told her of Kenny's death, she only said, "I'm sorry to hear that," never once looking in my direction or taking her eyes off the TV screen. Talk about a cold self-absorbed person. I knew I had to get away from her quickly so I stood up and walked out.

When I got to my mother's place, it was so quiet, not a sound could be heard. No radio, no TV, no voices, nothing but the sound of stillness in the air. As I opened the door with my key, the whole apartment was as if a blackout was in effect.

After striking a match, I was able to locate the wall switch for the light. Seeing my mother's face in the dim light, she looked so childlike, innocent yet deeply wounded. Her ashen face appeared to have aged twenty years. For several minutes, we just sat in deep silence before she told me the story of my brother's death earlier that day.

Shirley's brother Bobby, whom I had not seen in many years, had also lived in Detroit. From what Shirley and the police told my mother, Bobby came by the house dope sick, asking for money, which his sister refused to give him. Words were exchanged between Shirley and her brother. In a fit of rage, Bobby beat his sister up, and left. When Kenny came home from work, he sees Shirley all beat up and crying. She tells my brother what happened. He goes looking for Bobby. They had a fistfight in some backyard. Kenny got the best of him, kicked his ass bad with his hands. As Kenny was walking away, Bobby pulled out his knife, ran up behind my brother and stabbed him in the back several times. As Kenny was lying on the ground bleeding, Bobby took out my brother's knife and placed it in his hand.

This whole thing had to have taken place near their apartment because Shirley was on the scene in minutes of it happening. Kenny died in Shirley's arms in a dirty backyard defending the woman he loved so dearly. As for Shirley's brother being charged with murder, it never happened. The state of Michigan at that time had a justifiable homicide law that freed him of any charges. I could say okay, but when someone is stabbed in the back where is the imminent threat of danger? Perhaps, not being a NASA "Rocket Scientist" is the reason why I don't understand the Detroit Police Department's reason for not charging Robert Ford with the brutal murder of my brother.

The impact of Kenny's death ran deep in my family. My mother would cry about how she missed him, up until the time of her own death. Many nights in the years following his death, she and I would reminisce about when Kenny and I were kids.

The day of Kenny's funeral, Shirley jumped off the Bridge connection Boston to Cambridge, Massachusetts.

By the mercy of Allah, she didn't die that day. Back in Detroit, six men were in hot pursuit of Shirley's brother Bobby Ford. How he got away is still a mystery. All I can say is he was very lucky. Those six men were members of my family who also were living in Detroit. They were known to be short with words and patience.

At the funeral, many people wondered why Shirley, my Shirley (even though she was pregnant) didn't attend the service. I also still wonder about that, even now, in December 31, 2008, at the time of this writing. She did not even come to my mother's house after the burial.

In 1976, a childhood friend, who we'll call "Alice," reached out to a family member of mine to say Bobby Ford was seen in a certain housing project in a section of Boston called Roslindale. The family member just wanted to have a heart to heart talk with Mr. Ford, but Allah intervened and removed him. We can't bring the dead back, we just have to move on with our own lives and leave things to Allah.

In July 1971, I was arrested by absconding from Bridgewater. Rather than send me back to Bridgewater, Roxbury Court sentenced me to Deer Island House of Corrections for one year. While serving that sentence, my lovely daughter, Melanie Belim, was born October 15th, 1971, in the Boston City Hospital. She also was born with a bad case of eczema.

Upon my release on Parole in January 1972, I saw my pretty baby girl for the first time. She was so tiny lying there in that little crib, the doctor had the nurse put these mittens on her hands and her feet were covered as well. Her skin was so red and raw in many spots. Shirley missed her period the following month. By April we were at each other again. I was staying back at home with my mother, but I would visit daily to check on Shirley and the kids.

One Sunday, I came by the house and she was gone. No note, no nothing. She had gone to Chicago where her sister Rae lived. Her family assisted her in locating a place for she and the children. Each time I made an attempt to contact her through Rae I was told that Shirley and my daughters were fine. As for address or phone information, the answer was always the same. "Shirley and the kids are fine and she doesn't want any contact."

On November 28th, 1972 in Chicago, our second daughter, Katina Belim, was born. Our lives and those of our children would remain separate from mine up until 1993. By then, married and unmarried, each daughter would have children of her own. My two daughters would produce six Belim children, four grandsons and two granddaughters. But my lineage doesn't end there. There are three more Belim girls, Shera Z. Battey-Belim, Charlene N. Belim, and Chanel Belim. Five beautiful daughters and ten grandchildren, six grandsons and four granddaughters.

 catch

Chapter 38 ~ Going Back to New York

After finding out Shirley had returned to Chicago to be near her family, and being totally cut off from them, I knew what my plans would be.

Boston represented too much pain for me to deal with. The birth defects, surgeries, my Mom and Dad's shit, Bill the TV man, the Elder Adams. The deaths of father and brother, Shirley's shit. Leaving Boston was absolutely necessary for my well being. To stay would have been emotional suicide for me.

All those negative memories were stifling me, sucking me dry. I wanted, I needed, an opportunity to breathe. Some things are just inevitable. I knew the Big Apple was my calling, and I was going to answer that call, no matter what the cost. Sure, it may have been selfish, but life isn't always fair. Mom still had Bill on the Lay-A-Way plan. My Dad, brother and daughters were gone. Now it was time to do Charlie.

C<

Chapter 39 ~ In a New York State of Mind

My man Ernie was home and in a program on Massachusetts Avenue. The State Parole Board sent him there upon his release from Concord Prison. We were cool, going way back, along with Shorty, Mike C, Rico and Cully. So I went by that spot on Mass. Avenue. I immediately started in with talk of going to New York, not just to play the town, but to live there on our own as young up and coming Players and pickpockets. Ernie came up with "Triple P." It stood for "Pickpocket, Player and Pimp," in that exact order. We knew we were pickpockets and players, the pimping was just waiting for us to get to. We knew there was a woman in New York with each of our names on their lips and embedded in their hearts.

We planned our trip with precision. We could not leave town without a "Grubstake" (a bank) for hotel, bail and food, etc. I knew my baby, Star, and her friends would be a big help. But you don't leave home with thoughts of relying on someone else, especially when you're not being expected. Plus, we were not going to visit. We knew New York was going to be home for us. And every "tub must stand on its own bottom," and every man must be equipped to stand on his own two feet.

Ernie and I agreed we would hustle seven days a week to build our banks up to three-thousand-dollars each. We would each be responsible for our own money. It took us a little over a week to get our banks in order. Ernie and I played all over Cambridge, Brookline, Commonwealth Avenue, Kenmore Station, North and South Stations. Those spots got beat up bad. Had we had our own car, we would have gotten our banks together much sooner by playing those horse and dog racetracks in New Hampshire and Rhode Island.

Finally, our night to leave came for us. Both our Moms came to the bus station to see us off. We had to promise we would look out for one another, no matter what. When his Mom, Dad, sister and brothers were gone, he still had me as a friend. In 1989, while I was awaiting transfer to the federal penitentiary in Atlanta, Georgia, prior to his death, Ernie stayed with my mother and daughter Charlene.

Death is so much a part of my existence. We can't have life without expecting death at the end of the day. Ernie's day ended in Paterson, NJ. Now, three of my childhood friends are gone. I like to call them my brothers; they are Michael S. Collins, Daniel "Cully" Davis, Bryant "Shorty" Green. Though not biologically linked, we might as well have been. I pray that Allah continues to keep us all healthy and safe.

As our bus made its way down the highway from Boston that night with Ernie and I on it, I knew this wasn't just a trip. It was our Maiden Voyage to game and manhood. Each passing light and building we passed that night as we left the city represented a bad experience that had taken place in my life up to that point. All those operations, those tin man casts, the patched up eyes, Bill the TV man and the deaths of members of my family. Those experiences were flashing before me now. Yet, passing away at the same time before my mind's eye. Going to New York that night on the Greyhound bus represented rebirth. An opportunity to not only play the (Cannon) game, but help improve it, as well.

Back during the 1800s out in the Midwest, there were areas known as the Badlands. That's where all the outlaws hung out and felt safe. It was a haven for Crooks, Hoes and Gamblers. Tenderfoots were not allowed or welcomed. Many of those placed were without any form of, or very little, conventional law. Going to New York that night to two young Cannons was like going back in time.

We knew New York was a modern day badland, and Harlem was where Crooks, Hoes and Gamblers could go to hang out and feel safe. The PoPo was even down with the lick back then to some extent. We had long ago heard many of the stories of the legendary men and women who had stepped across 110th Street into Harlem to make their mark. The underworld that birthed the criminal mind within me was alive and kicking on that bus ride to New York.

We honestly felt we were modern day Cowboys (Crooks). That's how we pictured ourselves in our minds; two outlaws on a stagecoach drawing closer to Dodge City. Dodge City was a wild and wide open town in the 1800s. You could even get away with murder at high noon.

Harlem was still wide open when I got back to it in 1972. A man could still kill a man at high noon in Dodge City Harlem under the right set of circumstances and step back into the Gold Lounge, the Playhouse on 118th Street, and have no fear of arrest.

Knowing all those things ahead of time made that ride that night one of the most comfortable rides I have ever had in my life. Back then you could still smoke cigarettes in the last three rows of the Greyhound bus.

As Ernie and I sat back there smoking and thinking, we knew many wonders awaited us up ahead, which we would eagerly embrace with open arms.

Knowing we had no family in New York, Ernie and I were forced to lean on each other for additional strength. The only people I knew were a handful of prostitutes. Necessity made us that much closer as friends.

You could see the excitement in Ernie's eyes and hear it in his voice. He was elated beyond belief that he was finally given the opportunity to play New York City. We all have our own personal demons, bad memories, and I'm sure many of Ernie's got left behind at the station in Boston once we boarded that bus. For us, this trip was like being called up from the Minor League to play in the "Major League of the Cannon Game." It was like finally getting that long overdue opportunity to star in a major film in Hollywood. Two young men on a mission who were about to fulfill a dream, "Playing the Cannon in the Greatest City in the World: New York."

Ernie would come to rely much on my opinion and judgment because I had been to New York so many times before. For him, this journey represented his first major outing period, and he was thrilled. I had already mapped out in my mind exactly where we would stay once we got to the city. Ernie just could not believe that bars were allowed to stay open until four a.m. In many Harlem clubs the requirement was move off the bar to a table and you still got served.

When I first started coming to New York, the bus would come right down Seventh Avenue. Harlem, USA. On our maiden voyage in 1972, that is exactly how it came down Seventh Avenue.

I had fallen asleep as the bus pulled out of the bus station in Hartford, Connecticut. Ernie's anticipation and excitement would not allow him any sleep that night. By the time our bus hit the streets of Harlem, I was fast asleep.

At first, I thought I was having this dream that someone was calling my name, "Charlie, Charlie!" Then the next thing I knew, my whole body was being propelled forward. Then I felt this pressure on my arm. I awake to Ernie's loud voice saying, "We are here, we are here, Charlie!" as our huge bus came to an abrupt stop at a traffic light at the intersection of 135th Street and 7th Avenue.

Ernie shouted, "Charlie, look at all the people out on the street and look at all those Cadillacs double parked by that nightclub!" We looked out the bus window as we were held by the traffic light to see the famous "Smalls Paradise." Smalls was once owned by the famous Pro Basketball Player Wilt Chamberlain. Directly across the street was Mr. B's, another popular club. Many well known sports stars and entertainers could be found at those clubs along that part of Seventh Avenue. There was the Red Rooster, and the Reny (Renaissance) Bar, once owned by a member of the famed Harlem Globetrotters Basketball team. We had never before seen that many people (Blacks) so sharply dressed in one place at that hour of the night.

The scene from the bus window was like watching a scene at Times Square on New Year's Eve or the Macy's Christmas Day Parade, all at once. Ernie was so excited he started to stutter as he repeated, "Look, Charlie! Look at all the cars and people!" Finally, the traffic light changed and our bus moved on down the avenue in the direction of 125th Street. Now I was plastered to the window hoping to catch a glimpse of the Apollo Theater. Before leaving Boston, I had told Ernie how Star and her friends Butch and Cinnamon had taken me clothes shopping and then to see a show at the Apollo.

As we eased through the traffic at West 125th Street and Seventh Avenue, I quickly looked out the right side of the bus window in the direction of Eighth Avenue. Before I could focus clearly, Ernie was again up and screaming out my name, "Charlie, it's the Apollo Theater! Look, look!" The other people on the bus started to look as well now. Ernie was elated as a child in the M&M candy factory or the chocolate factory in Hershey, Pennsylvania.

Our bus headed west down 110th Street, and made a left turn onto Columbus Avenue. For us and many others like us back in Boston, all we were accustomed to was white folks and blacks, nothing in between. To see people emerging from bars and full supermarkets at 1:30a.m. was mind blowing to Ernie. He let it be known as our bus moved through the thick of night traffic on Columbus Avenue.

Approaching Ninth Avenue near Lincoln Center, we instantly became entangled in a maze of traffic and a sea of wild driving yelling Yellow Taxicab drivers. Each one cursing and honking their horns at each other as the traffic flowed like a snail down the avenue. Before the bus could pull into the tunnel-like entrance off 40th Street, Ernie had his luggage bags down from the overhead rack above his seat and was standing by the driver waiting to get off the bus. Time passes, but certain memories are forever etched in our minds. I honestly just closed my eyes and saw Ernie's smiling face standing by that driver, as the tears stream slowly down my face. So much of my life has deceased, never to return.

I gathered my two luggage bags and stepped onto New York soil. I knew we were only steps away from the Ninth Avenue exit doors. Honestly, I thought about setting both bags down right there and running out that exit door to search for that "Sexy walking and talking Star." The Star that not only glowed in the dark of night, but also glowed as the sun was at its Zenith above the clouds.

Reality is a hell of a tool when it's in the right person's hands. That is why I love and respect players (true to the Game ones, I mean). They quickly bounce back to reality. That is exactly what I did after checking and assessing myself. There would be ample time to check on Ms. Star.

Right now, it was about getting Ernie and myself a secure spot to lay at by the week.

I thought about the spot on 47th Street between 6th and 7th Avenues, as well as the Hotel President on 48th between Broadway and 8th. After a few minutes of deep thought, I decided against both. The spots were much too busy for my liking. We needed something that was much more secluded with an inside bath, two beds and cooking facilities.

Suddenly I knew the perfect place. It was an apartment hotel on 44th between 6th and 7th Avenues. It had all the amenities we would need for sixty-five-dollars a week. We paid two weeks rent plus one week security. Ernie's name was William Canada, I was Robert Greenday. Now that we had secured our spot, we could sleep safely.

The next morning, we left early to catch all of my girls at the Ham and Eggs Restaurant on 50th and 7th Avenue. When we walked in that morning, all three of my old friends were in their regular booth facing 50th Street. Butch and Cinnamon were facing me in the direction of the door. Immediately, I placed my finger to my mouth, indicating for them not to say a word as I tiptoed up to their booth.

Star was busy telling the girls about this trick she had the night before who wanted to eat her even though she said she was on her period. Slowly, I eased up behind Star, while she held her fork in midair. I licked the nape of her neck. She froze in mid-sentence, dropped her fork and screamed my name, "Charlie!" without ever turning to face me. As she attempted to stand, her whole plate of food went flying in the air. She could care less and everyone around her knew exactly how she felt about me.

No longer was I that hungry kid needing a bit to eat or a place to stay. A man, all twenty-one years of me, stood before her, all filled out and looking like new money fresh off the press. Star dove over her seat and kissed me with such force, sliding her tongue so deep down my throat until I almost choked. She damn near knocked me and Ernie down. She kissed, cried, screamed for every bit of five minutes straight, while holding onto me. Even Butch and her girl started to cry. Ernie broke the ice by saying, "Shit! I'm starved!"

Star's first question was, "You've come to stay, haven't you?"

I said, "Yes."

She dropped her head for a minute. I automatically knew wshy. She was ready to leave New York and go back to Hartford, Connecticut. Everyone introduced themselves to Ernie and he to them. I could tell he wasn't feeling Butch at all and I knew exactly why. It had to do with his sister Sam and her being gay. He just didn't like gay women, period.

Butch and Cinnamon left and we all promised to meet at the Oasis Bar uptown on Broadway on Saturday night. Ernie and Star liked each other. We ate and talked for at least an hour. Star had changed a lot. She was much too beautiful to be out prostituting herself. This woman had plenty of class. She now was readying up to leave and I was digging in for the long haul. Ernie and I had decided when we got up that morning that we would work until that Monday, and today was only Thursday.

After eating, we all walked back to our spot. Ernie wanted to chill and then go over to New Jersey to visit his Dad in Paterson. We agreed to meet by eight p.m. back at the spot.

As Ernie was leaving us, I turned to Star and asked, "So, what are you doing the rest of the day?"

She just smiled and said, "Having sex with you, of course."

ՃՑ

Black Robes White Justice *by:*   **Bruce Wright**

Illusions of Justice *by:*   **Lenox Hinds** *(Iowa University)*

The Browder Files *by:*   **Anthony T. Browder**

Bad Blood *(The Tuskegee Experiment) by:*   **James H. Jones**

From Superman to Man *by:*   **J. A. Rogers**

Assata Shakur *by:*   **Assata Shakur**

Stolen Legacy *by:*   **George M.G. James**

Miseducation of the Negro *by:*   **Carter G. Woodson**

They Stole It but You Must Return It *by:*   **Richard Brown**

The Isis Papers *by:*   **Dr. Frances C. Wesling**

The Gnostic Gospels *by:*   **Elaine Pagels**

Possessing the Secrets of Joy *by:*   **Alice Walker**

The Conspiracy To Destroy Black Boys *by:*   **Jwanza Kujufi**

Before Columbus *by:*   **Ivan Van Sertima**

Christianity, Islam and the Negro Race *by:*   **Blyden**

Glory of The Black Race *by:*   **El Jahees**

7 African Arabian Wonders of the World *by:*   **Khalid Mansour**

Blood In My Eye *by:*   **George Jackson**

The Autobiography of Malcolm X *by:*   **Alex Haley & Malcolm X**

The Holy Quran translated *by:*   **Yusuf Ali**

HOOD WARS by ESCO
ISBN# 978-0-9844071-4-9
Page count: **397** Price Book **$16.99**
Prison order price: **$11.00**

Nina and Toast are two disheartened enemies who vowed to "WARN AND PROTECT" each other over the course of an impending war. Eventually Nina feels betrayed, after a rush of slugs nearly claim her life. She goes on a manhunt tracking down Toast, revealing her own treacherous behavior to her inner circle. Unfortunately, her acts of desperation may soon get her killed!

Toast has too much to worry about than explaining his innocence to Nina. At the same time, he and his "FLUNKIES" are having a transformation of power. Toast must find ways to keep himself and his underlings safe from the most monstrous gang in the city. Plus the risk of death ten folds when Toast soldiers have a clash of ideas and a division of loyalty. Plunged into a world where HONOR and RESPECT is cut paper thin. Toast is not going to know who to trust.

Who will be left standing when the smoke clears at the end of this bloody tale of deception, betrayal and survival of the fittest? Will Nina be able to eliminate Toast before her own treacherous past catches up with her? Will toast find sanctuary away from the madness; or will he walk right into the line of fire set up by either friend or foe?

D.D. Ellis explosive novel HOOD WARS is non-stop action, filled with larger than life characters, and will keep you asking "What will happen next?"   It's a must read!!!

FIVE STAR REVIEW
Esco you got one. HOOD WARS truly a great read.
Finally a representation of a writer from Allah Born.
Very entertaining! Keep pushing, we're moving......

GOAT
Albany, New York

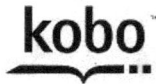

FALLEN ANGEL by FruitQuan
ISBN# 978-0-9844071-3-2
Page Count **333** Price Book **$15.99**
Prison order price: **$11.00**

From the Brownsville slums of Brooklyn, New York and Los Angeles, California all the way to the Federal Penitentiary, the hourglass is ticking, the streets are watching, and Gangstaz gotta KEEP IT GULLY!

With Albert Anastasia roots and links to the Biggie Smalls vs Tupac rival, Brooklyn's home of the legendary Mike Tyson is saturated with history...... Brownsville has a story to tell.

FIVE STAR REVIEW

Fallen Angel is a story of the games that are played on the streets; some people's reality. The characters in the book remind me of actual people that live & hang in the streets of the five boroughs (NYC). I found myself constantly picking up the book to read at every opportunity that I could.

FruitQuan did an excellent job characterizing Hurricane, the main character as well as the others (Mama Maxie, Pale Face etc). Hurricane reminds me of "Midnight" from Sistah Souljah's book "A Coldest Winter Ever". The story is written whereas you know Hurricanes every thought, whether you agree with those thoughts or not. So if you like a book with lots of family love, street hustle, action & fast money this is the book for you."

Crystal
Brooklyn, NY

WHAT'S NEXT by Courtney B. Walker
Drama, Pain, Heartache & Betrayal
ISBN# 978-0-9844071-2-5
Page Count **249** Price Book **$12.99**
Prison order price: **$9.00**

The author weaves a dynamic plot showing how one young woman's life undergoes drastic changes with each situation she faces, much of which leads to more pain and heartbreak. The character, Angel Reneé Walker, is unlike other people in the world. She can tell what lies ahead, all the drama, pain, heartache, and betrayal. It all began on the first day of her senior year when her mother's life was taken in a car accident. Since then, her world has turned upside down.

Angel finds herself in difficult situations, while her relationship with her father is at its breaking point. It seems that nothing can go right. She starts to give up on life, on everything. When she meets someone who makes her believe there is still a chance, she feels hopeful again. But like everything else in her life, will this love be destroyed? Angel will be tested when a dark secret shocks her and she finds out that the one person she trusted most in the world was involved in the tragic accident that took her mother's life. Is she destined for a life of despair and betrayal? What's Next reveals all.

FIVE STAR REVIEW

"I recently read "What's Next," and I was amazed. I thought that this book would be a self-help book to help young people deal with the trials of growing up. But I was wrong. It was real talk from the beginning to the end. The young Angel Reneé Walker goes through things that a lot of adults can't handle. She lives, learns and falls down. But most of all, she had to find a way out of the place where people hide to get away. I found that this book is inspirational and just what is needed in today's world for our young people, both guys and girls. Grief comes to us all, but not all of us make it through. The aspect I admire is how she maintains her social standing among her peers."

KAY JOHNSON
Brooklyn, NY

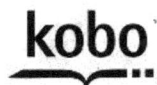

BROOKLYN ICE by Anthony Brewer
ISBN# 978-0-9844071-0-1
Page Count **305** Price Book **$14.99**
Prison order price: **$11.00**

Brooklyn Ice follows its main character Theresa Jones. A Financial Consultant and Attorney; known through academic, corporate and judiciary realms as Ms. Jones. She is known on the streets and by friends as B.G. (short for Baby Girl), and there is only one thing she loves more than her desire to acquire money or her zeal for drama - and that's Joseph Cohen.

Joseph who is cut from the old school cloth of stick up kids use to rob banks, drug dealers and payrolls. He started investing money early on and sent his virgin love to school while he styled under the guise of a Real Estate Agent. That was back in the day, but now, the laid back, more reserved J.C. comes to find his Baby Girl has adopted his old gun slinging ways and combined them with her education and unrelenting Brooklyn ways.

Tempted by millions in diamonds, Joseph has decisions to make. In a time of recession, the Brooklyn bad boys are coming out with hopes Joseph will let Brooklyn do what it has always done - get money. Ride with J.C. or BG; she will not only get you money, but she'll show you how to use it. You decide. But whatever you do, don't get it twisted. The school girl is no longer taking lessons: she's giving them...... There's a new Brooklyn bully. Who would think it's a female?!

FIVE STAR REVIEW

"BROOKLYN ICE by Anthony Brewer is an exciting, breath-taking, fast pace novel to read. This book will have you on the edge of your seat waiting for the next piece of excitement. This book is definitely a page turner. BROOKLYN ICE is packed with plenty of action..."

Barbara Morgan
ATL, Georgia

TERRORIST IN BROOKLYN by Anthony Brewer
Revolutionary or Conspirator
ISBN# 978-0-9844071-1-8
Page Count **254** Price Book **$14.99**
Prison order price: **$11.00**

Terrorism activity has picked up on American soil as a result of the construction of an 80 billion dollar American oil project in Iraq, leaving the Federal Bureau of Investigation with work to do. With Corporate buildings getting blown up, dead bodies appearing out of thin air and the Bureau short on answers all fingers point to Special Agent Black of CTU.

No one ever thought terrorism would be on the door step of Brooklyn residents as victims or practitioners, but what is discover will change Brooklyn forever.

It doesn't help matters when Sheppard's Private Contracting Security Agency (Mercenaries) who served in the Iraq, Afghanistan and Saudi Arabia killing with impunity, have come to America after MOST WANTED terrorist that fled from Iraq seeking refuge in Brooklyn.

Equally alarming are the African American faces with international ties that are popping up as suspects of terrorism. In the midst of Agent Black's investigation, he connects Muslim residents from local Mosques supporting none terrorist. What's worse he finds he is not only a suspect, but a MOST WANTED.

With all eyes on Special Agent Black, he will have to choose between clearing his name when suspected of terrorism activity or making a name for himself by standing for justice against terrorist no matter who the perpetrators......

SHOESHINE BOY by Charles Belim
ISBN# **978-0-9844071-6-3**
Page count **269** Price Book **$14.99**
Prison order price: **$11.00**

The "Shoeshine Boy" saga chronicles events in the life of a young kid growing up in Boston, Massachusetts. At age ten he's given an opportunity to shine shoes in a shine parlor deep within the "Mob" controlled section of Boston's notorious 'North End'. Unbeknownst to him, the shine parlor is a front for illegal betting from horses to the local 'nigga number' in his community of Roxbury.

The experiences and exposure of that summer will catapult the Shoeshine Boy into being dubbed one of Boston's most infamous 'Common Known and Notorious Thieves.' The Shoeshine Boy story is about his beginning.

"Payin' My Dues", **"Plastic Money"**, and **"Paper Money"** by the same author, will chronicle his rise, fall, and resurrection. Mr. Belim's resurrection as a new urban writer has given his readers a glimpse into the Black Underworld of trickery and deception.

LOYALTY REIGNS by Japlin Cureton
ISBN # **978-0-9844071-8-7**
Page Count **413** Price Book **$17.99**
Prison order price: **$11.00**

"Loyalty Reigns" exposes the raw and often ugly truth about survival in a world tainted by jealousy, rivalry, violence, drama and mayhem; disagreements settled only by bullets and blood. The question whose answer determines who lives or dies that day is, "Will Loyalty Reign or will the storms of betrayal make it hail?" Be for warned, it's not a fairy tale or a story for the squeamish or the faint-hearted, but if you're unafraid to be inoculated with a dose of reality, jump into a Destinations Cab and join Jap Cureton for an "adults-only" tour through the unforgiving world where only "Loyalty Reigns," and honor rules.

This story chronicles the act of deception where there is no honor amongst thieves; where mayhem thrives in a sinful world of MONEY, SEX, and POWER. Decrypt coincidences, coordinated murders, set-ups, perpetrated by Blueberry, and dishonest Agents will test ones quest of LOYALTY REIGNS!

Jap Cureton is presently at work on the second book of the "Loyalty Reigns" trilogy.

INDICTED by Lamont Christian
ISBN# **978-0-98440071-7-0**
Page Count **341** Price Book **$16.99**
Prison order price: **$11.00**

They say that there are two sides to every story and to every coin, but what most don't know is that there are two sides to a small section of the city's world Renown Island "MANHATTAN" and it all depends on which side you are on. Harlem always rung louder and there is only one thing that mattered above all and it's that "paper".

In this story of East meets west, the traditional fashion of how the sedative that is excreted from a syringe, through the eye of a needle and finally into the blood stream of heroin hungry veins, causes sides to clash. This eventually places the "self proclaimed king of Harlem" Lavell Collins in direct opposition with the eastside and that inadvertently puts Yvonne, Lavell's girlfriend in a freedom compromising, life altering situation.

INDICTED is a story that illustrates love, lost and the desperation that often justifies the behavior of those residing in Harlem and the various communities that mirror it. Places where addiction consumes the home, demoralizes the people and erodes the spirit. Like the many that came before it, INDICTED gives readers a unique and in depth look at a world where the social, economic mechanics, that has for generations plagued our culture, could be unfair and outright discriminative.

This goes beyond the 2014 version of Romeo & Juliet because it takes place in HARLEM where Lavell and Yvonne have to fight for everything, including the basic liberties such as life and love while fending for one another, even if it's by their own set of rules.

FANTASY BALL by ADENA
ISBN#**978-0-9844071-9-4**
Page Count **448** Book Price **$17.99**
Prison order price: **$11.00**

ABANDONED 310 MILLION YEARS AGO, IN WHAT IS NOW SOUTHWESTERN PENNSYLVANIA, A GROUP OF BALLS ARE SLOWLY UNEARTHED DEEP IN A FAMILY COAL MINE. THE FIRST TO BE DISCOVERED IS A NINE FOOT TALL YELLOW FANTASY BALL. NEITHER, NASA OR OTHER SCIENTIST CAN IDENTIFY WHAT THE IMPENETRABLE SPHERE IS MADE OF.

WITH NO APPARENT USE OR VALUE, THE OWNER OF THE COAL MINE PLOPS THE BALL DOWN IN HIS BACK YARD FOR HIS 13 YEAR OLD SON TO PLAY ON. YET IT IS THE AUTISTIC NEIGHBOR GIRL WHO USES HER GIFT OF MENTAL TELEPATHY TO OPERATE THE YELLOW SPHERE. SO JOIN CHAD AND VENUS ON THEIR SOMETIMES DANGEROUS, YET ALWAYS THRILLING, ADVENTURES THROUGH TIME AND SPACE IN THE FANTASY BALL; THE FIRST BOOK IN THE SERIES.

JO ANN
"SHE ROSE FROM THE ASHES"
ISBN # 978-0-9844071-5-6
Page Count: **376** Book Price: **$17.99**
Prison order price: **$11.00**

America, the most powerful country on earth, has produced some of the most prolific families on earth. One such family is the Douglass'. Spawned from England and hardened by the Civil War, the family history is intriguing (mixed heritage) ruthless, and unique. This story entails the first of the mixed heritage, Jo Ann Douglass, and the family members that blazed a burning trail through the civil war era and reconstruction. A taut, suspense filled story in which the protagonist joins the union army passing as a white man, and shares adventures with us as a war hero, feminist, Romantic Heroine, and business woman that happens to become the first black female woman of wealth, all the while harboring a viscous secret.

Travel with me down the pulse pounding, page turning road with
"Jo Ann."

Little known fact; over 250 women enlisted and fought in the civil war for both the Union and Confederacy as men, now comes the story of the only black women to do so!

ORDER FORM

Name:_____

Address:_____

State:_____

Phone# _____

Title(s) purchased:

_____

_____ Ship: $2.50

_____ Total $_____

Send Mail :

New Era Books

1211 Atlantic Ave, Suite 303

Brooklyn, New York 11216

Purchase on line: www.newerabooks.net   or call 347-651-6366

Always include alternative book selection for unavailable books

Book Submissions & Inquiries: newerapublication@aol.com

Free shipping with the purchase of any two books.

PRISON DIRECT

Prison Direct: Family and friends can send New Era books, posters, greeting cards directly to any inmate in State/Federal prison. New Era Books promotes education for this reason we sell books to the prison population at a discounted price. Order Prison Direct through newerabooks.com

Rehabilitation Begins With Education......

NEW ERA
BOOKS

VILLAGE
HEADQUARTERS

4REEL
ENTERTAINMENT

www.ingramcontent.com/pod-product-compliance
Lightning Source LLC
Chambersburg PA
CBHW061005280326
41935CB00009B/843